Matthew Elliott, British Indian Agent

Reginald Horsman was born in Leeds, England in 1931. He received his A.B. and M.A. degrees from the University of Birmingham, England, and his Ph.D. from Indiana University.

Now associate professor of history at the University of Wisconsin-Milwaukee, he is the author of many articles on American-British frontier relations. His book, *The Causes of the War of 1812,* appeared in 1962.

Matthew Elliott, British Indian Agent

Reginald Horsman
University of Wisconsin-Milwaukee

Wayne State University Press
Detroit, 1964.

TO LENORE

CONTENTS

ACKNOWLEDGMENTS

I wish to thank the many librarians who have helped me in he task of discovering material relating to Matthew Elliott. I am particularily indebted to the staffs of the Canadian Public Archives in Ottawa, and of the Burton Historical Collection in the Detroit Public Library. The staff at the Public Archives gave me every possible assistance in using their abundant resources, and Mr. James M. Babcock of the Burton Historical Collection made it a pleasure to work in the excellent collections under his care.

I would like to thank the *Mississippi Valley Historical Review* for permission to use the material in my article "The British Indian Department and the Resistance to General Anthony Wayne, 1793-1795," which appeared in that journal in September, 1962, and the *Ohio Historical Quarterly* for permission to make use of my article "The British Indian Department and the Abortive Treaty of Lower Sandusky, 1793," which appeared in July, 1961. I have made use of the former in chapter five of the present work and of the latter in chapter four. The University of Pennsylvania Press was kind enough to give me permission to expand on the material on Matthew Elliott which originally appeared in chapters nine and twelve of my book *The Causes of the War of 1812* (*Philadelphia, 1962*).

I would also like to thank the Research Committee of the Graduate School of the University of Wisconsin for travel support, and for a research grant in the summer of 1959.

R. H.

PROLOG

Although the British and their Indian allies had taken Detroit in the summer of 1812, their position was not an easy one in the coming winter. By October, only four months after the War of 1812 had begun, the British were faced not only with the problem of preparing to resist the Americans, but also with feeding and placating the Indians. The problem of supplying provisions proved a serious one, and the British decided to send a large body of Indians to live for a time near the rapids of the Maumee River in what is now the northwest corner of Ohio. There, some eight miles southwest of the present Toledo, were supplies of corn and cattle which had been deserted by the Americans at the start of hostilities. To lead the British Indians from Detroit, the obvious choice was Matthew Elliott, Superintendent of Indian Affairs at Amherstburg, the British post on the Canadian side of the Detroit River. Although now over seventy, Elliott was still the vital link between the British and their Indian allies in the Northwest.

Some fifty years had passed since Elliott, then a young Scotch-Irishman recently arrived in America, had first seen what is now the state of Ohio. At that time it was a land cherished by the Indians who hunted and planted unhampered by the all-encompassing American farmer. In the following years Elliott had seen American settlement pour across the Ohio River. In the distant days before the American Revolution Elliott himself had been in the vanguard of the movement, and had traded and lived with the Shawnee on the Scioto. In 1812 he was no longer young, but he was one of the lucky ones who were hardened rather than destroyed by the wilderness. He had fought, traded, and intrigued for over fifty years, but was now quite ready to fight another war against his old adversaries. Already he had assisted in the capture of Detroit, and at the end of October he prepared to take his old Indian friends to the rapids of the Maumee.

As they sailed down the Detroit River to Lake Erie and the mouth of the Maumee, those on the gun-boats and other vessels that carried the British party could see the Elliott home and three thousand acre farm, the finest in Upper Canada, standing proudly on the Canadian shore. At this Amherstburg home, soon to be ravaged by the Kentuckians, Elliott had left his young wife Sarah, but perhaps he had other memories as once again he led his Indians into the field. Ahead of him, already scouting along the Maumee, was his half-Indian son Alexander. Elliott had not only traded and fought with the Shawnee, he had also taken his first wife from among them. His son Alexander had been educated as a lawyer in Montreal, and had only been admitted to the bar in February of 1812. In November Matthew Elliott spent a cold month beside the rapids of the Maumee, surrounded by some 250 Indian warriors, while his son Alexander scouted through the surrounding territory. Unfortunately, Alexander was not as shrewd as his father, and his education in Montreal had not sharpened his knowledge of wilderness ways.

On November 22, Alexander and his Indian companions captured the famous Shawnee chief Captain Logan, and two other American Indians. This was a considerable coup, but Alexander and his party made a fatal mistake – they allowed the prisoners to go unbound. When an opportunity arose, Logan and his party seized guns, shot five of the seven in the British party, and escaped. Logan was fatally wounded, but this was no consolation to the grief-stricken Matthew Elliott, for among the slain was his son Alexander. Although the country was firmly in the grip of winter, Elliott did not leave him on the Maumee; he returned down the Maumee on a tragic, macabre journey with the corpse of his son. The elements themselves turned against him as, in his wife's words, he was "cast away in the ice, within 5 miles of the Enemy's Shore, with the Corpse of his eldest son." But Elliott was not deterred. He made his way to Amherstburg. On December 17 the rites were completed, and his son was finally laid to rest.[1]

This then was Matthew Elliott. For an entire generation his

life was tangled in the threads of the advancing frontier. He deserves to be rescued from the semi-oblivion into which he has faded.

Chapter 1

WILDERNESS TRADER

Matthew Elliott was one of that numerous band of Scotch-Irish who left their impoverished land to find fame and fortune in the New World. His origins are lost in the obscurity of the poor and illiterate. Born in County Donegal, probably in 1739, he crossed the Atlantic in 1761 to join a great host of his countrymen on the Pennsylvania frontier. He came to America as England swept the French from the North American Continent and he was not to die until the United States had acquired their independence through two hard-fought wars and had expelled the English from the country south of the Great Lakes.[1]

For the Scotch-Irish the Pennsylvania frontier was a land of opportunity in the eighteenth century. Fort Pitt was still only a small outpost in the wilderness when Elliott arrived in 1761, but one hundred miles to the east in Carlisle and along the Path Valley, settlers and traders were ready to continue their irresistible march westwards. It was not surprising that young Matthew Elliott should come to this area on arriving in America. His fellow countrymen dominated the region, and there were already Elliotts along the Path Valley in 1761. Although it was a far cry from the soft green fields of Donegal to the harsh wilderness of Pennsylvania, Elliott showed the usual skill of his compatriots in learning the ways of the new land. Frontier life was not easy, but neither was life in Ireland. At least there was now ample food for the taking, and a sense of change and excitement not to be found in the monotonous drudgery of rural life in northern Ireland. To an Elliott, whose family centuries before had dwelt upon the wild and bloody Scots-English border, the dangers of frontier life could have been as a homecoming. The French and Indian War, which had begun at the forks of the Ohio in 1754, was over when Elliott arrived in America. New France had fallen, England had control over the rich Ohio Valley, and the conclusion of European peace in 1763 was to give England her legal sanction to the western region. Before this was accomplished England discovered that the Indian tribes of the region were not prepared to acquiesce quietly in the new state of affairs. In the spring of 1763 an alliance of Indian tribes joined in an attempt to destroy English power west of the Appalachians, and for a time the attempt came perilously near to success. The only important posts to stand before the onslaught were Detroit and Fort Pitt. The settlers and traders who had advanced eagerly into western Pennsylvania in the wake of the French defeat now scurried back across the mountains as the Indians burned and scalped their way eastward across Pennsylvania. The British acted promptly to restore order. In June the British commander in chief, Lord Jeffrey Amherst, ordered two expeditions to the relief of the western posts. Colonel Henry Bouquet, a Swiss mercenary, was given the task of relieving Fort Pitt, and at the end of the month he began to gather his troops at Carlisle on the edge of Pennsylvania settlement.[2]

For Elliott, who had been absorbing knowledge of the new frontier in the two years since his arrival in America, this was the chance to take up the military activities which proved so attractive to him in the years to come. In later years he often asserted proudly that he had begun his British military career under Colonel Bouquet in 1763, although on this occasion, as befitted his youth and inexperience, Elliott was but a lowly volunteer. He made no great mark, but adapted himself with his usual quickness. In the following year he was referred to in a letter to Bouquet as "a person well acquainted with the Country."[3] In August 1763, Bouquet met and defeated the Indians some twenty-five miles west of Fort Pitt at the battle of Bushy Run, and then advanced to the relief of the fort. For the most part it was not Pennsylvanians but Bouquet's regulars who were present at Bushy Run, but Elliott was seldom lacking when a battle was in prospect. After the relief of Fort Pitt, Elliott probably served as a messenger and carried dispatches along the dangerous Forbes Road that connected Carlisle with Fort Pitt. It was in this period that Elliott became acquainted with his later trading

2

partner Alexander Blaine, who was serving as lieutenant in command at Fort Ligonier.[4]

Elliott's hectic and highly dangerous occupation came to an end at the beginning of October 1764 when Bouquet advanced westward from Fort Pitt to subdue the Indians of the Ohio country. Elliott accompanied this expedition, and saw the region that was to be so familiar to him in later years. Bouquet advanced across the Muskingum toward the Scioto, and by the second week in November had succeeded in obtaining a pledge of peace from the Indians as well as securing the release of a large number of prisoners taken in the preceding years. He then returned to Fort Pitt and to Carlisle. Apparently Elliott was already starting some trading activity, for in October on the Muskingum Edward Moran "hired nine horses to Mr. Elliott, who is to return them at Fort Pitt."[5]

Bouquet's successful action at Bushy Run, his relief of Fort Pitt, and Pontiac's failure to take Detroit, brought an end to Indian dreams of driving the English back across the mountains. The Ohio country was once again open to trade, although England attempted to curb settlement west of the mountains by her Proclamation of 1763. In the decade from 1765 to 1775, as Pennsylvanians advanced along the Forbes Road and Virginians pushed up along Braddock's Road to the forks of the Ohio, Indian traders based on Fort Pitt roamed westward through the Ohio country. It was in these years that Elliott gained the experience which was to serve him so well in the British-American conflicts of 1775 to 1814. He was not one of the great figures of this early period. While such figures as Baynton, Wharton, and Morgan, Simon Campbell, and George Croghan moved in exalted trading and political circles, Elliott pursued a quiet trade among the Shawnee in the Scioto region. He learned their language, their customs, and, of great value in his later career, he earned their respect. Like so many other traders of the Ohio region, Elliott left little individual mark on the history of the time. He was one of the many small traders who were preparing the wilderness for the coming of the settler.

In the fall Matthew Elliott travelled westward from Fort Pitt to winter among the Shawnee on the Scioto. Throughout the long winter he gathered furs and skins, and in the spring brought them east on the backs of his packhorses. From Fort Pitt the pelts were shipped to Philadelphia for sale. As he pushed westward through the Ohio wilderness, or sat in the smoke and heat of an Indian winter cabin, Elliott was no longer a plodding Donegal peasant but an American frontiersman on the raw edge of the frontier wilderness. In the years before the revolution, Elliott spent a good part of each year among the Shawnee towns scattered along Paint Creek, the region west of the main Indian town in that area, present-day Chillicothe, Ohio. Here there were sturdy log houses, and to the south a great plain which served the Indians as a cornfield. At Wockachaalli, some three miles northwest of Chillicothe, lived the British Indian agent Alexander McKee – Elliott's friend for the remainder of his life. Pecaweca and Blue Jacket's Town were located in the immediate vicinity. Pecaweca, which was north of Chillicothe, was called by the Welsh Baptist missionary David Jones "the most remarkable town for robbers and villains." It was in this town that Elliott kept a trading house in the period immediately prior to the Revolution.[6]

With their log cabins and cornfields, the Shawnee villages did not suffer in comparison with the British outpost of Elliott's trade operations, Fort Pitt. When the missionary David McClure arrived there in August 1772, the first sight that struck his attention, "was a number of poor drunken Indians, staggering & yelling through the Village." Though he described the fort as a handsome and strong fortification (it was dismantled in October 1772), he was less complimentary about the village itself, which stood about a quarter of a mile distant on the bank of the Monongahela River. This village of some forty log houses was the headquarters of the Indian traders, "& the resort of Indians of different & distant tribes." As a good missionary, McClure viewed the inhabitants of Fort Pitt as "very dissipated," and was shocked that "a great part of the people here make the Sabbath a day of recreation, drinking & profanity." Yet, the future of this wilderness outpost was plainly visible; in the hill across the river was a great open seam of coal.[7] After wintering on the Scioto, and returning through Fort Pitt, Elliott must have found the frontier center of Carlisle a crowded and most established community.

The steady round of existence which occupied Elliott from 1765 to 1774 came to an end in the latter year, and he never saw its like again. For some of the other inhabitants of the region, this span of time was not quite so peaceful. The land speculators and the great trading companies contended for control in the Ohio region, and used their influence to change British policy and to obtain lands and concessions from the Indians. After the British relaxed their policy of restriction of settlement to the east of the Appalachians in 1768, the next year saw the beginning of general settlement west of the mountains. The Scotch-Irish advanced along Forbes Road to Fort Pitt, gradually forging a chain of settlement along the entire route while other frontiersmen pressed northwestward from Virginia toward Fort Pitt along the old Braddock Road. Although the main impact of settlement in the early seventies was concentrated in western Pennsylvania, many frontiersmen began to manifest a distinct interest in the land further down the Ohio, in the "dark and bloody ground" of Kentucky. Again the Indians saw the axes flashing, the trees falling, and cabins rising on once rich hunting grounds. The inevitable "incidents" arose to plague the frontier, and the Indians again prepared to defend their way of life.

The Shawnee, who hunted in the Kentucky region, became particularly restless in the early seventies, and by 1774 Indian war again threatened the frontier and the livelihood of Elliott and his fellow traders. Lord Dunmore, the Governor of Virginia, decided to lead a campaign against the Shawnees. He advanced into the northwest in the fall of 1774, and defeated the Shawnee at the battle of Point Pleasant on October 10, 1774. Following this battle, which took place near the mouth of the Great Kanawha, Dunmore advanced into the Ohio country. His object was the Shawnee towns along the Scioto, and he marched to within fifteen miles of his goal before the Indians made a definite move for peace. They decided to negotiate rather than fight, and determined to send a messenger to inform Dunmore. Elliott by this time was well in the confidence of the Shawnee, and it was clearly not in his interest that Lord Dunmore should destroy the towns on which his fur trade was based. Thus it was Matthew Elliott who agreed to carry a conciliatory message to Dunmore's advancing army. With a flag of truce, and accompanied by several chiefs, Elliott came out to meet Dunmore. He requested that Dunmore should send an interpreter to the Indian towns to start negotiations. Dunmore complied with this request, which led to a re-establishment of peace between the Americans and the Shawnee.[8] It was of short duration, however. By 1774 a decade of controversy between the American Colonies and Great Britain was reaching a climax; a climax which was to change the course of Elliott's life.

In the winter of 1774-75 an uneasy peace settled over the western country. Elliott spent the winter in his usual manner, and lived and traded in the Indian towns along the Scioto. While Boston was aflame with resistance, frontier trade followed its normal paths. In the years immediately preceding the Revolution, western Pennsylvania had been more occupied with the internal problems of the American colonies than with the birth of the Revolution. Two of the greatest colonies, Pennsylvania and Virginia, had been contending for control of the rich land around the forks of the Ohio. News of the great events at Lexington and Concord reached Pittsburgh in the first week of May 1775. In the middle of that month a meeting was held, and those present swore their devotion to the cause of the colonies. This was a severe blow to the Virginian leader in Fort Pitt, John Connolly, who was strongly pro-British. He made determined attempts to enlist Royalist supporters, but finally became so obnoxious to the settlers that he was seized and imprisoned in June 1775. Virginia, rather than viewing this as a blow against England, viewed it as a setback to her hopes in the Ohio Valley. She protested the action, and Connolly was soon released. Shortly after he fled from western Pennsylvania and joined Virginia governor Lord Dunmore on a British vessel off Virginia.[9]

Elliott was soon to discover that it was impossible to remain merely a trader – one also had to assume the role of patriot or loyalist. If Indian warfare was to be added to the British-colonial struggle, then the role of the fur traders would assume vast importance. Elliott and his fellow traders could sway the tribes toward peace or war. Since they were in a position to provide the link between the British and American governments and the Indian warriors, both sides were anxious to secure the allegiance of the traders. For the fur traders themselves – among whom

6

shrewdness was an occupational necessity – the decision was not an easy one. It was not simply a question of jumping patriotically to one side or the other, and in the first two years of war there were many who tried to keep two irons in the fire. Elliott himself made no immediate decision – it seems quite apparent that like many others he would have rather traded and profited while the armies fought – but he found that a position of neutrality was not easy to maintain during a revolution.

The Continental Congress of the American colonies fully realized the devastation that would come to its vast, exposed frontier if the British gained the allegiance of the Indian tribes, and it quickly adopted a policy designed to control the Indians. In July of 1775, the frontier was divided into three districts, each with its own commissioners for Indian affairs. The Middle District was centered at Fort Pitt, and dealt with the tribes of the Ohio Valley. The commissioners for this district were a distinguished group – Benjamin Franklin, Patrick Henry, and James Wilson. Richard Butler was appointed under them as the district Indian agent. The commissioners themselves were responsible to the committee of Congress for Indian affairs. The policy was simple in intent, but complicated in execution. It was the hope of Congress that the Indians could be persuaded to remain neutral. [10]

While Congress was creating an organization to deal with Indian affairs, Elliott was beginning his involvement in the revolutionary struggle. Elliott later claimed that in July 1775 he refused an American request for him to recruit Indians for the American cause. There is no proof that any such specific offer was made, or that Elliott turned it down, but there is proof that in spite of his later assertions Elliott was supplying information to the Americans in the summer of 1775. He informed the American authorities at Fort Pitt of his visit to the British post at Detroit (for trading purposes) and gave them information concerning the strength of the post, reporting that it had about twelve guns manned by seventy good soldiers. He also informed the committee that the British had already raised over four hundred militia. [11] Elliott's actions and sympathies during 1775-76 are not easy to disentangle, because although he always later asserted that he was a true loyalist from the beginning, he had not yet definitely committed himself. His primary interest was still trade rather than war.

At this time Elliott was engaged in the fur trade in partnership with Alexander Blaine of Carlisle. While Elliott journeyed into the wilderness, traded with the Indians, and brought the furs and skins back to Fort Pitt, Blaine organized the eastern branch of the trade. He arranged for the sale of the pelts in Philadelphia, and supplied Elliott with all the goods necessary for carrying on the trade. The partners owned a string of some fifty horses, and these were used both to bring the pelts out of the Indian country to Carlisle and to carry goods westward. They also employed several men to handle the horses, help in the Indian country, and assist in all the details of the peltry trade – sorting, packing, shipping, and so on.

By the summer of 1775 successful Indian trade was becoming a complicated matter because of an increasing difficulty in obtaining the necessary supplies. Blaine wrote to Elliott in August and told him of the various difficulties he was encountering. As yet he had been unable to secure lead, powder, traps, or "silver truck" – the small trinkets and decorations with which the Indians loved to ornament their persons. The lead and powder was of course being taken for the Revolutionary army, and traps were unobtainable as the blacksmiths were all engaged in "making guns and all kinds of Warlike Instruments." The silver truck was unobtainable owing to a silver shortage. He had managed to obtain a supply of other trade goods – blankets, lace, ribbons, coats – from the efforts of his brother Ephraim in Philadelphia. Ephraim, who was to serve as Commissary General for the American army during most of the Revolution, had succeeded in obtaining the only part of a shipment of goods for the Indian trade that had not been taken by Congress. The Continental Congress was eager for goods as it had determined to hold treaties with the Indian tribes to keep them in peace and friendship with the American colonies. Blaine feared that no more goods would be sold until Congress had acquired what it wanted, and that even then goods would be obtainable only for cash. Yet, in spite of all this, Blaine urged Elliott to send the horses as soon as possible, as he would obtain all the necessary articles, including a supply of rum, by the fall.

Apart from recounting his problems in obtaining goods, Blaine also gave Elliott information on the state of the peltry market. On the whole he had been disappointed in his efforts to sell the peltries that Elliott had brought from the Indian country. Though he had spent ten days in Philadelphia, he had sold only the deer skins – at a price of 2/- per pound. The price for pelts had not been as satisfactory as Blaine had hoped. Alexander's brother Ephraim had been somewhat more successful. He had managed to sell all the furs; the racoon at 2/- and the beaver at 9/- per pound. Alexander Blaine was still hopeful of a rise in prices, and urged Elliott to send all the kid skins he could obtain, as he expected they would bring a good price in the fall. Blaine had decided to save money by investing in an indentured servant and sending him to Elliott. He had obtained "a good Scolar" with three years to serve for a price of £15. Blaine considered this a good investment, for it would cost that to pay the wages of a hired hand for nine months. He emphasized to Elliott that the servant had been "well educated," and requested that "youl please spare him a little at first." This is not the last indication that Elliott could be a hard taskmaster.[12]

In the fall of 1775, as the tribes gathered at Fort Pitt for a treaty with the Continental Congress, Elliott went about his normal business. He spent this first winter of the war living peacefully on the distant banks of the Scioto. That October the Shawnees, Wyandots, Munsees, and Senecas (to the number of about four hundred) made an agreement with Congress at Fort Pitt. Although there was disagreement at the conference between the Iroquois and the Delaware, the chiefs stated that they would remain neutral. Indeed, this first winter of the war was a quiet one on the American frontier. The frontiersmen went about their business free from attack. Elliott left for the Shawnee towns early in the fall, and for a time was incapacitated by a serious illness. [13] He was undoubtedly not made any happier in October 1775 when Ephraim Blaine wrote from Fort Pitt and told him that some of his horses had been requisitioned for the purpose of bringing flour for the Indian treaty, and had been injured. Ephraim said he would have to hire other horses to bring an assortment of goods that had been collected by Alexander Blaine from Carlisle to Fort Pitt. Elliott was requested to send horses from the Shawnee towns in five or six weeks to collect these supplies. [14] While world-shaking events were occurring in Philadelphia, and the colonies were completing their estrangement from England, trade along the Ohio continued in its normal paths. As the year of Revolution passed into the year of Independence, Elliott was buried deep in the country of the Shawnee.

In February of 1776, Alexander Blaine wrote to Elliott and questioned him concerning his plans for the spring. There were rumors of a great campaign against the British post of Detroit, and if Elliott were going to be home in time Blaine intended to take steps to hire out their horses for the expedition. [15] As it turned out neither Elliott's early return nor the campaign materialized, and the Elliott-Blaine horses were dedicated to more prosaic tasks.

It was not until June 1776 that Elliott finally came out of the Indian country to Fort Pitt, and he returned with a very successful haul of peltry. When they were finally sold in Philadelphia at the end of June they brought the partnership a profit of practically £800. Prices had risen since the previous summer. The 4,941 pounds of fall skins sent by Elliott sold at 2/9 a pound, and the 702-1/2 pounds of summer skins at 3/9. Beaver now brought 15/- rather than the 9/- of the previous summer.[16] Elliott had reason to congratulate himself on his operations during this first winter of the war.

Yet Elliott could not retain immunity from the events going on around him. Ideally, he may have liked the idea of trading and taking advantage of the war to increase his profits, but as a friend of the Shawnee he was in a key diplomatic position. The Indian situation was becoming critical by the summer of 1776. Throughout the first half of the year the Continental Congress had endeavored to pursue a policy of peace in regard to the Indians; if the tribes could be persuaded to remain neutral the frontier would be safe from the horrors of Indian warfare. It was through Fort Pitt that the Americans attempted to negotiate with the Ohio Valley Indians who threatened the Virginia and Pennsylvania frontiers. Richard Butler, the Indian agent for the Middle District, was replaced by George Morgan in April 1776. Morgan, as a member of the famous fur trading house of Baynton, Wharton, and Morgan, had been one of the most prominent fur traders of the Ohio Valley in the years preceding the Revolution. Morgan arrived in Pittsburgh at the end of April, and spent the spring and early summer in an attempt to urge a policy of peace among the Indians and to summon them for another council at Fort Pitt. Morgan made several attempts to persuade the Shawnee to negotiate with the Americans. After sending trader William Wilson to urge them not to visit the British at Detroit but to come into Fort Pitt for a treaty with the Americans, Morgan himself visited the Shawnee towns in June. Though the Shawnee promised to attend the treaty if possible, Morgan could obtain no definite commitment. Morgan then returned to Fort Pitt in July, reported to the Indian commissioners, and in August visited Philadelphia to discuss the state of affairs with the Continental Congress. [17]

For the frontiersmen, the summer of 1776 was an anxious time. They knew that the British were meeting with the various Indian tribes at Detroit in an effort to persuade them to fight on the British side, and that the Americans were most anxious to persuade the Indians to pledge neutrality. As a result, yet another messenger was sent into the Ohio country to invite the tribes to a treaty – on this occasion Matthew Elliott, who had recently returned from the Shawnee towns. At the beginning of August Elliott was sent as special emissary to the Shawnees and Delawares. His task was to invite them to a treaty at Fort Pitt. [18] For the rest of his life Elliott kept this whole episode a deep secret. In later years, after he had joined the British, he frequently asserted that he had refused to aid the Americans from the very beginning of the Revolution.

Elliott left Fort Pitt early in August, carried a message to American agent William Wilson at the Delaware town of Goschochking (in what is now eastern Ohio at the junction of the Tuscarawas and Wolhonding Rivers), and then hurried on to the Shawnee towns on the Scioto. There, where he was so well-known, he called the chiefs together, and delivered the American request for the presence of the Shawnee at a treaty at Fort Pitt. The Americans wanted the Indians to come in as soon as possible. The turmoil in the Ohio country became quite obvious in the middle of the negotiations when Elliott's position became precarious owing to the arrival of an unfriendly band of Mingoes,

11

Wyandots, and Caughnewagas. A young Indian warned Elliott that this party was about to seize and possibly kill him. Elliott spent most of the night hidden outside the town, and just before daylight took refuge in a cornfield where he passed most of the next day. That night he returned in secret to one of the Shawnee dwellings, and eventually was told that he could appear openly as the Mingoes had said they would not harm him. After all this, Elliott still could not obtain a definite answer from the Shawnee. They told him that the decision regarding an American treaty was to be left to the Wyandots. Elliott then returned east, and arrived at Goschochking on August 23. There he heard more bad news; a message had arrived saying that the Wyandots would soon be going to visit the British at Detroit. Elliott pressed on east, and on August 31 was able to report all he had learned to the commissioners at Fort Pitt. He told them that he thought Indian war was inevitable, and that if the Indians did attend a council, they would come in great numbers with the intention of destroying Fort Pitt and the adjoining village. He also reported that a general confederacy was being formed among the Indians, and that this confederacy was preparing for war. He had no gleam of hope for the American commissioners. [19]

Elliott's dire warning produced considerable alarm among the Indian commissioners at Fort Pitt. On the same day that Elliott reported, they sent his information to the Congressional Committee for Indian Affairs, and stated that it justified putting the frontier into a state of defense. They feared a treaty would at best only delay Indian war. The committee did not wait for a reply from Congress. They immediately sent letters to the state authorities of Pennsylvania and Virginia, and to the Committees of Safety in the western counties, warning them that there was an acute danger of Indian war. [20]

Though Elliott's warnings of Indian war proved correct in the following year, his forebodings concerning the treaty at Fort Pitt turned out to be unjustified. Though the British tried to prevent it, Six Nations, Delawares, Munsees, Mohicans, and Shawnees, assembled at Fort Pitt in October to the number of nearly 650, giving assurances of their desire to preserve peace with the United States. The treaty did succeed in giving the United States a temporary calm, but the peace was illusory. The Shawnees and the Wyandots were soon to join the British in active warfare, and even by the time of the treaty, outbreaks were beginning along the Virginia and Pennsylvania frontiers.[21] The following year was to bring general warfare.

Up to this point in the Revolution Elliott had made every effort to continue his trading activities, a task that had become increasingly difficult. He knew that Indian war could not be long delayed, and that such a war would be ruinous to trade. Moreover, he was undergoing new pressures in the summer and fall of 1776. In the summer, Congress asked Elliott for his Indian goods (blankets and general supplies) for the use of the army. The Indian commissioners at Fort Pitt also made this request. Elliott refused, and claimed that he had promised to supply the Indians with the goods then in his possession.[22] As a general Indian war became more likely, this course of action infuriated the American frontiersmen. Yet, in the fall of 1776, Elliott pressed on with his trading activities in spite of the increased frontier tension. His determination was not unconnected with the prevailing price for pelts. At the end of September Alexander Blaine wrote to tell him that the price for skins was now very high, and that he was most optimistic about future prospects. He told Elliott that his brother Ephraim expected to become the victualler for the troops raised from Pennsylvania, and he urged Elliott not to be too forward in selling any of their goods, as he thought there would soon be a good market for them.[23] Elliott and Blaine were not averse to selling flour, liquor, and other goods in addition to pelts, as long as there was a good profit to be made.

By October, Elliott's friends had full knowledge of his intention to venture again into the Indian country, and Ephraim Blaine warned him that neither his goods nor his person would be safe at such a time. Reports of murders were arriving regularly from down the Ohio.[24] All this had no effect on Elliott. By the middle of October, he was ready to set off west. On this occasion he was not leaving with the best wishes of the Americans at Fort Pitt. His object was to trade goods wanted by the colonists to Indians who were already beginning the border skirmishing preparatory to full scale warfare. Elliott was fully aware of the opposition this move would arouse. He wrote to Alexander

Blaine: "I am greatly blamed for going to the [Shawnee] Towns but I am in Hopes there is no danger for me for I am to be escorted by a party of the Shawanese down and up." It was not Elliott's safety that the colonists were worried about. They feared that the Indians with whom Elliott was trading would soon be ravaging the American frontier. "I am sorry the Publick makes so free with my character," wrote Elliott, "but as I am convinced you know me too well and that all these assertions will not prejudice you against me." After Elliott had arrived in the Indian country, trader William Wilson gave him more information on the frontiersmen: "it is the opinion of maney people here that you are not for the good of the Contrey – Mr. Morgan has expressed Sum disgust at you, the Reason I have not yet Learned." Wilson himself was able to console Elliott, as well as show an understanding of his motives, with the time-honored sentiment that "if sum of those had the same opertunity of helping themselves they would." Wilson had no doubts concerning Elliott's willingness to risk both the dangers of the Ohio country and the animosity of his countrymen – he had heard that skins were now bringing 3/- and 4/- and he intended to follow Elliott if he could find the goods with which to trade.[25]

This trip was a fateful one for Elliott. In later years he consistently maintained to the British authorities in Canada that he left Fort Pitt in the fall of 1776 with the intention of going to Detroit to join the British. He was backed in this by the statement of the British Indian agent and loyalist Alexander McKee, who swore that Elliott had told him before he left Fort Pitt that he intended to go within the British lines.[26] These statements conflict sharply with those made by Elliott when he left Fort Pitt that fall. It is true of course that Elliott was unlikely to announce to all and sundry that he was leaving to join the British, but the circumstances were such that if he did intend to join the British he did a remarkably clever job of dissimulation. Certainly there is no hint in his correspondence at the time or by any of his friends that he intended to join the British. In the letter he wrote to his partner Alexander Blaine just before he left for the Shawnee towns he stated that he expected to distribute his trade goods and gather his pelts quickly, and that if this materialized he would be back by Christmas. He wanted his

14

partner to meet him at Pittsburgh to collect the skins and take them east for sale. He also wanted Blaine to send one of their hired hands to the Shawnee towns to assist him in the return to Pittsburgh. This last request was particularly subtle if, as he later stated, Elliott intended all along to join the British at Detroit. There is no doubt that Blaine acted upon it, since one of their hands wrote to Elliott at the Shawnee towns by the end of January to tell him that he was ready to come down to the towns if conditions were satisfactory. Moreover, Elliott informed Blaine that he had left twenty-six horses at Pittsburgh in addition to twelve horse-loads of deer skins in Joseph Speers's cellar. If Elliott was deserting his partner by fleeing to the British, it was hardly likely that he would leave a string of twenty-six horses in Pittsburgh.[27]

Before he left Pittsburgh, Elliott had to obtain permission from the Indian agent George Morgan. This was given him on October 14, though he did not actually leave Fort Pitt until November.[28] He slowly made his way westward with his string of pack horses, a Negro slave, an indentured servant, and "a female Indian companion." The escort of Shawnee had apparently not materialized. By November 12 Elliott had reached the Tuscarawas River, in what is now eastern Ohio, where the towns of the Moravian missionaries and their Indian converts were located. From this time on, Elliott's life was strangely entwined with that of these missionaries, who had moved to this region in the years before the American Revolution. The Christian Indians were surprised to see Elliott, "a man known for many years as a trader," since the Ohio traders were fleeing the territory before the threat of Indian war. When he told them that he was on his way to the Shawnee towns along the Scioto, they warned him of the great danger he might face from the Sandusky Indians. There were both Wyandots and Mingoes (the Ohio Seneca) at Sandusky, and all of them were ready for war. Elliott ignored the warnings of the Moravians. He assured Blaine before he left Fort Pitt that in his opinion the present danger was not great, although he was "almost certain there will be hell to pay next Spring." Elliott pressed on westward, but shortly after he left the Moravian towns, a party of hostile Senecas from Sandusky arrived, picked up Elliott's tracks, and followed him westward.

15

They caught up with him, seized his goods and the Negro, and bound Elliott and his servant. Two of the Christian Indians followed the Sandusky Indians in an effort to save Elliott's life. They arrived when Elliott and his servant were already bound, but managed to persuade the warriors to spare their lives and free them.[29]

Elliott now made every effort to recover his lost property. As the Indians had told Elliott that they were acting under the orders of British in Detroit, it was quite obvious where he would have to go to find redress. Now practically destitute, Elliott went first to his friends at the Shawnee towns to spend the winter. By next spring he was ready to make his way to Detroit. Elliott's servant later swore that Elliott determined to do this to try and purchase goods on credit, and return to the Shawnee towns to recover his losses.[30] Like so many of the statements concerning Elliott, this seems no more than a half truth. If Elliott was looking for credit, he stood far more chance of getting it in Pittsburgh than in Detroit. Elliott undoubtedly went to Detroit to discover what chance there was of recovering his lost property. There also seems little reason to doubt that it was after he lost his property, not when he left Pittsburgh, that he decided to visit the British at Detroit.

Elliott's difficulties were not yet over. To his infinite shock his visit to Detroit resulted in his arrest as an American spy in March 1777. The trunk that was taken with him unfortunately contained not only letters from his partner, but also correspondence with George Morgan and William Wilson. Both of these men were known as American Indian agents (though fortunately for Elliott his own efforts on behalf of the Americans in 1775-76 remained a secret), and while these letters did not incriminate Elliott directly they at least produced suspicions of guilt by association. As a result Elliott returned to Pittsburgh by a long route: Governor Henry Hamilton of Detroit decided to send him to Quebec on suspicion of being a spy. At Quebec it was decided that there was no real proof that Elliott was a spy, and he was given permission to return to Pittsburgh on parole. This journey was accomplished by sea. Elliott travelled through New York and Philadelphia, both in the possession of the British at that time. Such were the problems of communication that it was not until early in 1778 that Elliot returned to Pittsburgh, almost a year after he was arrested in Detroit as a spy.[31] He was to have little rest, for within a few weeks he was to flee the American colonies.

Frontier conditions had radically altered since Elliott had last seen Fort Pitt. Indian war was now a reality. The isolated Indian attacks which were already troubling the frontiersmen when Elliott left for the Shawnee towns had turned into a full scale offensive by the summer of 1777. Encouraged and provisioned by Governor Henry Hamilton at Detroit, the Indians had swept out of the Ohio country from the late spring of that year to attack the frontiers of Virginia and Pennsylvania. During the summer the raids took a heavy toll. Organized American resistance was not great, though at the beginning of June 1777 Brigadier General Edward Hand arrived at Fort Pitt to take charge of the post on behalf of the Continental Congress. Congress had sent a general but they could not spare the troops; they were to follow later. Meanwhile, Indian devastations increased. During the summer Hand hoped to carry the war into the Indian country, but repeated difficulties and delays reached a climax in October when the campaign had to be abandoned when the expected Virginian forces did not arrive. However, Hand was determined to attempt a sortie, and his opportunity came in the winter of 1777-78. News arrived that the British had established a magazine at the mouth of the Cuyahoga (near the site of modern Cleveland), and that in the spring they would use it to supply the Indians for raids against the American frontier. Hand decided to lead a mounted expedition to destroy it. The expedition was a complete failure. It brought not tragedy but pathos. Hand led a party of some five hundred men through the flooded land south of the Cuyahoga. Conditions were so bad that the party became completely disheartened, and determined to return without accomplishing the object of the mission. Before returning, the troops attacked two small parties of Indians. Total casualties: four squaws, one old man, and one boy killed, and two squaws taken prisoner. On his return, Hand requested Congress to replace him. His request was granted in the spring of 1778.[32]

17

While the army floundered, the Indian department labored under suspicion. George Morgan, the Indian agent at Fort Pitt, had quite obviously failed in his task of keeping the Indians in a state of neutrality. His failure was so disastrous, although through no real fault of his own, that doubt was now thrown on his integrity as well as his competence. By October 1777 the accusations had reached such a point that Morgan was confined to his house in Pittsburgh while his conduct underwent investigation. At the same time grave suspicion was thrown upon John Campbell, Alexander McKee, and Simon Girty for their pro-British sympathies. All three of these men were well known to Elliott. The Congressional investigation into the conduct of Morgan resulted in his absolute acquital in March 1778, but in the meantime Elliott had returned to Fort Pitt. His subsequent actions stem quite naturally from the events of the previous year and a half.[33]

Elliott was undoubtedly most anxious to obtain retribution for his losses to the Seneca. He certainly could not do this from Fort Pitt, though it might be possible from Detroit. If instead of being arrested as a spy, Elliott could be welcomed into the British camp as a loyalist fleeing from the rebels, he could perhaps obtain retribution for losses inflicted by Indians acting under British encouragement. Moreover, the American position on the frontier looked precarious at the time Elliott returned to Fort Pitt. The previous summer had brought Indian raids all along the border, and while there had been a temporary cessation during the winter months, it seemed quite obvious that the attacks would be renewed in the spring. The possibility of trading westward out of Fort Pitt was hardly an attractive one. Certainly Hand's "Squaw Campaign" did nothing to enhance the hopes of firm and effective American military action. Elliott in fact had very little to gain by remaining in Pittsburgh. The war hardly seemed to hold out much hope for the Americans. Elliott had come home by way of New York and Philadelphia, and had found both of them in British hands. The American troops had spent the winter in the bitter cold of Valley Forge. The American colonies offered little to a realist and a man with an eye for gain. Elliott was to stay for only a few weeks.

On this occasion Elliott had the opportunity to travel in

influential pro-British company. Alexander McKee, who had been under suspicion since the beginning of the Revolution as a pro-British sympathizer, was perhaps the most influential Tory at Fort Pitt. In the years before the Revolution he had served not only as a trader among the Shawnee but also as a British Indian agent. He was a good friend to Elliott, and as a man of wide influence among the Indians would be a valuable addition to the British cause. At this time McKee was living in his house below Pittsburgh on the Ohio, at the mouth of Chartier's Creek (the spot now known as McKee's Rocks). When Elliott returned to Pittsburgh, McKee's problems were reaching a climax. McKee had been implicated in pro-British activities at the time of the accusations against Morgan in the fall of 1777, and his position had become increasingly precarious during the winter. In February General Hand ordered him to present himself to the American Congress at York (where it was meeting after having been driven from Philadelphia) because of the suspicions of his pro-British activity. McKee claimed that he was too ill to go, and remained at his home outside Pittsburgh.[34]

Elliott visited McKee when he returned to Pittsburgh, and probably warned him that there was a plot to have him ambushed on the way to York. Be that as it may, both McKee and Elliott decided to flee from Pittsburgh. With them went Simon Girty, Robert Surphit (who was McKee's cousin), and a man by the name of Higgins. The most famous of this group was Simon Girty, who became a byword for infamy among the American frontiersmen, though he remained a subordinate of McKee and Elliott for the rest of his days. Girty was born in Pennsylvania in 1741 of an Irish father and an English mother. He had been bred to violence. When Simon was a boy his father was killed by an Indian in a drunken brawl. His mother married again, and during the French and Indian War the whole family (including Simon's four brothers) was captured by the Indians. In the presence of his wife, and probably in the presence of the sons, Girty's stepfather was burned at the stake. For three years Simon was held by the Senecas. He became expert in their language, and in the years before the Revolution often served as an interpreter at Fort Pitt. Two of his brothers – James and George – became interpreters for the Shawnee and the

Delaware respectively; the tribes in which they had been held during their captivity. Simon, however, was always the most famous of the brothers. Simon Girty, Matthew Elliott, and Alexander McKee became names of abhorrence to the American frontiersmen in the following years.[35]

The flight of the Tories was made on the night of March 28, 1778, from McKee's home below Pittsburgh. General Hand moved too slowly to arrest them – the troops he sent arrived the next morning. Elliott and his friends were already moving west into the Ohio country. The American authorities conjectured that Elliott must have brought dispatches to McKee from Canada. Although it is not impossible, there is no proof of it, and it seems unlikely that the British would have entrusted dispatches to a suspected spy. Both McKee and Elliott had ample reason to leave Pittsburgh, and it seems likely that they fled before McKee could be placed under closer confinement.[36]

Elliott never again lived in Pittsburgh. The life he had built both there and at Carlisle came to an end. Some of his pre-Revolutionary friends accompanied him in his flight, others were later to join him within the British lines, but many never again entered his life. The Elliott-Blaine partnership came to an abrupt end, and there is no record that any settlement was ever made between the two associates. In Elliott's subsequent claims to the British for reimbursement for his losses, the existence of Blaine was conveniently forgotten. It is difficult to give a precise estimate of Elliott's economic status at the time he left Fort Pitt, for not only is it impossible to separate his assets from those of Alexander Blaine, but there is also good reason to suppose that Elliott inflated his losses in his later claims. The final claim that Elliott submitted to the British (in August 1787) was that he had lost personal property and real estate to the value of £1332 Sterling as a result of his flight from Pittsburgh. This consisted of merchandise valued at £900, sixty-two horses, and one Negro slave. The merchandise, the slave, and fifteen of the horses he claimed were lost when he was captured by the Seneca Indians in the fall of 1776. An earlier claim, which was not granted, gave a far larger estimate of the value of the goods he lost as a result of the attack by the Indians in 1776. In this earlier claim he estimated his losses from this attack at £1475.

16.0. He asserted that twenty horses were lost rather than fifteen, and filed claim for the loss of an indentured servant not mentioned in his final claim. He also gave a far more detailed breakdown of his losses than in his final claim. If this detailed breakdown is compared with a still earlier list, further discrepancies appear. Before leaving Pittsburgh in the fall of 1776, Elliott was obliged to submit a list of the goods he was taking to George Morgan, the American Indian agent. The quantities on this list are less on practically every count than on the later claims made to the British government. One is left with the choice that he was either underestimating to the Americans the goods that he intended to trade to the Indians (for fear of their confiscation), or that he was later overestimating the goods he had possessed in order to receive a larger reimbursement from the British government. It is quite possible he was doing both.[37]

Yet, whatever doubts surround the individual figures submitted by Elliott, it is clear from his claims that he lost most of his assets when attacked by the Indians in November 1776. He claimed comparatively little for any assets he might have had in Pittsburgh or further east. This being the case, Elliott, apart from any altruistic loyalist feelings he might have had, certainly had good reason to flee to the side that might restore to him the assets he lost in 1776. It quickly became apparent that he was prepared to throw himself wholeheartedly into the struggle against his old friends on the frontier as the small party of loyalists passed beyond the frontiers of Pennsylvania and into the Indian country in the spring of 1778.

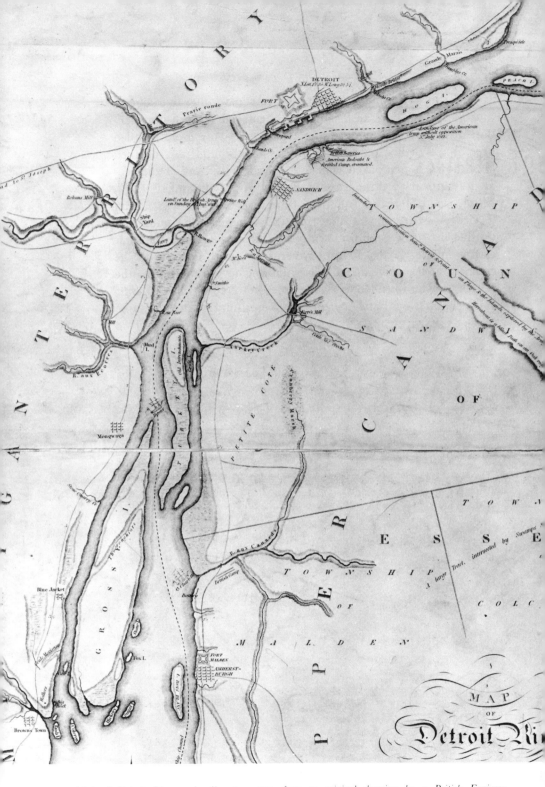

Map of Detroit River and adjacent country, from an original drawing by a British Engineer. H. S. Tanner Sc. Philadelphia: Published by John Melish, Chestnut Street, 2 August 1813. Entered as the Acts Directs.

Chapter 2

WAR ON THE FRONTIER

After leaving Pittsburgh, Elliott and his friends quickly showed their allegiance to the British. They travelled along familiar
paths to Goschochking, the main town of the Delawares on the
Tuscarawas. There they met in council with the leaders of the
Delawares, and told them that the Americans were determined
to kill all the Indians. They then urged the warriors to rise up
in an all-out war. The Delawares had kept the peace in the early
days of the Revolution, and now the efforts of chief Captain
Pipe to obtain agreement with the loyalists were temporarily
thwarted by White Eyes, who desired peace. White Eyes also
sent a message to the Shawnee, and asked that tribe to ignore
these pro British arguments.[1]

On April 4, 1778, McKee wrote from Goschochking to the
British commandant at Detroit, Henry Hamilton, and told him
what had happened. He also gave information on American
plans. No expedition of any consequence could be undertaken
by the Virginians from Fort Pitt through the Delaware villages
toward Detroit, wrote McKee, but he had heard that there was
to be an attempt against the Indian villages on French Creek
(Rivière au Boeuf). Hamilton was delighted to send news of
these events to Guy Carleton, the British commander in chief,
and he praised McKee. He told Carleton that McKee was a
man of good character, had great influence with the Shawnee,
was well acquainted with the country, and probably would be
able to give further useful information. He was far less complimentary about Elliott, and commented that Elliott was "the
young man who was last summer sent down from this place
a Prisoner – This last person [Elliott] I am informed has been
at New York since he left Quebec, and probably finding the

23

Change in affairs unfavorable to the Rebels, has Slipped away to make his peace here.''[2]

Though Hamilton sent a man to conduct the loyalists safely through the Indian country to Detroit, they did not immediately come into the British post. They first went to visit their old friends the Shawnee along the Scioto, and had arrived in Detroit by June. This town of over two thousand inhabitants was the post from which the British controlled the Indians of the Ohio country and directed their onslaughts against the American frontier. Henry Hamilton had taken up his position as lieutenant-governor at Detroit in November 1775, and from the early summer of 1777 he had considerable success in gaining the allegiance of the Indian tribes.[3] McKee and Elliott had joined the side which was already successfully waging Indian warfare.

Elliott's position in the summer of 1778 was not entirely a happy one. He had severed his bonds with Pennsylvania, and in June the Supreme Executive Council of that commonwealth included "Matthew Elliott, Indian trader," in the list of those who would be considered guilty of high treason if they did not deliver themselves up by August.[4] In addition, his position in Detroit left much to be desired. Hamilton did not trust him, and though McKee and Simon Girty rapidly acquired positions in the British Indian department – McKee as a captain and Girty as an interpreter – Elliott was not employed by the British until later in the year. Eventually he was given the opportunity to play a minor role in a major British project.

While Elliott and his friends had been making their way through the wilderness to Detroit, the Americans had at last made an effective move in the war in the west. The infant settlement of Kentucky, at this time still part of Virginia, was dissatisfied with the extent of the protection it had been given against the marauding Indians. To ease the pressure, the famous Kentucky leader George Rogers Clark obtained permission from Virginia to lead an expedition into the Illinois country. In June 1778, with a small army of some 175 men from southwestern Pennsylvania, Kentucky, and the Holston settlement of Tennessee, Clark left the falls of the Ohio (present-day Louisville) and advanced into the Illinois country. On July 4 he took Kaskaskia, and later in the same month Cahokia and Vincennes yielded peacefully to the Americans.

This threat to British control over the Indians and to their trade in the Illinois country could not be ignored by the British. Hamilton and his superiors determined on an expedition against the Americans in that area. At the beginning of October Hamilton led his force from Detroit on a most arduous journey to Vincennes. As much as possible the force travelled by water; down the Detroit River, into Lake Erie, up the Maumee, a back-breaking portage to the Wabash, and then down the Wabash to Vincennes. Hamilton left Detroit on October 7, and finally reached Vincennes on December 17. The post surrendered without resistance. On this expedition Elliott was first able to bring himself to the notice of the British authorities by serving as a scout. While Hamilton occupied Vincennes from the latter part of October 1778 to February 1779, Elliott led Indian parties eastward to discover the intentions of the Americans. His first effort to move into the Ohio country with a party of Shawnees and Miamis resulted in failure. The Indians who were with him thought they had been observed and would go no further than the falls of the Ohio. As a result, Elliott was back in Vincennes by January 15. He remained there only a few days. On January 20 he requested permission to proceed to the Shawnee towns, and then eastward toward Fort Pitt in an effort to secure information regarding American movements which he had failed to obtain on his earlier attempt. Possibly the opportunity to visit his old friends and haunts in the Shawnee towns partially explained his eagerness for service in the Ohio country. Whatever Elliott's reasons it was a wise move, for Hamilton's control of Vincennes was to be of short duration.

On February 6 George Rogers Clark left Kaskaskia and travelled overland across the cold, flooded ground to attack Vincennes. After a brief siege from February 22 to 24, Hamilton surrendered. Elliott was fortunate enough to be still absent; he was also fortunate that he did not return while Clark was besieging the fort. One group of Indians that did return from a scouting expedition to the falls of the Ohio at this time was surprised by Clark's men outside Vincennes. The five Indians who were captured were tomahawked in full view of the defenders of the fort. Elliot was perhaps lucky in another way, for Hamilton's capture, journey to Virginia, and eventual repatriation to Quebec meant that he was effectively removed from the Detroit theater of the war. Hamilton's opinion of Elliott, colored by his first belief that Elliott was an American spy, was not a good one, and his removal was to Elliott's advantage. From 1779 on, Elliott appeared regularly on the pay lists of the British Indian department at Detroit, beginning at the rate of 16/- New York currency per day.[5]

It was not until the fall of 1779 that Elliott had his first real chance to distinguish himself, and he did it in a manner which caused great anger on the American frontier. One of the main problems for the American frontier defenders was an acute shortage of powder. To bring powder over the mountains from the east by pack-horse was a long and difficult process, and the frontiersmen had been in dire straits from a shortage of powder at the start of extensive Indian raids in the spring of 1777. At that time relief had been afforded by the efforts of Captain George Gibson and Lieutenant William Linn and their men, who had been commissioned by Virginia to journey down the Ohio and Mississippi to bring powder from the Spanish at New Orleans. Their safe return in the spring of 1777 added twelve thousand pounds of powder to the frontier stock at a time when it was desperately needed. It was from this supply that George Rogers Clark drew when he advanced into the Illinois country.

By the spring of 1778 the supply of powder in Fort Pitt was once again severely depleted, and Governor Patrick Henry of Virginia sent Captain David Rodgers to bring more powder to the besieged frontier. Arrangements had already been made for the purchase of the powder through Oliver Pollock in New Orleans, and he had sent it up the river to St. Louis. Unfortunately, this was not realized, and Rodgers, who set out in June 1778, went all the way to New Orleans before going to St. Louis. Owing to this long and difficult journey, the Rodgers party of some forty men did not leave St. Louis until the summer of 1779, at which time they advanced cautiously up the Ohio on two flatboats. The voyage was tedious and uneventful until the party reached the mouth of the Licking River, near the site of the modern Cincinnati. Here an opportunity for glory as well as labor presented itself; as they sailed close to the Kentucky

shore, the Rodgers men noticed several Indian canoes crossing
the river further upstream. The Indians showed no sign that they
had noticed the American party, and Rodgers decided to bring
off a coup by landing his force and annihilating these frontier
raiders. The boats nosed into the mouth of the Licking. Rodgers'
party landed, and plunged into the dense woods to surprise the
small Indian force.

The woods were not as they seemed, for Matthew Elliott and
Simon and George Girty, along with a large force of Shawnees,
Wyandots, and Mingoes were hidden in the undergrowth. As the
Americans advanced, a sudden volley of gunfire ended their
hopes of an easy victory. Some fell, and the rest fled through
the woods, pursued by the Indians; about thirteen finally got
away, some of these wounded. Rodgers, severely wounded, was
left behind in the forest. He was never seen again. The total
number of men in frontier engagements was never large, but in
sparsely settled frontier settlements a loss of thirty or forty men
was bitterly felt. That night Elliott and his Indians crossed over
to the north bank of the Ohio; the scalps hanging from the belts
of the warriors measured the extent of their success. From this
time forward Major Arent De Peyster, who had just assumed
command at Detroit, showed a marked respect for the abilities
of Matthew Elliott.[6]

The winter of 1779-80 was a bitter one – the most severe of
the war – and snow lay deep in the Northwest. To the American
frontiersmen these conditions brought definite advantages. While
the Indians hunted or sheltered in their lodges they did not carry
death and destruction across the Ohio. The period of calm was
needed, for the coming of spring would bring renewed warfare to
the frontiers of Pennsylvania and Kentucky. The Kentuckians
did not wait to be destroyed. They had learned that scattered
settlements could not withstand the Indian onslaught. To provide
more effectively for defense, the frontiersmen constructed forts
throughout the Kentucky region. When danger threatened, the
Kentuckians flocked into the forts (or "stations"), and presented
a concerted defense to the Indians and their British leaders.

At the beginning of March, 1780, Elliott and the Girtys,
along with Alexander McKee, returned to Detroit from the Shawnee country where they had spent much of the winter. They

reported that the Americans "had quite surrounded the Indian
Hunting ground of Kintuck, by having built small forts at 2
days journey from each other."[7] The efficacy of this method of
American resistance was soon to be tested by the British, for
with the coming of spring they again led the Indians on the war-
path. In May they decided to send an expedition from Detroit
to capture the fort established by George Rogers Clark at the
falls of the Ohio.

De Peyster, the commandant at Detroit, gave the leadership
of this expedition to Captain Henry Bird, an old army officer
who had previously been stationed at Sandusky. On May 25,
1780, Bird led a force of some one hundred and fifty whites and
several hundred Indians southward out of Detroit. The Indians
were led by McKee, Elliott, and Girty. The force took several
cannon, and on its way south attracted more Indian warriors
until they numbered nearly one thousand. This was a formidable
force to throw against the scattered Kentucky settlements.

The army followed a familiar route; down the Detroit River,
up the Maumee, across to the Great Miami, and down the Great
Miami to the Ohio. Here the British party ran into difficulties,
for McKee and Elliott were unable to persuade the Indians
to go down the Ohio to attack Fort Nelson at the falls of the
Ohio. Rather than attack that fortified garrison, the Indians
wanted to go up the Licking River into Kentucky to attack some
of the more vulnerable Kentucky settlements. The warriors prevailed, and Bird was forced to change his plans. His force advanced up the Licking to its forks, and then went overland to
attack Ruddell's Station. The Indians alone would have had
considerable difficulty breaching the defenses of the station, but
when Bird came up with his cannon the Kentuckians had no
hope. The station surrendered on Bird's promise that the settlers
would be preserved from abuse by the Indians. In return they
gave up their slaves and other property. Bird's promise was not
completely fulfilled, for the Indians could not be restrained from
slaughtering some of the defenders when the fort yielded. The
officers of the Indian Department eventually restored order, and
some three hundred Kentuckians were taken prisoner.

After this success the British force moved on to attack nearby
Martin's Station, and here too the Americans were obliged to

surrender. There was little bloodshed, although the movable property was of course all taken. Bird had hoped to proceed through the Kentucky country destroying the settlements, but he was now running short of provisions. The Indians had hindered him by slaughtering the cattle at both the captured stations, and by roaming the country destroying what they could find. Bird was now unable to replace the provisions his force had consumed, and he was forced to retire. The damage to infant Kentucky had been great, but it would have been far greater if the Indians could have been organized to support the general plan. Elliott, McKee, and the Girtys did what they could – it had been a credit to the Indian department that so many Indian warriors had been raised for this campaign – but as so often happened, the Indians could not maintain the same discipline as regular troops. They had their own traditions of warfare, and though the Indian department could influence them it could not suddenly transform them into grenadiers. In the next thirty years the military and the Indian department were frequently to clash over the nature of the control exercised over the Indians by the Indian department.[8]

Bird now brought his force back to Detroit. It had been a successful campaign. The British harassed Kentucky, captured over three hundred prisoners, and carried off large quantities of movable property and a number of slaves. Bird's party was welcomed back to Detroit on August 4, 1780. The campaign had also been a satisfactory one for Elliott. He had shown his usual efficiency, and had also begun to build his personal fortune for the period after the war. It was on Bird's expedition that Elliott began to obtain the nucleus of the slave force that was to help increase his prosperity. The methods of Elliott and of the Indian department in general were well-revealed by the story of Mrs. Agnes La Force, one of the prisoners brought back from Kentucky by the Bird expedition.

Mrs. La Force had been taken prisoner along with thirteen of her slaves, and she appealed for them to be given back to her. The situation was brought to the attention of the commander in chief, Sir Frederick Haldimand, who ordered the commandant at Detroit, Arent De Peyster, to discover who had the slaves and reclaim them. The former task proved simple, the latter was im-

His later comment was that Elliott "acted the complete hypocrite." possible. De Peyster had to inform Haldimand that though the owners were known the slaves could not be produced. The fact was that the slaves had been divided among the members of the Indian department and the Indians. Simon Girty and Alexander McKee had one each, and Elliott had two. The rest had been divided among the other Indian officers and the Indians. De Peyster was not prepared to risk alienating the Indian officers by ordering the restoration of the slaves, and there is no record that Haldimand was ever able to secure action in the affair. The subject was apparently allowed to fade into oblivion, and the Indian officers retained these slaves and added others from further raids.[9]

The Bird expedition was Elliott's main activity in 1780, apart from the regular routine of the Indian department, and the coming of winter again brought comparative peace to the hard-pressed American frontier. It did not last. Early in the following spring of 1781, Elliott, acting under the De Peyster's orders, again led a marauding party of warriors down into Kentucky. If Elliott had ever been captured it is unlikely that he would have lived to tell the tale, but once again his undoubted skill in the wilderness served him well, and he escaped unscathed after marauding and burning his way through the Kentucky country.[10]

After serving with the Shawnee throughout the spring of 1781, Elliott turned to his main task of the year. He was ordered to remove the Christian Indians from their homes and farms along the Tuscarawas River, and take them westward to be placed more closely under British control. These were the Christian Indians who had saved Elliott's life in November 1776.

The Moravian missionaries and their Indian converts were in an unfortunate position in the Revolution. In the years before the outbreak of that conflict the Moravians, by dint of great efforts, had gradually built up a prosperous and peace-loving settlement along the banks of the Tuscarawas River in what is now eastern Ohio. There were several hundred converts occupying three villages, scattered for a distance of some fourteen miles along the banks of the river. The main village was Gnadenhütten

30

(about seven miles south of the present New Philadelphia), six miles south was Salem, and to the north of Gnadenhütten was Schönbrunn. Here the Moravians and their converts fared well, cultivating extensive fields and owning large herds of cattle.[11] Their downfall came because of their strategic position between the American frontier of western Pennsylvania and the British outpost of Detroit, and from their injudicious participation in the conflict. The Moravians were in an excellent position to gather information about the moves of the respective forces, and the Moravian leaders David Zeisberger and John Heckewelder favored the American cause. For some time before 1781 they had been supplying information concerning British movements to the Americans at Fort Pitt. This practice brought disaster in the summer of 1781, for De Peyster decided that the Moravians were a menace and sent a force under Matthew Elliott to remove them. In August, after Elliott and his party had reached the Tuscarawas River, Zeisberger proved there was good reason for De Peyster's action. Zeisberger wrote to Colonel Daniel Brodhead, the American commander of Fort Pitt, and warned him that a party of some two hundred and fifty Indians led by Matthew Elliott were approaching the American settlements, and that they would probably advance on Wheeling, Fort McIntosh, and Fort Pitt. As a result of this warning a party of Indians which had been sent forward to attack the American settlements was repulsed. They did, however, get wind of the fact that Zeisberger had warned the Americans, and this news only increased the British determination to remove the Moravians.[12]

Elliott first arrived at the village of Salem on August 10. At that point he had with him a few loyalists and French-Canadians, and about one hundred and forty Indians, mostly Delawares and Wyandots with some Shawnees, Ottawas, and Chippewas. This Indian force soon increased to some three hundred men. On his first evening at Salem Elliott dined with missionary John Heckewelder and his family. He apparently went out of his way to be pleasant to Heckewelder. He spoke of the good work of the Moravians, of their services to him before the war, and he presented Heckewelder's child "with sundry articles of merchandize for clothing." Heckewelder was unmoved by all this. His later comment was that Elliott "acted the complete hypocrite."

Heckewelder was puzzled that Elliott had brought two horse-loads of goods with him on the expedition, and asked Elliott's servant, Michael Herbert, the reason. Herbert replied that Elliott had said while they were packing the two horseloads "that with these goods he expected to make the greatest *speck* he ever had made; that the Moravian Indians had at each of their towns great stocks of horned cattle, which when once distressed by the warriors, he could purchase of them for a song; (a few dollars per head,) while he would get forty dollars a head at Detroit." Heckewelder also mentioned that Elliott had "for a trifle bought up every new pair of shoes belonging to us." Elliott, though he was engaged in warfare of one kind or another for the rest of his life, was at heart a trader. He was never happier than when making a "speck." It was perhaps as well that during the four weeks he spent among the Christian Indians he was never seen outside his tent without a dirk in his hand.[13]

The British force passed only a day at Salem before moving up the river to Gnadenhütten. They then set up camp at the west end of the village. David Zeisberger entertained Elliott, and agreed with Heckewelder that he behaved in a friendly manner; also like Heckewelder he concluded that this was merely guile. The principal chiefs who accompanied Elliott were the Wyandot Half-King (Pomoacan) from Sandusky, and Pipe with his Delawares. On August 20 the first move was taken to effect the business in hand. On that day the Half-King spoke to the missionaries and their Indians, telling them that they should come and settle nearer to him at Sandusky. On the following day the Moravians replied. They said that they would give a definite answer sometime before next spring. At this point the matter might have come to an end – the Half-King appeared satisfied – but Elliott, who at the conference was half-hidden behind Captain Pipe and the Delawares, urged them to press the Half-King to question this answer. The Half-King therefore expressed his dissatisfaction, and several days later on August 25 spoke again to the Christian Indians and said they had set too distant a time to give an answer to the British. Once again the missionaries and their charges resisted the pressure. They told their oppressors that they had to have time to harvest their crops, otherwise their women and children would perish. The Half-King again appeared satisfied, but Elliott, who was of course under orders, would not and could not yield to the requests of the Christians. For a time Elliott even lost ground when the Wyandots took the British flag from his camp and burned it. But Elliott was not one to display weakness. He told the Wyandots: "If you go home without these ministers, expect no favor from your English father; if you fail to seize them, I will leave this place and report your faithlessness. Then you will not have a father, but a powerful enemy at Detroit; and the English and the Americans both against you, what awaits your tribes but destruction?"[14]

By the end of the month the villages were in a considerable state of tension. The British Indians were not certain what to do; some advocated killing the missionaries and dispersing the Christian Indians. In Gnadenhütten some of the converts were weakening, and some advised the British Indians to seize the missionaries, for then the Christian Indians would all follow. Conditions worsened. Zeisberger later complained that "We also had to see harlotry openly carried on and could do nothing to prevent it." On September 1 the missionaries from Salem and Schönbrunn were ordered to come to Gnadenhütten; some came from each place, leaving one or two behind. From this time on the Indians became increasingly wild, either by accident or design. They now began to shoot the cattle and pigs, and these dead carcasses strewn about the village added to the horror of the missionaries' situation. On September 3 the missionaries were seized and stripped of their clothing, and their possessions were plundered. Over the heads of the missionaries rang out the fearful "Death Hallow" and it seemed their last moment had come. They were now led to Elliott's tent. He said he wanted to show them compassion, and said it was not intended that they should be treated in this manner, though there were express orders from the commandant in Detroit to bring them away by force if they resisted. Zeisberger did not believe him, and thought Elliott responsible for the whole affair. Elliott now provided the missionaries with old clothes so that they were not entirely naked. The tragedy came perilously close to farce when Brother David was given Sister Senseman's old nightgown to put on; Sister Senseman, who was in Schönbrunn with her newborn son, had little time to worry about her plundered possessions.

The missionaries were then removed to the huts of the Wyandots. They were not bound, but were given no covering. Their own Indians brought them some blankets. Next, the missionaries and their wives who were left in Salem and Schönbrunn were rousted out. Mrs. Senseman was forced to travel through the pouring rain with her baby born three days before. On September 6 the missionaries were freed, but only after they had agreed to the demand for removal. By September 11, the missionaries and Indians were all gathered at Gnadenhütten – some four hundred of them – and Elliott directed their removal. The Christians left their corn growing in the fields, and were forced to desert the settlement they had laboriously built up. The party descended the Tuscarawas to the Walhonding, arriving at the Delaware town of Goschochking on September 14. Here Elliott left the party; the missionaries and their Indians were now in the tender charge of the Half-King and his warriors. To Heckewelder this was an improvement. He later wrote in his diary: "We thanked God, when Elliott departed from us."[15]

This whole episode is a black one on Elliott's record, particularly when one considers that he owed his life to these same Christian Indians. The general gloom is not relieved by Elliott's version of the transaction which was sent by McKee to De Peyster. After leaving the Moravians at Goschochking Elliott made his way back to the upper Shawnee villages on the Mad River (in the present Logan County, Ohio). He arrived there on September 25, and reported that the party he accompanied to the Moravian towns "were detained there a long time and amused by the Moravians who were secretely sending Intelligence and endeavouring to bring the Enemy upon them to cut them off." Though the Wyandots planned to place the Christian Indians at Upper Sandusky, McKee advised against this, saying that they would be still too near to the Americans. He also advised that the six white teachers should be removed from the Indians. Zeisberger, he suspected, was employed by the enemy. McKee's comment on him, which was presumably given to McKee by Elliott, was that he "appears to be a Jesuitical old man;" a good Scotch-Irish insult.[16]

While Elliott was journeying to meet McKee in the Shawnee

villages, the Moravians were being driven from Goschochking up the Walhonding River and across to the Sandusky. Finally the Wyandots left them on the Upper Sandusky River, about sixty miles from its mouth, and here the Moravians settled down for a bitter, hungry winter. At the beginning of October De Peyster sent word to McKee that he wanted the Moravian missionaries to be brought into Detroit. The Christian Indians would have to stay with the Wyandots, as they would consume too many provisions at the British post. Elliott journeyed from the upper Shawnee towns to Sandusky to tell the Wyandots and Delawares at Sandusky of De Peyster's orders. The Indians responded quickly, and by October 18 Elliott was back to McKee with the news that Captain Pipe would take in the Moravian teachers without delay. On October 25 the Moravians left their new home and proceeded to Detroit by way of the Maumee.[17]

In the meantime Elliott was busily engaged on another task – that of distributing supplies to the Indians. The British had decided that rather than have the Indians come to Detroit and spend days obtaining supplies and consuming as many other provisions as possible, it would be better to send the supplies away from that main British center. The rapids of the Maumee had been chosen as a suitable distribution point, and, in particular, that spot known as Roche de Bout, about a mile above the present Waterville, Lucas County, Ohio. The missionaries and their escorts, who had cut overland from the Sandusky, arrived at the rapids of the Maumee toward the end of October. There they waited for Elliott, who was coming from the Shawnee villages to distribute supplies among the Indians. These supplies had been brought from Detroit by boat, via the Detroit River, Lake Erie, Maumee route which was to be the source of supply for the Indians of the region during the next fifteen years. The missionaries remained several days on the Maumee, waiting to see Elliott. From him they obtained more supplies, and on October 31, leaving behind them Captain Pipe – who was too drunk to continue – they set off for Detroit. At Detroit the missionaries were interrogated by De Peyster, but he could find no proof against them and sent them back to the Sandusky River for the winter. [18]

In early spring the Moravians were once again summoned to Detroit to be examined in regard to their communications with the Americans. Though they had undoubtedly supplied information, De Peyster found insufficient proof to proceed against them. Yet, he would not allow them to return permanently to Sandusky. They were obliged to settle on the Huron (Clinton) River, near what is now Mt. Clemens, Michigan. There they were to stay from the spring of 1782 until 1786, and there they built the village of New Gnadenhütten. Many of the Christian Indians did not go to this new home on the Huron; in the early spring of 1782 nearly one hundred of the converts returned to their villages on the Tuscarawas to obtain corn. In March 1782 they were fallen on by a body of Pennsylavia militia under the command of Colonel David Williamson and massacred. The work begun by Elliott the previous summer had been completed, and the Americans had added the final horror to the saga of the Christian Indians.[19] On the Huron River the Moravian missionaries began their work once again. This was not the last they were to see of Matthew Elliott, but from now on it was to be under more auspicious circumstances.

The Revolution was now entering its last phase. Cornwallis had surrendered at Yorktown in October 1781, and the British were moving toward an acknowledgment of American independence. Yet on the western frontier the war swayed brutally backward and forward. The victories won by Clark in the Illinois country in 1778 and 1779 had since been dissipated by the Americans, who had failed to follow up their early successes, and as the war entered its last summer of active fighting the pendulum swung clearly to the side of the British. Elliott was active in both of the decisive engagements in the western country in this last summer of the war.

In the spring of 1782 the Americans determined to deliver a firm blow to the Indian villages before the raiding parties could once again devastate the American frontier. Ambitiously, they decided to enter the heart of the Indian country to attack the Wyandot and Delaware villages on the Sandusky River. The force that was raised to accomplish this task was one of Pennsylvania militia under the command of Colonel William Crawford, a man of fifty, a friend of Washington, and a well-known leader of frontier Pennsylvania. He had under him nearly five hundred men, chiefly Scotch-Irish. The Americans assembled early that May at Mingo Bottom (now Mingo Junction, Jefferson County, Ohio) on the Ohio River. They set out on May 25, moving northwest from the river into the Indian country. They headed with painful slowness toward the object they had in mind; it was to take them ten days to reach the Sandusky. They were not unobserved. Indian scouts followed their advance and carried the news not only to the Sandusky villages but also to De Peyster in Detroit. He immediately dispatched a force of Butler's Rangers under the command of Captain William Caldwell, another Pennsylvania Irishman, to aid the Indians in resisting the American attack. He sent Matthew Elliott to command the Indians. It was not until June 3 that Crawford's party reached the first Wyandot village on the upper reaches of the Sandusky. It was deserted. Crawford, now apprehensive of Indian preparedness, advised withdrawal, but he was overruled by a majority of his officers who decided to march one more day toward the main Wyandot town. It was one day too many.[20]

On the next morning, when trader John Leeth learned that Crawford's army was only fifteen miles away, he set out from Upper Sandusky toward Lake Erie. After travelling about three miles he met Matthew Elliott "hurrying forward with all possible speed." About twelve miles further on he met the main British force also advancing rapidly to meet the Americans. Elliott arrived at the gathering place of the Indians in the full regalia of a British captain, and was greeted enthusiastically by the assembled warriors. As the American scouts advanced they were met by the outlying forces of the Indians; in the van were Pipe's Delawares, accompanied by Wingenund and by Simon Girty. Before Crawford could move into position in response to the warnings of his scouts, the Indians quickly took possession of a strategic grove. The first encounter occurred about noon on June 4, and general fighting flared up during the afternoon. The Americans quickly drove the Delawares from the grove, and moved into it as the main British force advanced. The Wyandots, previously held back by Elliott, were now sent into the struggle, and were joined by the main Caldwell force. Elliott sent the Delawares to flank the Americans to the right and assault them in the rear. This maneuver was successfully accomplished, and the Americans were hard pressed. The firing continued until nightfall brought a temporary cessation of hostilities with the Americans still in possession of the grove.[21]

At daybreak the following morning the firing resumed, and continued in a somewhat sporadic manner for most of the day. By the afternoon the British position looked particularly strong, for some one hundred and forty Shawnees joined the British forces. The Americans were now in a most precarious situation. To the north were a strong force of British and Wyandots, and on the south (the American escape route) the Delawares were now reinforced by the Shawnees who took up a position on the Delaware west. The Americans decided to wait for the coming of darkness, and then to attempt to escape to the south. They were amazingly lucky. Though an attempt at a silent retreat quickly degenerated into something approaching a rout, the Indians did not immediately pursue the retreating force nor did they warn the main British force of what was occurring. As a result the main pursuit did not take place until June 6. It was led by Lieutenant John Turney of the Rangers since Captain Caldwell was wounded early in the action. Although the Indians kept up the pursuit until the seventh, the Americans managed to fight them off. The American losses were heavy for a frontier engagement, but not as heavy as they might have been, considering the annihilation the American force had faced. The total of dead eventually reached about seventy, although at first only some three hundred Americans returned to Mingo Bottom. The rest were scattered in the retreat, and found their way back to American settlements in ones and twos during the following days. British losses were light. The figures reported by Turney to De Peyster were one ranger and four Indians killed. Turney bestowed praise on the conduct of the British forces: "too much cannot be said in praise of the Officers, the Men and the Indians no people could behave better, Capt. Elliot and Lt. Clinch in particular Signalized themselves." No blame was placed on Elliott for the Indian mistake in allowing the Americans to break out of their position. He had fought bravely himself, and had handled his Indians skilfully for most of the battle. Unfortunately for the British, the Indians were not always predictable.[22]

This striking British success was marred by a tragic episode. The seventy Americans who died did not all die on the field of battle, for the precipitate American retreat left many stragglers to fall into the hands of the Indians. It was only three months since the Christian Indians had been mercilessly slaughtered along the Tuscarawas, and the Sandusky warriors had not forgotten. Among the Americans separated from the main body was the commander, Colonel William Crawford. For two days he attempted to evade the pursuing Indians, but eventually was captured. The Delawares determined to torture the American commander, and their two war chiefs – Captain Pipe and Wingenund – took him to the Delaware town of Tymochetee, on Tymochetee Creek (near the present village of Crawford, Wyandot County, Ohio). On June 11 the Delawares prepared to exact revenge for the Moravian massacre. To Elliott's credit he made an attempt to intercede on Crawford's behalf, but it was to no avail; Elliott and Simon Girty found themselves witnesses to Crawford's death. The American commander was tied to the stake in such a manner that he could move around it. After his ears were cut from his head, he was tortured by fire for a space of some four hours, chiefly by the women and children of the Delaware. Simon Girty is reputed to have replied with a jest when Crawford asked the British interpreter to shoot him. Finally Crawford died; a burnt sacrifice to the bitterness of this frontier conflict. The Delawares had avenged the death of their Christian compatriots on the Tuscarawas.

The British did all they could to prevent a repetition of the Crawford affair, though this was in truth the price that would have to be paid if the Indians were to be used as allies. Indians had their traditions of warfare just as the whites had theirs. De Peyster wrote from Detroit to tell commander-in-chief Haldimand that he had sent messages throughout the Indian country threatening to withdraw the British troops if the Indians did not desist from such "horrid cruelty." Haldimand declared his abhorrence at such events, and asked De Peyster to convey this to the Indians. Yet all this could not assuage the shock which traversed the whole American frontier. For once it was not a nameless trooper, but a friend of Washington and a military commander who had died at the hands of the Indians. These events of the Revolution – the frontier raids, the massacre of the Christian Indians, the torture of prisoners – could not be erased by the ending of the war. This western aspect of the conflict was not to end until the remnants of the northwestern tribes straggled on to the lands beyond the Mississippi. The Revolution in the west was not merely a case of America fighting for her independence from England, it was also one brief episode in the continuous struggle between frontiersman and Indian for the land of the Mississippi Valley.[23]

After the death of Crawford, Elliott returned again to his beloved Shawnee towns. He travelled west to Wapatomica on the Mad River (near the present Zanesfield, Logan County, Ohio). Considerable agitation had been caused there by an American prisoner's report that Cornwallis had surrendered. Elliott, who was never hampered by too great a respect for the truth, told the Shawnee that the American had lied. In the following weeks Elliott served at Wapatomica, although he was absent briefly to carry a message to the Sandusky River. By the middle of July the British were ready for another campaign. Caldwell, who had recovered from his wounds, led a British and Indian force eastward with the intention of attacking Fort Henry at Wheeling. While he was advancing eastward, news reached him from Wapatomica that George Rogers Clark was marching north to exact revenge for the Sandusky affair. Although this information subsequently turned out to be false, Caldwell and his force now returned to Wapatomica and prepared to meet Clark's supposed invasion. McKee and Elliott used all their influence to gather the Indians together.[24]

The British now marched over thirty miles south from Wapatomica to Piqua, which had been abandoned by the Shawnee at the time of Clark's expedition in 1780. The Indians who gathered here to resist Clark soon amounted to a large force of some eleven hundred warriors; Shawnees, Delawares, Wyandots, Munsees, Mingoes, Ottawas, and Chippewas were all represented. McKee reported that he had three hundred more within a day's march. However, most of these Indians dispersed when it became obvious that the reports of Clark's advance were false. The British were left with some three hundred Wyandots, Ottawas, and Chippewas.

At this point Caldwell decided to advance into Kentucky, attack some of the forts, and gain prisoners and information. The advance began early in August, and the British followed approximately the same route as that used by Captain Henry Bird in 1780, when both McKee and Elliott had been among the party. They entered Kentucky along the Licking River, and the force of two or three hundred Indians and thirty rangers advanced on Bryant's Station, which was located about five miles northeast of Lexington. The station was surrounded on the night of August 15, and the British began their attack at dawn on the following day. The siege continued until the morning of August 17, but unlike the Bird expedition of 1780 Caldwell's force had no cannon, and the fort proved too strong for the British force. Caldwell decided to withdraw after inflicting considerable damage on the crops and livestock around the fort.

Up to this time the expedition had been a fairly routine affair with few casualties on either side, but all this was changed when the Kentuckians decided to pursue the British force with some one hundred and eighty men under Colonel John Todd. Although a hundred Indians had left Caldwell's force, he still had an army of nearly two hundred and fifty men. The Kentuckians confidently pressed after the retreating British force and overtook it on the Licking River on August 19. The Kentuckians charged, faltered, and met disaster at this battle of Blue Licks. The rangers and Indians rushed from cover to drive the Kentuckians from the field. Nearly seventy of the Americans were killed, including the commander, Colonel John Todd. It was a harsh blow to the sparsely-settled area, and the battle of Blue Licks was long remembered in Kentucky.

The British suffered only slight losses; ten Indians and one member of the Indian department killed. Elliott once again had been in a victorious campaign. By 1782 he had removed the stigma of being a suspected spy, and had managed to be present at all the major British western victories of the Revolution. As the British force withdrew to Wapatomica, Elliott was now sent by McKee to carry news of the victory to De Peyster. He found that the war in the west was nearing its end, for De Peyster had already received orders to act only on the defensive owing to the prospects of peace. The order had reached De Peyster too

41

late for him to stop Caldwell advancing into Kentucky, and seventy Kentuckians had died.[25]

For the remainder of the war the British stayed on the defensive in the Northwest while they awaited the news of a definitive peace. The Americans were less inclined to declare a truce, particularly after the disaster of Blue Licks, and in November 1782 George Rogers Clark led another expedition into the Indian country. On this occasion the Americans attacked Chillicothe, the main Shawnee town on the Great Miami, at the site of the present Piqua, Ohio. Though the Indians withdrew, Clark and his men destroyed the town and other villages in the vicinity. They also destroyed the British supplies at Lorimer's store, which was located at the portage at the head of the Great Miami. Throughout the winter the British encouraged the Indians to act on the defensive, and Elliott was mainly employed in transferring British stores. In the following spring he was also employed in bringing into Detroit the prisoners who had been redeemed from the Indians.[26]

Though the British were acting on the presumption that the war was coming to an end, it was not until the summer of 1783 that definite steps were taken to pacify the Northwest. The American Congress officially proclaimed the end of hostilities with Great Britain on April 11, 1783, and on May 5 Ephraim Douglass was ordered to carry news of the peace to the Indians of the Northwest. Douglass had traded out of Fort Pitt in the years before the Revolution, and had been a friend of Elliott's until the war had sent them their separate ways. Douglass finally left Fort Pitt on June 7, 1783, and travelled west to the Sandusky River. He hoped that the Indians would come to him there from the Maumee and from Detroit, and that he would deliver the American message to them in formal council. In this way he could tell the Indians that the British had ceded all the land to the Mississippi. The Indians proved reluctant to answer the summons of the Americans, and on June 17 Douglass wrote to Elliott asking him to use his influence to persuade the Shawnee to come to listen to the American message. As Elliott was already employed in telling the Indians to go into Detroit to hear the British version of the peace, he did nothing to further Douglass's plans. Instead he forwarded the letter to De Peyster in

Detroit. De Peyster decided that Elliott should be used to conduct Douglass to Detroit so that the American would not have the opportunity to "do mischief among the Indians."

As Douglass was achieving nothing at Sandusky he decided to go to Detroit at the end of June. On June 30 he set out in company with Captain Pipe of the Delawares. They travelled twenty miles on the first day, and after going another twenty on July 1 they met Elliott, who had been sent by De Peyster to bring them into Detroit. He immediately conducted them to the Maumee, some seven miles distant, and there they spent the night. On the following day they proceeded to Detroit, where they arrived on July 4. At Detroit Douglass still could not accomplish the objects of his mission, since De Peyster would not allow him to meet in separate council with the Indians. On July 7, the American messenger left Detroit and proceeded to the British post at Niagara, where once again he was unable to obtain permission to speak in council to the Indians. He returned east, thwarted in his attempt to establish direct contact with the tribes of the Northwest.[27]

The lack of British cooperation with Douglass boded ill for American pacification of the Northwest in the years following the war. If the British were determined to retain influence in the area ceded to the United States, then it seemed inevitable that there would be further difficulties. The main problem was that in ceding all the land of the Northwest to the United States the British had ignored their Indian allies. Though the Indians had played an important part in the war, they played no part in the peace. Territorial sovereignty over their lands had been forfeited to the Americans, who could be expected to press relentlessly for actual possession. A clash between the Indians and the Americans was inevitable, and Great Britain had the task of deciding the role she would play in this struggle. That England resolved to retain influence in the Northwest was fortunate for Elliott. He could now expect further opportunities to display his talents.

43

Chapter 3

LANDOWNER AND FUR TRADER

Matthew Elliott, like many other loyalists, had to rebuild his life in the years after the Revolution He had more advantages than many, for his talents as a leader of the Indians again became necessary when the first shock of the American victory had been absorbed. In the meantime he concentrated on recouping his losses, for his official employment under the British temporarily came to an end, and he was thrown on to his own resources. As might have been expected, he turned once again to the life of an Indian trader, and also attempted to ground his fortunes firmly on the possession of land. He proved more successful as a landowner than as an Indian trader in the years after 1783.

By the close of the Revolution Elliott had already acquired certain assets. Not only had he obtained possession of a number of Negro slaves on his raids into Kentucky, he had also contrived to engage in some trade on his own account during the war. As a result he had acquired some of the cattle he needed to stock a farm. As yet, however, he had little land, though he had taken possession of a town lot down by the Detroit River.[1] The opportunity to possess more land came from the efforts of a group of loyalists who had been connected with the Indians during the Revolution. After negotiations during the winter of 1783-84, the Wyandots and Ottawas in the Detroit vicinity agreed to cede a tract of land some seven miles square at the mouth of the Detroit River to a group of Indian officers and interpreters who had served with them in the war. The land was located at one of the choicest spots in Upper Canada, some eighteen miles below Detroit on the opposite bank of the river and commanding the approach from Lake Erie into the Detroit

River. It was ideally situated on the line of communication between Detroit and the Maumee valley, and gave access to the whole country stretching down to the Ohio and along the Wabash. Among the nine men given this land by the Indians were Matthew Elliott, Alexander McKee, Henry Bird, William Caldwell, and Simon Girty. Bird, Caldwell, McKee and Elliott were to do most toward developing the grant, and of these Elliott was to prove by far the most successful, both in acquiring the most desirable location and in farming it.[2]

The immediate problem for the grantees was to secure some acknowledgment from the British government of their right to take possession of land obtained privately from the Indians. In the years after the Revolution the British government in Canada developed its land policy in a somewhat piecemeal manner. In July and August of 1783 General Haldimand had been given the power to make land grants to British subjects of the former American colonies who wished to remain on British soil; reduced field officers could obtain a maximum of one thousand acres and ex-captains seven hundred acres. By the close of the 1780's these possible allocations were increased to five and three thousand acres respectively. Though the British government was willing to listen to applications for land, it was definitely opposed to the idea of individuals obtaining lands from the Indians. Yet in this respect as in others during this period, the officers of the Indian Department proved to be a law unto themselves. Haldimand ordered a cessation of Indian grants to private individuals in the Detroit region, but the lieutenant-governor of Detroit, Jehu Hay, reported to him in July 1784 that almost all the land on both sides of the strait between Lakes Erie and Huron, was already claimed, and that much of it had already been settled on and improved.[3]

Faced by a *fait accompli* Haldimand decided to allow the Indian officers to take possession of the land they had obtained at the mouth of the Detroit River. When the officers agreed to a division of land in August 1784, Elliott received very favorable treatment. Though the initial allocation was small, Elliott was able to expand considerably in the following years. Bird, Caldwell, McKee, and Elliott were each allotted "six acres in front" on the Detroit River directly opposite to Bois Blanc Island. They actually occupied some ten acres each. Elliott was given the allocation nearest to Lake Erie, and his home and farm were soon to become a landmark for those approaching Detroit via the Lake Erie-Detroit River route. There in the years after 1783 Elliott gradually built up the farm and home that became a show-place in Upper Canada before they were ravaged by the Kentuckians in the War of 1812. This settlement of Indian officers was the beginning of Amherstburg, and in the 1790's was to be the location of the British post of Fort Malden.[4]

For several years the Indian officers were left quietly in possession of their new settlement along the Detroit River, but by the close of the decade the whole question of their right to be there, and of the extent of land they could occupy, once again concerned the British government. In July 1788 the area later to become Upper Canada was divided into four districts – Lunenburg, Mecklenburg, Nassau, and Hesse. Hesse, which included the settlements around Detroit, stretched from Long Point to Lake St. Clair. The government established Land Boards in each district to consider applications for grants. Any large application had to be forwarded with the recommendation of the Board to the Governor and Council for decision. Elliott and the Indian officers could now look forward to a favorable hearing, for among those named to the Land Board of Hesse was Elliott's old friend Alexander McKee.[5]

McKee rapidly took advantage of his new position when in June of 1789 the government ordered the establishment of the township of George Town immediately opposite to Bois Blanc Island. The Hesse Land Board was informed by McKee that this area had been ceded by the Indians to the Indian officers, that General Haldimand had approved this transaction in 1784, and that Bird, Caldwell, McKee, and Elliott occupied the whole frontage facing the island of Bois Blanc. As a result of McKee's presentation of the officers' case, the Land Board decided that the establishment of George Town could not proceed, and referred the whole matter back to Lord Dorchester. In September Dorchester wrote to the Land Board to say that though he understood the area opposite to Bois Blanc was the best possible site for a town in the district, they could establish the town at some other spot on the strait should circumstances make it impossible to use the preferred site.[6]

Throughout the 1780's there had been no precise definition of the extent of the claims of the Indian officers, though they had been given a definite right to frontage on the strait and it was known that the original grant from the Indians had extended some seven miles inland. In July 1790, the Land Board brought up the problem that if the grants or claims of the Indian officers opposite to Bois Blanc extended inland for seven miles they would encroach on the cultivated farms of other settlers. Elliott informed the Board that although the original deed to the Indian officers did specify seven miles inland, none of the claimants under the deed wished to oust settlers already established in the area. In fact, as the major part of the land claimed by Elliott and his associates had not yet been settled by any others, he was quite willing to grant away any small portion that was settled, if this would enable him to establish a more solid claim to what remained. As yet, though the Indian officers had been given the right to the frontage on the strait, they had not been given any official government grant of the major part of the cession from the Indians. Elliott's statement to the Board helped his claims considerably, for the Board decided to start its survey of the lands along Lake Erie at the eastern edge of the unoccupied lands of the original Indian grant to the officers. This gave at least a tacit acknowledgment of their right to the Indian grant. Moreover, in December 1790, the Land Committee of the Council at Quebec said they would not insist on the laying-out of George Town opposite to the island of Bois Blanc, as the right of the Indian officers to the area had been shown.[7]

The development which finally allowed Elliott to settle his claims beyond all power of dispute came in August 1791, when the Province of Quebec was divided into Upper and Lower Canada. Under this royal order in council, any settlers who held lands under the authority of the former Quebec government were to surrender their land certificates to the government of Upper Canada and receive a fresh grant in exchange. Upper Canada was now to have its own Lieutenant-Governor, Executive Council, Legislative Council, and Legislative Assembly. At first the administrative center was Newark, but in 1797 the town of

York (Toronto), which had been laid out in 1794, became the permanent seat of the government. Elliott's claim for three thousand acres as an ex-Revolutionary captain was entered only two weeks after the establishment of the new government. He asked that this acreage should be granted to him in addition to the lands he already held that fronted on Bois Blanc, since that land was a gift from the Indians and not an official government grant. By this time Elliott had fenced or in some way improved some eight hundred acres, and was rapidly becoming the most important farmer in the Detroit district. He did not directly engage in farming himself, but ran it as a plantation with a steward or overseer to supervise his Negro and Indian slaves.[8]

In May 1792, the Land Board of Hesse took up Elliott's claim for three thousand acres, and though they immediately granted him two hundred, they sent his claim for the remainder to the first lieutenant-governor of Upper Canada, John Graves Simcoe. The lieutenant-governor was in the meantime concerned with the problem of establishing a town at the western end of Lake Erie. Although the previous attempt to establish a town opposite to the island of Bois Blanc had been blocked by the prior claims of the Indian officers, the government of Upper Canada now went ahead and achieved a compromise between its desires for the organization of the area and the prior claims. In January 1793, the whole question was taken up in council by Simcoe, and William Caldwell appeared to present the case of the Indian officers. After hearing his argument, the council resolved that a new township, to be called Malden, would be created out of the land granted to the Indian officers in 1784, and that McKee, Elliott, and Caldwell would be the patentees of this township and could exercise the option of making up their quotas (three thousand acres) from land within its bounds. Any person who had settled under the authority of Lieutenant-Governor Hay of Detroit in the 1780's, and who had made improvements, was to be confirmed in possession to the extent of two hundred acres, but any new applicant for land in the township would have to obtain a recommendation from the patentees. McKee was designated principal patentee, and the only one who could act alone; Elliott and Caldwell could make joint recommendations. Within the township, land fronting on the strait just to the north of Bois Blanc was reserved for a government fort, and two-sevenths of the total land of the township would have to be reserved under Simcoe's proclamation of February 1792. This designated one-seventh of each township to be set aside for the support of a Protestant clergy, and one-seventh for the future disposition of the Crown.[9]

Elliott's position had now been immeasurably strengthened, and in July 1793 he received his grant of three thousand acres within the township of Malden. His home overlooking the Detroit River was now the center of a large plantation to which he had an indisputable right. In the following years Elliott was to add to this nucleus, and by the time of his death he owned over four thousand acres in the vicinity of Malden. Elliott certainly could not complain of the treatment he had received from the British government. The proceedings of 1793 established him as one of the most prominent landowners in Upper Canada, only fifteen years after he had been sent down from Detroit on suspicion of being an American spy, and only sixteen years after he had actually been working for the Americans.[10]

It was perhaps fortunate that Elliott succeeded in firmly establishing his prosperity on a land basis, since his endeavors in a field in which he was supposedly expert proved less successful in the years after the Revolution. Elliott once again became a fur trader when an uneasy peace returned to the Northwest. The winter of 1783-84 was particularly harsh – by March of 1784, the snow was still four feet deep in the vicinity of Detroit. Elliott, spent part of the winter in Detroit, and part in the Shawnee towns in the vicinity of the Mad River. In February he went by sleigh over the deep snow to visit the settlement of the Moravians on the Huron River north of Detroit. With the war over, Elliott reversed his attitude toward the Moravians, and in the following years repaid them to some extent for saving his life and gave reparation for his attitude toward them during the Revolution.[11]

In the summer of 1784, while establishing himself at the mouth of the Detroit River, Elliott obtained permission from Haldimand to trade out of Detroit, and was recommended to the good offices of Jehu Hay, lieutenant-governor of that post. By the summer of 1784, Great Britain had done nothing to relinquish her posts in the Northwest in accordance with the treaty of 1783. Afraid of Indian war, and desirous of retaining control over the Indians as well as over the fur trade south of the Great Lakes, England was prepared to risk the wrath of the American government. As American settlers began to push down the Ohio, and the American government began to acquire the lands to the northwest of that river, British traders still left Detroit and traded into the valley of the Maumee, and on to the upper reaches of the Wabash and the Great Miami. Elliott now spent his winters on the upper reaches of the Mad River, near the Shawnee town of Wapatomica. As he had done before the Revolution, Elliott went into partnership. His new partner was Captain William Caldwell, a man whose life up to then had been similar to Elliott's. He had been born in Ireland, settled in western Pennsylvania, and had been a loyalist in Butler's Rangers during the Revolution. Elliott and Caldwell had acted together in the defeat of Crawford in 1782, and in the spring of 1784 they were joined together in the land project at the mouth of the Detroit River. With the Americans thrusting across the Ohio and the Indians becoming increasingly warlike, the partners, like so many others in Detroit, were to find that trading presented many difficulties.[12]

In the period from 1784 to 1786, Elliott and Caldwell made an ambitious attempt to succeed in trade. Their center of operations was Detroit, but their trade had ramifications stretching east to the mouth of the Cuyahoga and to Pittsburgh, and south to the Shawnee towns in the Mad River-Great Miami region. They depended not only on the fur trade (though Elliott devoted most of his time to this aspect of their operations) but also dealt in other commodities in the Detroit market. The partners took particular advantage of the trade that developed between Pittsburgh and Detroit in the years after the Revolution. From the American viewpoint, Detroit was an illegally held post, but this did not prevent the Pittsburgh trading establishments from making advantageous trade connections with the Detroit firms. The key to the activities of Caldwell and Elliott was the Pittsburgh firm of David Duncan and William Wilson. The two firms entered into an agreement in 1784, and from that time Caldwell and Elliott depended on the Pittsburgh partners for supplies of flour, cattle, bacon and other provisions. These items were often scarce in the Detroit region, and Duncan and Wilson advanced a considerable amount of credit to their Detroit partners. Caldwell and Elliott sold provisions in the Detroit region, and also used the supplies for the purposes of trade among the Indians. Their main base east of Detroit was at the mouth of the Cuyahoga River (the site of the present Cleveland, Ohio). There the partners had a storehouse, and kept a fairly large supply of provisions. Matthew Elliott could best use his abilities, however, in the villages of the Shawnee, and Elliott spent his time between his home at the mouth of the Detroit River and trading expeditions along the Maumee River country, or to the Shawnee villages on the upper tributaries of the Great Miami River.[13] Elliott moreover did not confine his activities to trading, since from his strategic position in the Shawnee villages he was able to watch the growth of Indian resistance to American policy in the Old Northwest, and what was more important, was able to give them a British point of view. Elliott had fought the Americans in the Revolution. If they now advanced across the Ohio Valley, Elliott's life as an Indian trader would come to an end, since his trading activities were now inevitably entwined with political ideas.

American Indian policy in the years immediately after the Revolution was dominated by considerations of Indian support for the British during the Revolution, and by the American desire for the rich lands northwest of the Ohio. The frontiersmen had long since pushed into western Pennsylvania, and down the Ohio to Kentucky. They were now ready to settle the area south of the Great Lakes. As an old enemy of the Americans, and as a fur trader, Elliott had every reason to resist the American advance into the Northwest.

In the fall of 1783, Congress had decided that treaties would have to be signed with the Indian tribes of the Northwest. The Indians were to be told that the lands west to the Mississippi had been ceded by the British at the treaty of Paris in 1783. Although America would not compel the Indians to retire to the north of the Great Lakes, she would require the Indians to cede much of the modern state of Ohio. This would be reparation by the Indians for their hostility during the Revolution. In line with these ideas, the American Government dictated treaties to the Indians of the Northwest in the years between 1784 and 1786. In October 1784, at Fort Stanwix in New York, the Six Nations ceded all their nebulous claims to the land west of Pennsylvania. After the Fort Stanwix treaty the American commissioners travelled west, and in January 1785 met representatives of the Wyandots, Delawares, Ottawas, and Chippewas at Fort McIntosh in western Pennsylvania. Once again a treaty was dictated to the Indians, and these tribes were forced to yield all their lands except those in northwestern Ohio. They were to be enclosed within an area bounded by the Cuyahoga River on the east, a line across central Ohio on the south, the St. Mary's and the Maumee on the west, and Lake Erie on the north. Within the area yielded to the Americans were the Shawnee villages on the upper tributaries of the Great Miami, including those on the Mad River, where Elliott's operations were centered.

The Americans, however, knew quite well that they had yet to deal with the Shawnee, or with the tribes even further to the west along the Wabash. During the previous ten years the Shawnee had been a greatly-feared frontier tribe. Their activities in Dunmore's War and in the Revolution had convinced the American frontiersmen of their capabilities for resistance, and the Shawnee were now exceedingly dissatisfied at the cessions made at Fort Stanwix and Fort McIntosh. The Shawnee had never really stopped fighting at the close of the Revolution. The treaty of Paris in 1783 brought an end to none of their basic problems. The threat to their lands became greater as a result of the end of the Revolution and the British cessions. Thus the first summer after the war – that of 1784 – saw bands of Shawnee raiding the American frontier just as they had so often done before. Indians from the villages on the Mad River raided as far as the frontiers of Virginia in the fall of 1784, and Elliott once again saw American prisoners brought into the Indian villages. He was even given one of the American captives in the spring of 1785, but the threats of the Indian woman who claimed the American soon persuaded Elliott to relinquish his prize.[14]

After Fort McIntosh, the Americans were anxious to negotiate with the Indians further to the west, and in July and August of 1785, American commissioners sent messages asking the Indians to meet at the mouth of the Great Miami on the Ohio on October 1. The Indians were reluctant to come. They knew of the manner in which the treaties had been dictated at Fort Stanwix and at Fort McIntosh, and they had no desire to acknowledge the American right to all the land west to the Mississippi. Moreover, the British authorities in Canada had encouraged Indian resistance. As far back as September 1783, the British had informed the Indians in a general council at Sandusky that the Indians were still the sole proprietors of the land northwest of the Ohio River. The very fact that the British had not withdrawn from the Northwest posts encouraged the Indians to believe in the strength of the British and the weakness of the Americans. The Shawnee looked with distrust and emnity upon the Americans in the spring and summer of 1785, since the advance of the American farming frontier was incompatible with the Indian way of life. The Shawnee war chief Captain Johnny told the Americans in May 1785: "we can almost hear the noise of your axes felling our Trees and settling our Country," and he threatened that should the Americans cross the Ohio, "we shall take up a Rod and whip them back to your side of the Ohio."[15]

In spite of Indian resistance, plans for the treaty were continued, though it was soon apparent that it would be quite impossible to hold it at the beginning of October 1785. Moreover, the Wyandots, Ottawas, Chippewas, and Potawatomis refused to come. They said they had not yet had time to understand fully the events that had transpired at Fort Stanwix and Fort McIntosh, and did not want to hold a new treaty until the following spring at Detroit. At Detroit, of course, events would be under the eye of the British. The Shawnee reluctantly decided to attend the American treaty, and on January 14, 1786, some one hundred and fifty men and eighty women arrived at the mouth of the Great Miami from its upper reaches. When on the following day the commissioners asked the Shawnee why they had not come to negotiate with the Americans in 1784, they replied that the British had prevented them by stating that the Americans were going to cheat them. The treaty council echoed those of

1784 and 1785. The terms of the treaty were dictated to the Shawnees, and only one slight modification was allowed when the Indians said they were being left with no land on which to live or raise corn. The dictation of terms brought a stirring reply from Chief Kekewepellethe:

> To-day you demand hostages till your prisoners are returned. You next say you will divide the lands. I now tell you it is not the custom of the Shawnese to give hostages, our words are to be believed, when we say a thing we stand to it, we are Shawnese – and as to the lands, God gave us this country, we do not understand measuring out the lands, it is all ours.

The American commissioners held firm, and Kekewepellethe was obliged to beat an ignominious retreat. The treaty at the mouth of the Great Miami (Fort Finney) designated the lands upon which the Shawnee could live. In essence, they ceded everything east of the Great Miami to the United States, including the Shawnee towns on the Mad River. The cession meant that the Shawnee were giving up the main area in which they lived; all of what is now southern and eastern Ohio had been obtained by the United States in the years from 1784 to 1786.[16]

Although the Shawnee had been browbeaten into signing the treaty at the mouth of the Great Miami, the inevitable reaction came with great rapidity; that it was so soon in coming was owing to the presence of Matthew Elliott in the Shawnee towns on the upper reaches of the Great Miami. Elliott's part in encouraging Indian resistance, even though Great Britain and the United States were now at peace, became increasingly obvious at this time. When an American emissary journeyed through the Shawnee towns in March and April 1786, he discovered that Elliott held frequent councils with the Indians, "and that the Shawanese in general were not well disposed to the Americans." This was an understatement. The result of Elliott's councils became apparent at the end of April. On April 29, 1786, the Shawnee informed the British in Canada of their dissatisfaction with the treaty they had signed with the Americans. They said they had signed the treaty because the Americans had assured them that it contained the best possible terms, but that on returning to their towns they had discovered the true meaning of the terms granted to them. They left no doubt as to the source of their enlightenment:

> We inform you how they have deceived us, by telling us
> the King of Great Britain had ceded the whole country
> to them, and we were not sensible of the error we have
> committed till our friend Elliot explained it to us.

As a result of Shawnee disillusionment with their treatment at the American treaty, the Shawnee renewed their attacks on the American frontier with increased ferocity in the spring and summer of 1786. The northwestern Indians were rising in disgust at the dictated treaties of the post-war period, and in the hope of saving their homes and hunting grounds northwest of the Ohio.[17]

Although the American frontiersmen were infuriated by the Indian onslaughts, they had difficulty persuading the American government to take offensive action in the Northwest. The main problem was the wretched state of the nation's finances, which made any elaborate offensive against the Indians impossible. Moreover, some in Congress opposed the idea of an expedition, and maintained that the raids were being carried out by isolated bands of hostile Indians and that the majority of the tribes were friendly. To the frontiersmen, this was arrant nonsense, and they demanded protection for their homes and their families. Although Congress was not prepared to take definite offensive action, the state governments did not feel the same reluctance. Governor Patrick Henry of Virginia authorized the local authorities in Kentucky to take measures for their own defense, and at the beginning of August 1786 the Kentuckians decided to take offensive action against the northwestern Indians. George Rogers Clark was appointed commander in chief, and Benjamin Logan second in command. Arthur St. Clair, who was later to lead his army to disaster in the Northwest, protested in Congress that the proposed expedition would be a breach of faith toward the Indians, and that Virginia should disband her troops. However, while Congress debated the merits of defending the American frontier, the Kentuckians acted.[18]

Although Clark now led an unsuccessful expedition against the Wabash tribes, Benjamin Logan led his Kentuckians successfully against the Shawnee towns on the upper reaches of the Great Miami, and along the Mad River. The blow was a great shock to the Shawnee and to Elliott. Logan's men burned down seven of the Shawnee towns, destroyed the crops, and killed a number of Indians. In the town in which Elliott lived ten Indians were found dead, including the chief. One of the Indians suffered death by fire as the Americans returned to an eye for an eye policy. This attack was the death blow to Shawnee hopes of holding central Ohio. They established themselves along the Maumee, in what is now the northwestern corner of the state. Elliott had moved from the Scioto to the Great Miami; he was now to confine his activities to the Maumee region.[19]

Elliott had played an important part in encouraging Shawnee resistance to the Americans in the years following the Revolution, and he now found that the general unrest and active warfare was not conducive to the success of his trading activities. With American settlers pushing across and down the Ohio, and the Indians engaged in desultory warfare, Ohio was no longer the trading paradise of an earlier day. The ideal traders' frontier was moving to the west. In the years after 1783, trade south and east of Detroit became increasingly precarious for the Detroit traders. By the summer of 1786 Caldwell and Elliott, though continuing activities as far east as the Cuyahoga River, were in considerable difficulties. By the following spring these difficulties reached a point of crisis when Duncan and Wilson of Pittsburgh began to press for the payment of outstanding debts. David Duncan was particularly infuriated that Caldwell and Elliott had left a string of their horses in Pittsburgh with Duncan and Wilson since the previous November, and had neither paid for their keep nor showed any sign of collecting them. At the end of May in 1787, he wrote to tell the Detroit partners (as one of the less successful frontier spellers he addressed them as "jantallmin") that unless they sent for their horses he would sell them. This threat had little effect, and he repeated it at the end of July. Elliott and Caldwell did eventually send Indians to collect their horses, but apparently the Indians took them without payment!

The affair of the horses was merely a symptom of far more

serious matters. The firm of Elliott and Caldwell began to collapse in the spring of 1787. That May, David Duncan and William Wilson appeared before a notary public in Detroit, and tried to prevent Elliott and Caldwell from making delivery of eighty head of cattle they had sold in the town. The objection of the Pittsburgh partners was that these cattle had been obtained from them, and Elliott and Caldwell had not yet paid. Duncan and Wilson also protested any future sale of goods in which Duncan and Wilson had an equal interest. By selling these goods, the two Detroit partners tried to keep off other pressing creditors.

This state of affairs continued throughout the summer. Caldwell and Elliott continued to sell goods in which Duncan and Wilson had an interest in order to keep other creditors at bay. Duncan was furious, and wrote of "their Vilianny" but he could do little about it. Though Duncan and Wilson eventually had a summons served on Caldwell and Elliott, it was too late. In midsummer the Detroit partners called a meeting of their creditors in Detroit, told them they were bankrupt, and assigned all their remaining property over to a small group of firms to be managed for the benefit of all their creditors. It appeared that they owed 18,000 and had assets of less than £800. Most of this money was owed not to Duncan and Wilson, who had been so bitter over the result of their partnership with Caldwell and Elliott, but to Robert Ellice and to Alexander and William Macomb. For a number of years the trustees for the creditors attempted to manage the remaining assets of Caldwell and Elliott, but for the most part they had to write off their heavy losses.[20]

While his creditors suffered, Elliott came out of this whole episode remarkably unscathed. He retained his farm and his slaves at the mouth of the Detroit River. He was to gain a legal hold on some three thousand acres in the early 1790's, and his talents were soon to win him back a position in the Indian department. Moreover, at the end of this potentially disastrous year, his claim to the British government for losses suffered during the Revolution was at last resolved in his favor. In December 1787 the government decided to grant Elliott a total of £520. Though this was only a third of his original claim for losses, it was still a considerable sum, and quite enough to enable him to improve the plantation he was developing at the mouth of the Detroit. Moreover, the failure of his trading concern apparently did not seriously injure his reputation, for when the District of Hesse was created in Upper Canada in 1788, Elliott received one of the appointments as Justice of the Peace for the District. Thus the illiterate Irish immigrant of thirty years before took his place on the judicial bench. This was not appreciated by the inhabitants of Detroit. In a long memorial on October 24, 1788, in which they objected to various aspects of the manner in which they were governed, they included an objection to the illiteracy of the justices: "Tho' Mr. Maisonville and Math. Elliot can mechanically sign their names they can neither read nor write." This was a problem until the end of Elliott's life. Whether at his home on the banks of the Detroit, or leading the Shawnee through the woods south of Lake Erie, Elliott always kept a clerk by him for the purpose of taking down his dictation. He would then painfully inscribe his name at the bottom of the letter.[21]

As the 1780's came to a close, Elliott was soon to find better occupation for his talents than sitting on the judicial bench. He had kept up his contacts with Alexander McKee in the years after the Revolution, and as Indian difficulties heightened McKee was once again able to find employment for his old colleague. The last years of the 1780's had brought renewed negotiations between the Americans and the Indians. In December 1786, a general Indian council at Detroit requested the American government to sign a new treaty. Realizing that their only hope lay in union, the Indians, under the leadership of Joseph Brant, placed their trust in a confederacy. They hoped to convince the American government that no single tribe had the right to cede land without the consent of the others. The Indian request for a new treaty eventually came to fruition at Fort Harmar in 1789. Unfortunately for the Indians, the treaties signed at Fort Harmar were a repetition of those signed earlier in the decade. The Six Nations, Wyandots, Delawares, Ottawas, and Chippewas agreed to confirm the cessions they had made at the treaties of Fort

Stanwix and Fort McIntosh, and in return received large additional payments. They agreed to do this, however, only under strong pressure from the American negotiator, Arthur St. Clair. Many of the Indians were disgusted at the failure of the negotiators to gain concessions from the United States (particularly a boundary along the Ohio River), and in the spring and summer of 1789 the western tribes again spread destruction along the American frontier. When the new government of the American constitution came into power in the spring of 1789, it was faced with a complete breakdown of the Indian policy of the Confederation. Though the new government would have liked peace, it would have to fight if it wished to settle the Old Northwest. The government could not hope to negotiate with the Indians until by a military victory it had demonstrated its ability to negotiate from a position of strength. In the years from 1789 to 1794, the American government tried to subdue the Indians of the Northwest. This environment of war and turmoil was ideal for Elliott, and in 1790 he regained an official position under the British as Assistant Agent of Indian Affairs at Detroit. His superior was Alexander McKee, and the two friends of the Shawnee were to direct Indian affairs on the Detroit frontier in the key years before the Treaty of Greenville.[22]

Chapter 4

RENEWAL OF WAR

By 1790 the American government had decided that it would have to strike into the heart of the hostile Indian country. The objective was one of the great centers of the western Indians – the point at which the St. Mary's and St. Joseph rivers combined to form the Maumee (the site of the present Fort Wayne, Indiana). Here were some seven villages of the Miami, Delaware, and Shawnee. Kekionga, or the Miami Village, as this spot was often known, also served as a gathering point for Indians preparing to attack the frontier of the United States. If the Americans could deliver a strong blow against Kekionga, it would awe both the tribes scattered along the Maumee to Lake Erie (particularly the Shawnee) and the tribes scattered along the Wabash. In July 1790, Arthur St. Clair, governor of the Northwest Territory, and General Josiah Harmar, commander of the American troops along the Ohio, met at Fort Washington (now Cincinnati), and planned a two-pronged attack. One force would proceed from Vincennes against the Wabash villages, while the main blow would be delivered against Kekionga by a force from Fort Washington under General Harmar. Throughout the summer the preparations for this attack proceeded laboriously.[1]

While the Americans prepared to fight, the British were weighing the situation from their strategic location at Detroit. Throughout the summer, although anxious to know the results of the American efforts, McKee and Elliott endeavored to maintain peace in the Old Northwest.[2] The American preparation lacked precision, and the troops that eventually set out toward the Maumee and the Wabash were inadequately trained and poorly equipped. The western wing of the attack accomplished practically nothing. Though the Americans advanced from

Vincennes along the Wabash, the Indians had deserted their villages, and the expedition was unable to bring them to battle. As usual the Indians knew well in advance when the ponderous American armies were on the march. The army under Harmar, consisting of nearly fifteen hundred men, encountered a similar problem. The expedition finally left Fort Washington on September 26, but it was three weeks before it reached what is now Fort Wayne, Indiana. When the Americans arrived they found that the Indian villages were deserted, and they proceeded to burn all they could.[3]

In the meantime the news of the advancing American army had reached the British in Detroit, and on October 18 McKee ordered Elliott to watch the progress of the American army. Elliott arrived at the Auglaize (the junction of the Maumee and Auglaize rivers) on October 21. Soon after he arrived, two Indian runners arrived from Kekionga bearing two scalps, and they brought messages requesting other Indians to join the forces opposing the Americans. They also brought the news of a victory for the Indians. The Shawnees and Potawatomis had surprised part of the American force, and claimed to have killed three hundred men with the loss of only one Indian. Understanding that another action was about to take place, Elliott left the Auglaize on October 23 and advanced to within forty miles of Kekionga by nightfall. His object was both to secure information for McKee, and also to aid the Detroit traders who were fleeing with their property from the scene of the American attack. That night an Indian runner brought news of another engagement into Elliott's camp. Harmar, withdrawing from the Indian villages, had hoped to give some justification to his expedition by sending out a force under Major John P. Wyllys on October 22. Although this force surprised some Indians, it was then attacked by the main Indian army and suffered a loss of over one hundred and eighty men. The runner who brought news of this engagement to Elliott made a very reasonable estimate of two hundred American dead, and told him that it was the Shawnees, Miamis, Ottawas, and Delawares who had engaged the Americans.

Elliott was thus able to inform McKee that the Americans

61

had lost some five hundred men. This was roughly double the actual American losses, but exaggerated or not, the Indians rejoiced at having inflicted a decisive defeat on the American forces. Their burnt villages seemed a small sacrifice beside the scalps of the Americans. Elliott told McKee that he had seen upward of one hundred and fifty scalps among the few Indians who were going to the Auglaize for provisions. While again probably an exaggeration, there were certainly enough scalps to inspire the Indians of the Northwest to further resistance. The Indians had probably gathered some six hundred warriors to resist Harmar's advancing army of over fourteen hundred troops. Elliott estimated that in neither of the two actions did the Indians bring more than two hundred warriors to the attack, and of course the Americans also did not manage to bring anything like their full force into either of the engagements. Even though the Indians had lost their villages and provisions, they could well claim a victory. Actual American losses amounted to over two hundred and sixty, while Elliott estimated that the Indians had lost not more than ten warriors. The engagement meant that the American hope of quickly subduing the Indians had gone, and Harmar limped back into Fort Washington on November 3. The necessity for an effective American expedition had become even more pressing.[4]

The British had not yet resolved on the correct policy to be pursued toward the American-Indian hostilities south of the Great Lakes. The coming into power of a new American government, determined to put an end to the Indian hostilities, threatened British control of the Indians south of the Great Lakes, and also threatened to bring the Americans far too near to the posts held by Great Britain. Elliott's report to McKee on the defeat of Harmar, which eventually was sent to Lord Dorchester and to England, had also contained the information that the Americans intended to take Detroit in the spring. This information was supposedly gleaned from American prisoners taken by the Indians. During the winter of 1790-91 the fear that American victory in the Northwest would be disastrous to British control over the Indians, and over the Northwest posts, led Lord Dorchester to espouse the idea of British mediation to bring peace between the Indians and the Americans. In February 1791, he informed George Beckwith, who was acting as British agent in the United States, that he would be willing to use his good offices to effect a peace, and he also asked the Superintendent of Indian Affairs, Sir John Johnson, to discover from the Indians their terms for a peace based on "equity, justice and policy." The British government in England took up this idea of mediation and pressed it upon its representatives in America during the following years. Yet not all of Dorchester's ideas were so pacific. The month before he adopted the idea of mediation, he wrote to the military commanders in Upper Canada, saying that he lamented the American-Indian hostility and would like to put an end to it, but also stating that should the information regarding an American attack on Detroit prove true, war would then have to be repelled by war. Although England had officially given up the Northwest posts in 1783, she was now prepared to defend them by force.[5]

While his superiors pressed ahead with plans for British mediation in the American-Indian conflict, Elliott helped to ease his conscience in the winter of 1790-91. The Christian Indians, removed from the Tuscarawas by Elliott in 1781, had spent several years near what is now Mt. Clemens, Michigan, but in 1787 returned into the Ohio country and settled at Pequotting on the east bank of the Huron (Pequotting) River, near what is now Milan, in Erie County, Ohio. Here, east of Sandusky Bay, they hoped to find peace. Once again they were disappointed, since, as in the Revolution, they were settled in the British-American no-man's-land, and by the winter of 1790-91 had become exceedingly afraid of the dangers of a general Indian war. In January 1791, they were given the opportunity to lay their case before the British. In that month, Elliott, who with McKee was visiting the Wyandots at Sandusky, travelled over the snow to see them. Elliott, more cautious than truthful, told them he knew nothing of the possibility of an Indian war, and the Moravians asked him to question McKee on the matter. If war was to come they wanted the British to find them a place to reside in safety. To the surprise of the Moravians Elliott promised not only to do this, but also gave the Moravians

hope that should they be forced to move, they would receive the
support of the British government. Elliott had long been remembered, most unpleasantly, by the Moravians for his activities during the Revolution, but David Zeisberger was forced to
observe that he was now "in every way friendly and showed
himself altogether eager to be of service to us."[6]

Elliott was true to his word. He carried the case of the
Moravians to McKee, and McKee arranged for them to settle
along the Detroit River. In April 1791, the removal of the
Christian Indians began. As McKee had received no reply to
his request to use a government ship for the removal, the Moravians hired a vessel from John Askin, the prominent Detroit
merchant, to carry their supplies. The Indians themselves came
in some thirty canoes. Elliott returned again in mid-April to
Sandusky Bay to help in the removal. Elliott and McKee offered
to let the Indians settle for a year on their plantations at the
mouth of the Detroit River, and use them as they wanted. Well
might David Zeisberger write in his diary: "Such things the
Saviour brings to pass, who can do all he will in heaven and
on earth." The Moravians reached the mouth of the Detroit
early in May. The missionaries stayed in the homes of Elliott
and McKee, and the Christian Indians spread out between them,
on McKee's land. In the following months the Moravians worked
hard, planting their crops and building a large meeting house
which was finished by the middle of June. Materially they were
doing well, since Elliott and others were able to employ them in
their harvests, but spiritually they were once again troubled. The
notorious Simon Girty lived up to his reputation by making the
Christian Indians drunk, and by paying them in rum for helping
him on his farm. By August the Christians were exceedingly
disturbed by the close proximity of distracting influences, and
again desired to move.[7]

In October 1791, the Moravians again told McKee of their
desires, and he gave them hope that he would again be able to
assist them. He was still awaiting a reply from the British government in Canada as to the eventual disposition of the Moravians. In December the Moravians once more asked Elliott to
intercede for them with McKee – they wanted a tract of land on

which they could plant and settle in the spring. Elliott suggested, saying that it was also McKee's advice, that they should merely find a suitable spot and settle; no one would drive them from it. Elliott indeed appeared a reformed character at this time. On Christmas Day he even attended the service of the Moravians in their meeting house at the mouth of the Detroit, and the Moravians spent the winter in his home.

At last plans were made for a fresh removal of the Moravians. It was agreed that they could settle on the River Thames, and throughout the late winter and spring Elliott visited them to arrange the details. The Moravians were constantly amazed by the change of attitude on the part of those who had caused them to suffer during the Revolution. In April 1792, they set out for their new home on the Thames River, near what is now Thamesville, in Kent County, Ontario. It seemed that they had at last found peace after eleven years in the wilderness, but eventually they were disappointed. The spot they had chosen for settlement was that on which twenty-one years later the British and the Americans were to fight the battle of the Thames. Yet, they no longer viewed Elliott as the ogre of the Revolution but as their benefactor of the Detroit River. [8]

The aid to the Moravians took only a small part of Elliott's time in 1791 and 1792. For the most part he was engaged on a more normal task of acting for the British among the Indians of the Northwest. During the winter of 1790-91 the United States rebounded from the shock of Harmar's defeat, and the British authorities in Canada decided if possible to mediate in the Indian-American controversy. In the spring of 1791, with the resumption of navigation and the return of the Indians from their winter hunting, Elliott and McKee once again worked earnestly to preserve British influence on the Maumee. The British authorities were most apprehensive of the possibility of an American attack upon Detroit, and the Indian Department was given the task of warning of any such move, and of discovering suitable spots to which the troops in the posts of Niagara and Detroit could advance to meet any American threat. Moreover, at the foot of the rapids of the Maumee was located the storehouse and the living quarters from which McKee and

Elliott distributed supplies to the Indians of the Old Northwest. This spot became increasingly important in the years before 1795, and in the spring of 1791 it was a way-station for the tribes passing along the Maumee to resist the Americans.[9]

While McKee stayed at the rapids to greet and supply the Indians, Elliott passed between the rapids and Detroit and organized the passage of Indians through the British post. It was not unusual in this period for Indians to travel from Saginaw Bay or from Michilimackinac to join their brothers along the Maumee, and Elliott had to ensure that the Indians passed through Detroit without drinking too much rum or rioting. The Indian Department was optimistic in the spring of 1791. At the beginning of June, Elliott told the commander of the British post at Detroit that by the time the whole Indian force was collected, it should consist of some two thousand five hundred fighting men. Many of these Indians stopped off to get supplies from McKee at the foot of the rapids, and warriors gathered all along the Maumee. On June 9, the Moravian Indians at the mouth of the Detroit were shocked to receive a message from Kekionga saying that they should go there to help fight for their land against the Americans. The Indians at Kekionga threatened that if the Christian Indians did not come of their own free will, they would come to root them out. Christianity should be put aside until the war was over. On the following day the Moravians described their plight to Elliott, who had come from Detroit to visit his farm. He reassured them, said that the message had come from the Delawares, and that it was not at all necessary for the Christian Indians to be distressed by it. The government would protect them from harm even if they did not go to resist the Americans.[10]

On July 1, McKee spoke to the nations at the foot of the rapids on the occasion of delivering to them their annual presents. He asked them the terms on which, consistent with their honor and interest, they would be prepared to make peace with the United States. As a result of his request the Indian nations formulated their demands for a boundary. The line they proposed was one running up the Ohio from the mouth of the Tennessee to the mouth of the Muskingum, then up that river to the portage which linked it to the Cuyahoga, and then in a direct line across country to Venango. The western Indians were prepared to concede to the Americans some land to the north of the Ohio River, but they wanted to retain all of the modern state of Ohio west of the Muskingum. Joseph Brant and deputies from the western nations were conducted by Elliott along the Maumee to the mouth of the Detroit River on July 8. The deputies then proceeded on the long journey to see Lord Dorchester in Quebec, and on August 17 Brant stated to Dorchester the terms on which the Indians would make peace with the Americans. Dorchester replied that the King would be pleased to mediate between the Indians and the Americans. On September 2, the first British Minister in the United States, George Hammond, was told that he was to take any opportunity to offer mediation between the Americans and Indians, as Great Britain considered herself to have strong commercial and political interest in the restoration of peace. Instructions to Dorchester later in the month (he left Canada before they arrived) told him to continue to observe strict neutrality in the American-Indian dispute, and asked him to bring the war to an end if he could, though he was to try and obtain possession of their hunting grounds for the Indians – this meant most of their land northwest of the Ohio.[11]

The Americans of course were not interested in the idea of a British mediation which would leave most of the rich lands of the Old Northwest to the Indians, and throughout 1791 while the British planned mediation the Americans planned a military expedition. In January 1791, Henry Knox, the Secretary of War, reported to the President that the defeat of Harmar had made another expedition essential, or the Indians would be encouraged to increase their depredations. He further suggested that an object of the expedition should be to establish a post at the Miami Village (Kekionga). The planning for this expedition proceeded slowly. At the beginning of March, Congress gave its approval, and the governor of the Northwest Territory, Arthur St. Clair, was put in command.[12]

While St. Clair's preparations laboriously proceeded, two small expeditions were sent to dissuade the Indians from any aggressive action. At the end of May, Brigadier-General Charles Scott attacked Indian towns along the Wabash, and this maneuver was repeated (further to the east) by Lieutenant-Colonel James Wilkinson. Wilkinson had less success than Scott, but for a time at the end of July, a swarm of Indians came down the Maumee toward the mouth of the Detroit to avoid the expected American army. Elliott came with them, and told the Christian Indians that they should send them all back again, "for they were always wishing to go to war." An English officer with Elliott was less pleasant, for after being told by a Christian Indian that these Christians could not go to war because they loved all men, he retorted "Ye will soon be compelled to go to war, and if ye will no so do a crown will be put upon your heads with the tomahawk."[13]

The main American expedition under St. Clair prepared slowly during the spring and summer. Its supplies, training, and timing were all inadequate. Throughout the summer and early fall the British in Detroit and the Indians to the south awaited the long-expected American army. There was no surprise involved – other than the fact that the Americans were taking such a long time to attack. In the middle of September, St. Clair finally made his first advance from Fort Washington when he sent a detachment to construct Fort Hamilton, on the east side of the Great Miami, some twenty-five miles north of Fort Washington. It was not until October 4 that the main body of the army moved northward. They advanced with painful slowness, constructing other forts as they went, and by November 3 had reached a point some one hundred miles north of Fort Washington. At dawn on the following morning, there was a complete disaster. The Indian tribes who had so long awaited this new expedition, and who had been well aware of its laborious progress in their direction, fell upon the American force and utterly routed it. The exultant warriors chased the panic-stricken American troops from the field, killing some six hundred and thirty, including the second-in-command, Richard Butler. This was the high-point for the Indians of the Old Northwest. The morning they sent the painfully collected American force flying in complete confusion it seemed that the white advance could be emphatically stopped. Elliott, who as usual had followed the Indians as an observer, returned to the mouth of the Detroit on November 15 with a typical estimate of casualties – about one hundred per cent too many. He announced the American losses as some twelve hundred killed. American prestige had reached a new low in the Old Northwest.[14]

The winter of 1791-92 saw the British government finally form its plans for mediation in the American-Indian conflict. On March 17, 1792, British Foreign Secretary Lord Grenville wrote to George Hammond and gave him a full plan for the proposed British mediation. In essence he suggested that the Indian boundary given to Dorchester in August 1791 should form the basis of a permanent American-Indian settlement. The resulting Indian territory in the Northwest should be guaranteed by both Great Britain and the United States as a neutral barrier state. Hammond did not present this formal offer of mediation, as he was certain it would be refused, but the idea of a neutral barrier state remained a definite hope of the British government.[15]

It was at this time of crisis in the Old Northwest that there was a change in the governmental structure of Canada. In August 1791 the old province of Quebec was divided into Upper and Lower Canada. The first lieutenant-governor of Upper Canada was Colonel John Graves Simcoe, an exceedingly able and energetic army officer who had won a considerable reputation as commander of the Queen's Rangers during the Revolution. His arrival at Montreal in June 1792 was to give a new vigor to the administration of Indian affairs in Upper Canada, and was also to precipitate a clash between the energetic Simcoe and the Governor in chief, Lord Dorchester.[16]

With the coming of spring in 1792 Elliott was immediately well-employed in distributing supplies to the Indians along the Maumee. His task was more than usually onerous, as McKee had gone east to receive instructions and discuss the possibilities for British mediation. At the Auglaize that May, the Indians presented their problems to Elliott. They announced that owing to the incursions of the Americans into their country they had left the headwaters of the Maumee and had come to settle in the vicinity of the Auglaize. They understood that the Americans were raising another army and were determined to persist in their efforts to take the country. The Indians – a thousand warriors and their wives and children – announced they were now in great distress owing to the shortage of provisions. They had been obliged to give many of their supplies to the Indians who had come to help in the defeat of St. Clair. They therefore wanted the British to supply their needs.[17] From this point the Indians became increasingly dependent upon the British for supplies. The constant councils and the extraordinary gatherings along the Maumee in these years were only made possible because the British were prepared to meet the Indian need for provisions.

In this summer of 1792, the British were placed in the position of having to issue supplies if they wished to retain influence. The Indian families along the Maumee were in great distress owing to the shortage of provisions, and throughout the summer they requested the British in Detroit to supply their wants. The normal method used by the British was to ship the supplies from Detroit, along the Detroit River, into Lake Erie, and then up the Maumee River to the foot of the rapids where McKee and Elliott had their headquarters. From that spot the supplies could easily be distributed to the Indians of the whole region. Elliott spent most of the spring and summer arranging the shipment of supplies and travelling between Detroit, the rapids, and the Auglaize.[18]

While Elliott was in a most practical way enabling the Indians to stay assembled to meet the Americans, McKee was in Montreal discussing British Indian policy with Simcoe. McKee arrived in Montreal on June 11, and immediately went into conference with the lieutenant-governor. Simcoe obtained from McKee all possible information to substantiate the claims of the Indians to such lands as the British government thought that they should retain. Simcoe and McKee also drew up a memorandum which was submitted to the British Minister in the United States (along with the proofs of Indian claims) sketching their idea of a suitable settlement to the Indian boundary question. They not only supported the idea of a buffer state, based on the Indian suggestions to Dorchester of August 1791, but also suggested that Great Britain should retain jurisdiction over Detroit. Though Simcoe wanted a cessation of American-Indian hostilities, he wanted peace on terms which would be impossible to the Americans. There seems little doubt that it was McKee who pointed out the advantages of holding onto the area along the Maumee; the route vital to British control of the Indians of the Old Northwest.[19]

After his talks in Montreal, McKee returned to the Maumee to meet with the Indians. His presence there was becoming necessary, for the Indians had decided to hold a great council at the Auglaize in the early fall. The northwestern Indians were now in a most confident mood. Twice they had turned back the American armies, and on the second occasion had inflicted a crushing defeat. They wanted once again to discuss possible terms for peace, but they now felt that they were arguing from a position of great strength. McKee arrived at the foot of the rapids in August, and in September received a new suggestion from Simcoe – a suggestion which Simcoe thought was well-designed to obtain the buffer state which they had planned in Montreal. Simcoe asked McKee to impress upon the Indians that they should spontaneously solicit the good offices of the British government in securing a peace: "It is to be extremely desired that this solicitation should be the result of their own spontaneous Reflections." McKee was also to make certain the Indians understood that the British government could undertake no offensive action on their behalf, and was urged to do his utmost to counteract any assertions "of self-interested and venal traders" that Great Britain would sooner or later engage in war with the United States in defense of the western Indians.[20]

The British Indian agents were thus strictly instructed at the time of the 1792 council to insist that Britain would not go to war on their behalf, and there seems no reason to suppose that either McKee or Elliott flouted these instructions. It is of course exceedingly doubtful whether the same could be said for the traders who were interested in the maintenance of British control south of Detroit, and British fears in this regard are well-demonstrated by Simcoe's urging of McKee to counter the assertions of the traders. Great Britain in 1792 was interested in peace between the Americans and the Indians, and Simcoe and his subordinates in Upper Canada hoped to effect a peace which would leave an Indian buffer state in the Northwest through which British agents and traders could still exercise control. They were anxious that the Indians should not achieve a peace without British mediation, for this would lessen British influence among them. [21]

The general council of the Indian nations took place at the Auglaize from September 30 to October 9, 1792. The decisive victory over St. Clair encouraged the Indians to increase their demands regarding a boundary. Instead of the Muskingum line suggested the previous summer, they now wanted peace on the basis of a boundary along the Ohio River, and agreed to offer to meet the Americans at Lower Sandusky in the spring to accomplish such a peace. Joseph Brant of the Mohawks did not arrive until the council was breaking up, and was then informed of the decision of the confederacy. The "spontaneous" request of the Indians for British aid in establishing a peace was formally given in November when the Six Nations met in council. On behalf of the Indians they requested the British to attend the coming treaty at Lower Sandusky with all the records and treaties pertaining to the Indian claims. Although the United States would not accept formal British mediation, Secretary of State Thomas Jefferson agreed that the British agents could attend the coming treaty to explain the American offers to the Indians.[22]

After the hectic procedure of supplying the many Indians travelling to the Maumee in the summer and fall of 1792, Elliott settled into his routine tasks in the winter of 1792-93. He spent much of his time travelling along the Maumee route, though with many away hunting there were now far fewer Indians to take care of. Yet, even in months when there was no massing of armies to meet the Americans, there was still a constant flow of prisoners or scalps passing along the Maumee. In this winter of 1792-93, Elliott devoted some time to the ransoming of a young American boy, Oliver Spencer, who had been brought to the Auglaize as a prisoner.

Young Spencer's connections in the United States had enquired about him through the British Minister, George Hammond. Hammond wrote to Simcoe, and Simcoe asked the commandant at Detroit, Lieutenant-Colonel Richard England, to do all he could to recover the boy. England applied to the Indian Department, and eventually McKee sent Elliott to try to obtain him. In February 1793, Elliott set off for the Auglaize on this somewhat thankless task. The Indians proved most reluctant to give him up, and eventually Elliott had to pay £60 New York currency before the Indians would release their prisoner. Many years later Spencer still remembered Elliott with intense dislike. Spencer remarked that Elliott received him "with considerable hauteur," and that he tried to act as though he were buying Spencer's freedom out of humanity rather than on the express orders of Simcoe. According to Spencer, Elliott uttered "a sardonic laugh" when James Girty, the brother of the famous Simon, threatened to cut off Spencer's ears. Spencer's description of Elliott was not of the most flattering type: "Elliot's hair was black, his complexion dark, his features small; his nose I recollect was short, turning up at the end, his look was haughty, and his countenance repulsive." Spencer was perhaps influenced by Elliott's "ungentlemanly remarks, and disparaging observations about the Americans," and by the fact that rather than taking Spencer all the way to Detroit Elliott left him in care of a band of Indians. One of these Indians stabbed Spencer, and though the wound was not serious Spencer carried word of Elliott's ill-treatment of him to Simcoe. Yet, Spencer was one of the lucky ones, for many prisoners never lived to be ransomed.[23]

While Elliott went about the details of Indian administration, plans for the following summer were being laid by the British officials in Canada. The United States had agreed to the request of the Indian confederacy for a treaty in the following spring, and the British officials were concerned with how they could best influence the proceedings on behalf of the Indians. The permission that had been obtained for British agents to be present at Lower Sandusky simplified matters, and Simcoe appointed McKee and Colonel John Butler to attend on the British behalf. The British meant to have more than a moral suasion over the Indians, for Simcoe refused American agents permission to

73

purchase supplies in Canada for the use of the Indians in the coming treaty. Instead, Great Britain would supply the tribes with the necessary provisions. For a treaty to be held between the Americans and the Indians on American soil, Britain intended not only to have her agents present, but also to supply the Indians with all they needed during the proceedings.[24]

The Indians also laid their plans during the winter. Fortunately for the American settlers the frontier was for the most part quiet, since the chiefs were restraining their warriors until America's decision regarding the invitation to Lower Sandusky.[25] The American Secretary of War, Henry Knox, replied in December 1792 to the Indian request for a treaty. He said the United States would be happy to meet the Indians, but he did not mention the boundary for which the United States would be prepared to negotiate. [26] the Indians now spent the winter in making arrangements for the coming treaty negotiations. The western tribes decided that they should meet in council before the gathering at Sandusky in order to confront the Americans with an appearance of complete unity. As early as February 1793, the western tribes informed the Six Nations that they would meet in council at the foot of the Maumee rapids in the spring, and they requested the Six Nations to attend. Yet, even in this message calling for unity before the treaty, there were distinct signs that the Indians would be unable to maintain it. The western nations expressed surprise that the reply of the Americans agreeing to the treaty made no mention of the Indian *sine qua non* – the Ohio boundary – and they therefore suggested that the Six Nations had not understood, or had not adequately explained to the Americans, the result of the Indian council during the previous fall. They wanted the Six Nations to come to the rapids to concert ideas, and also so that even before the Indians went to the treaty council they could ascertain whether the American commissioners had the power to make peace on the terms required.[27]

The Six Nations were not at all happy with the way in which the western Indians were directing the affairs of the Indian confederacy. In a letter to McKee in March 1793, Brant expressed the view that the Americans genuinely desired peace, and thought that the western nations should be most careful to restrain themselves. Moreover, the Six Nations themselves held a council at Niagara before their representative Brant and his entourage departed for the Maumee, and came to the conclusion that a reasonable line would be that suggested to Lord Dorchester at Quebec in August 1791 – the Muskingum line, which would yield land to the north of the Ohio. Brant also expressed the very reasonable point of view that places already settled by the Americans, such as Gallipolis or Marietta, could be yielded to the United States even though they were not within the general boundary so long as the permanent boundary was definitely marked. Plans for the Indian council at the rapids thus matured in an atmosphere of distrust and disagreement between the Six Nations and the western tribes.[28]

The British in Canada were of course most interested in the development of the Indian plans for the 1793 treaty, and they decided to provide the provisions for the preliminary Indian council as well as for the treaty at Lower Sandusky. At the end of April 1793, when Simcoe reported to McKee on Brant's ideas for a Muskingum boundary, he expressed the opinion that Brant's ideas seemed just, and that this arrangement would form the basis of an Indian barrier until the American commissioners had left Lower Sandusky with a signed treaty.[29] Simcoe ignored the fact that Brant's line disregarded the Ohio boundary decided on by the general Indian council in the previous fall.

While the British and the Indians matured their plans, the United States had no great hopes for the coming council at Lower Sandusky. Jefferson later said that these negotiations of 1793 were only entered into "to prove to all our citizens that peace was unattainable on terms which any one of them would admit."[30] The United States would have liked peace in the Northwest, but the government did not believe that they could obtain the land they wanted until they had defeated the Indians in battle. The problem of instructions for the American commissioners was a difficult one, and it was not until after cabinet discussions that this question was finally resolved. The great problem was whether the United States would consider retreating from the boundaries obtained during the 1780's. In essence,

these boundaries had given the United States a good part of
what is now the state of Ohio – everything east of the Cuyahoga
and the Muskingum, and southern Ohio west to the Great Miami.
The United States did in fact retreat a little in the instructions
finally given to the commissioners. At the end of April, Benjamin
Lincoln, Beverley Randolph, and Timothy Pickering, who were
to represent the United States, were told that the United States
would be happy if they could obtain confirmation of the boundaries established in the 1780's. If this were accomplished the
United States was prepared to confirm the Indian right of soil
to the remaining Indian lands in the Northwest, and to pay
liberally for the agreement. The commissioners could even consider retreating slightly from the line confirmed at the treaty of
Fort Harmar in 1789 if this would establish peace. They could
not retreat too far, because the United States had already sold
much of the land gained in the 1780's. The commissioners were
to negotiate as much as possible with the separate tribes, in
order to discourage the idea of a confederacy. They were also
told to try to complete their negotiations by August 1, and
immediately to inform General Wayne of the result. In this way
the military campaign could be carried out if, as expected, the
negotiations should fail. Wayne himself was ordered to have
everything ready for a campaign by July 20 or, at the latest,
August 1.[31]

By the spring of 1793, the participants in the proposed treaty
of Lower Sandusky were seeking at least four different objectives.
The western Indians hoped to secure a boundary that would
give them permanent possession of the lands northwest of the
Ohio. Joseph Brant and the Six Nations hoped to secure a
boundary that would give the Indians possession of most of
the Northwest, but would yield land in what is now southeastern
Ohio. The Americans hoped to secure a treaty that would bring
peace to the Northwest, and that in essence would confirm to
them the boundaries of the treaty of Fort Harmar – that is,
giving the Americans much of what is now eastern and southern Ohio. The British would have been happy with either the
Muskingum or the Ohio boundary for the Indians – the essential

condition being Indian unity on one or the other – and it was hoped that the creation of this boundary would prepare the way for the establishment of the remaining lands of the Old Northwest as a permanent Indian preserve. Moreover, a broad difference was that both the Indians and the British hoped in the coming treaty to gain acceptance of the idea that the Indians could negotiate as a united confederacy holding their lands in common, while the Americans hoped to emphasize the idea of the different Indian tribes having rights to particular tracts of land.

The American commissioners finally arrived at Niagara on their way to the west in the latter part of May 1793. There they were to stay for six weeks, until Lieutenant-Governor Simcoe informed them that they could go forward.[32] The delay was made necessary by the long-drawn-out preliminary proceedings on the part of the Indians. McKee had already expressed the fear that it was unlikely that the Indians would be ready to meet the commissioners until the middle of June, and this fear was borne out in the following months. The Indians remained in their villages engaged in the planting of corn and in other preparations for the summer until the latter half of May. McKee awaited the Indians at the rapids, while Elliott dealt with the problem of supply in Detroit. McKee was worried that the provisions he had brought with him for the Indians were insufficient, and he wrote to Elliott in Detroit asking him to secure as much again. For a time this produced a minor crisis, as Colonel England, the commandant at Detroit, stated he did not have the power to issue these extra provisions without the consent of Simcoe. It amounted to an extra twenty barrels of pork and twenty of flour, together with salt, rice, and peas. Finally, under considerable pressure from the Indian Department, Colonel England agreed to issue them without Simcoe's sanction. He then wrote to Simcoe to tell him what he had done, and won Simcoe's approval.[33] At a later date the eagerness of the Indian Department to supply provisions to the Indians was to cause considerable friction between them and the military.

On May 17, Joseph Brant arrived at Detroit with seventy of the Six Nations and Delawares from the Grand River. He immediately wrote to McKee, asking him to gather the chiefs of the western Indians from the Glaize to the rapids for the purpose of holding a private council. Brant arrived at the foot of the rapids on May 22, and was most disappointed to discover that none of the Indians had arrived. He sent a runner to summon them. McKee also sent a message to the Glaize, and discovered the reason for the delay. The Indians there had procured six or seven barrels of rum and had stayed to drink it. However, by the time McKee's messenger arrived on May 27, they were all sober and able to travel. They informed McKee that they were preparing to set off the next day, and that they were very happy that the British would supply them with provisions. The British problem of supply had been simplified, for Colonel England informed McKee on May 27 that he had written to Simcoe for permission to issue such provisions as might be required, and that in the meantime he would on his own responsibility give out all necessary supplies.[34]

By the second week of June most of the important chiefs from the Glaize had arrived at the rapids, and in the meantime Elliott in Detroit was busy sending down not only provisions but also the Indians who were coming through that post to attend the council at the rapids. This presented the usual problems of moving the Indians through Detroit without incidents, and the endeavor was not always successful. On June 4, England routed Elliott out of bed to quell a disturbance, and Elliott sat up all night supervising a party of Indians. The next day he sent on this party of thirty with provisions. From this point on, all Indians who arrived at Detroit were sent as quickly as possible to the foot of the rapids. They were usually sent on their way with provisions issued by Elliott on application to the military commander. The British agents did not merely supply the Indians and arrange for their journey to the council, they also did all they could to summon them from distant parts. On June 19 Elliott informed McKee that he had sent tobacco and wampum to the Saginaw Indians to hurry them on their way as quickly as possible. He had already sent for Indians in the region of Michilimackinac. In these councils of the early 1790's Indians attended from all over the Northwest – the Maumee, the Sandusky, the Wabash, Canada, the Saginaw Bay region, and the vast area west of Lake Michigan. The success of such general councils depended a great deal on the fact that the British would supply these Indians when they arrived, and on the fact that the British agents helped to summon the Indians to the place of meeting. Elliott told McKee that "I shall use all my endeavours to forward every Indian that comes this way with the greatest dispatch."[35]

Moreover, the provisions that were issued were not always the ubiquitous pork and peas. The boat that left Detroit for the rapids on June 19 carried, among other supplies, five barrels of powder, and one thousand pounds of ball and shot. This was required by the Indians for hunting, but it naturally also proved a great aid in establishing a stock of weapons with which to resist the American advance. The ease with which provisions could be supplied increased as the summer progressed. England informed McKee on June 20 that he now had been given a latitude that would enable him "with some ease" to attend to McKee's requisitions, and on June 22 Simcoe told McKee that he had informed Colonel England to lose no time in supplying him with provisions for the Indian councils.[36]

Simcoe's orders meant of course that the members of the Indian Department were able to judge for themselves the amount of provisions that was needed to keep the Indians happy and faithful, and throughout June and July Elliott organized the shipment of supplies from Detroit to the rapids of the Maumee. He was able to inform McKee on June 24 that all the Indians were now past, or would be the next day, except those from the Saginaw and Michilimackinac regions. On June 29 McKee wrote from the foot of the rapids to tell Simcoe that the number of Indians "from *distant quarters*" now amounted to nearly one thousand. This of course meant that the need for provisions became even greater, and at the end of June and the beginning of July nearly every day saw fresh supplies leave for the rapids – on the twenty-fourth, eighteen head of cattle; on the twenty-fifth, fifty bags of Indian corn and six barrels of pork; on the twenty-eighth, forty barrels of pork, forty of flour, forty of peas, and one hundred and thirty bags of corn.[37]

While the Indian Department ensured that the Indians would

79

actually gather for the council, and would be well-supplied, the council itself was not proceeding smoothly. From the point of view of the Indians and the British, the unfortunate development was an increasing rift between the Six Nations and the western Indians. Brant was not pleased that the Indians had not gathered when he arrived, and he became less pleased as time went on. In the first two weeks in June he recorded in his journal that evil reports were being spread against him to the effect that he was a traitor, and had only attended the council to receive money. Although he called a council with the Shawnees, Delawares, Miamis, Wyandots, and some of the Lake Indians (Ottawas, Chippewas, and Potawatomis) on June 15 in order to try to remove the bad impression, the evil reports continued. He was particularly perturbed that the Shawnees, Delawares, and Miamis were on many nights holding private councils to which the Six Nations were not invited. Although Brant was being excluded from the secret deliberations, there seems little doubt that the British Indian Department was in the confidence of the western tribes. McKee eventually approached Brant to ask him if he agreed to the idea of sending a deputation to meet the American commissioners at Niagara to ask them if they had the power to establish a new boundary. Brant expressed his approval, adding that the principal chiefs should go, and on July 1 the chiefs of the other nations came to Brant to make a formal proposal for a deputation. On the following day the deputation set out for Niagara. McKee explained in letters to Simcoe that the general confederacy was anxious to know whether the commissioners had the necessary authority to draw a new boundary (in particular one along the Ohio), and that the Indians were also concerned at the presence of a powerful body of troops in the Northwest (Wayne's force). McKee's opinion was that the Indians would not make peace unless the Ohio boundary was given, and all American forts to the north of the Ohio were demobilized. He expressed the fear that if the commissioners came to Sandusky without the authority to conclude an agreement in this form, it might incite the tribes to hostile action.[38]

McKee's fears concerning the outcome of the treaty council had already been voiced by Simcoe. During the weeks in which the American commissioners were detained at Niagara, it became very apparent to Simcoe that the United States was not prepared to deviate to any great extent from the boundary that had been established at Fort Harmar in 1789. Simcoe became convinced that there was little likelihood of a peace, and he realized that neither the commissioners nor Wayne really expected one. Simcoe's anxiety to make the forthcoming treaty greatly to the advantage of Great Britain was undoubtedly increased when in May 1793 he received and proclaimed the news that England and France had been in a state of war since February.[39] From this time on, the efforts of the British authorities in Canada to bolster Indian resistance and to secure an Indian-American agreement to Britain's advantage became far more overt.

Simcoe placed great faith in Alexander McKee, and the letters that passed between the two men clearly indicated the extent to which Simcoe entrusted power into the hands of the Indian Department. On June 22, Simcoe sent instructions to McKee and John Butler to guide them during the proceedings at Lower Sandusky. He told them that they were not to act as mediators, but that on the request of the Indians they should interpret maps and treaties. They should also make use of their influence over the Indians by inclining them to accept offers if they were of benefit to the Indians, and to reject them if they were contrary to their real interests. They should of course be cautious, and as had been usual in the Indian Department in the past, it was preferable that they should give advice privately to some of the chiefs. If it became necessary to express disapproval at a general meeting, it was better to do this by silence rather than by words. Simcoe expressed the desire for a safe and solid peace, and for the complete attachment of the Indians to Great Britain. In his instructions to the Indian interpreters who were also going to Sandusky, Simcoe added a little more. He told them that "The union of the Indian Nations" was the great object of their being sent to Sandusky. They should work for this end, and were to persudade the Indians "to adopt such measures as Col. McKee shall from time to time direct as necessary for their common benefit and preservation."[40]

It is striking how under the pressure of events in the spring of 1793, and with the news of the war against France, Simcoe more and more moved into the position of using the Indian Department as a direct organizer of the Indians within American territory. Undoubtedly his main object was still peace, but it was a peace which would leave the Northwest as a British and Indian preserve. On June 23, Simcoe wrote a confidential letter to McKee in which he expressed the hope that if a treaty were signed, the confederacy should guarantee the boundaries of the Indian buffer state sketched by McKee and Simcoe at Montreal in June 1792. Five days later he expressed the opinion that detaching Kentucky from the Union and attaching it to Canada would give the Indians perfect security, and while this might prove difficult, the attempt should not be out of sight for a moment.[41]

The deputation of the Indians from the rapids quickly proceeded to Niagara, and on July 7, in the presence of Simcoe, met with the commissioners of the United States. Brant spoke on behalf of the confederacy. He asked why the United States was presenting a warlike appearance in the Northwest, and whether the commissioners had the power to settle a boundary. The commissioners replied that Washington had forbidden hostilities until the result of the treaty was known, and that they had been given the authority to draw a boundary line. Brant promised that the deputation would take this message to the confederacy on the Maumee. Brant was by no means a good spokesman for the confederacy at this point – his willingness to give up land to the north of the Ohio was not matched by his western brethren. McKee wrote to Simcoe on July 5 that unless the American commissioners would agree to an Ohio boundary, it was likely that war would ensue. Simcoe himself was concerned by the apparent disagreement between the Six Nations and the other tribes, and while Brant was at Niagara, Simcoe tried to impress upon him the necessity for a strong union of the Indians.[42]

In the middle of July, both the commissioners and the Indian deputation set off west along Lake Erie to the vicinity of the Indian council. The American commissioners had grown increasingly impatient at the delay, and had requested permission to go to Detroit to be nearer the Indian gathering. Simcoe had refused this request, but he did grant them permission to go to the mouth of the Detroit River.[43] From there they could easily communicate with the Indians on the Maumee, and it was presumed they would travel from there to Sandusky when the Indians were ready. The commissioners sailed from Fort Erie on July 14, and it was decided that Elliott's house would be the most suitable accommodation for them while they were at the mouth of the Detroit River. On July 21, the commissioners arrived at Elliott's. Although Elliott himself had left for the rapids with provisions four days before, the commissioners were well taken care of by his many slaves. The commissioners later testified both to Elliott's hospitality and to his prosperity. General Benjamin Lincoln commented that Elliott "has the best farm I have seen in the country by far." While the commissioners stayed in the house, others in the party, including a group of Quakers, encamped in tents "on the pleasant Green" fronting Elliott's house. This green ran down to the Detroit River, and helped to make the house a show-place in this period. The American commissioners immediately informed McKee of their arrival – they had become used to the idea of dealing with the American Indians through the British Indian Department – and once again settled down to wait for the news that the Indians would proceed to Lower Sandusky.[44]

At the foot of the rapids the Indian council was encountering difficulties. On July 21, the deputation that had been to Niagara returned to the Maumee, and it immediately became apparent that the rift in the Indian confederacy was becoming a gulf – with Brant and the Six Nations, joined by the Ottawas, Chippewas, and Potawatomis on one side, and the Shawnees, Miamis, Wyandots, and Delawares leading the opposition. Many thought that the deputation to Niagara had not presented the Indian case with sufficient force. Moreover, in council on July 26, another clash developed because the Lake Indians thought it would be better to hold the council with the Americans at the mouth of the Maumee, rather than at Sandusky. Brant was willing to go along with this idea, but it was strongly opposed by the Wyandots, who had their main villages in the Sandusky region. The threatened impasse was avoided when Captain Johnny, the Shawnee chief in whom Elliott and McKee placed their main trust, spoke out on behalf of the Shawnee and urged that they should complete the business of the council and prepare a message for the commissioners. It is not difficult to see McKee's urging behind this request. Yet, when in answer to this plea the tribes withdrew to consult, they formed two separate councils; the Six Nations with the Lake Indians in one group, and the Shawnees, Wyandots, Miamis, and Delawares in another. After this separate consultation Captain Johnny spoke again, and said that the boundary would have to be that of the treaty of Fort Stanwix in 1768 (the Ohio River). The opinion of the Six Nations was not asked, and a Wyandot chief proceeded to frame the message while Lieutenant Prideaux Selby, who was attached to the Indian Department as an aide to McKee, wrote it down. Brant did not agree with the message and would not sign it. The message reflected the confidence of the western tribes after the defeat of St. Clair. It told the commissioners that if the United States wanted a lasting peace, she should immediately remove all her people from the Indian (north) side of the river. The Indians asked the commissioners whether they were authorized to fix the Ohio as a boundary, explaining that the deputation which had gone to Niagara had failed to give adequate expression to the desires of the confederacy.[45]

On July 28 a deputation of between twenty and thirty Indians – including principal chiefs of the Shawnees, Delawares, and Wyandots – set off for the mouth of the Detroit River. They were accompanied by Matthew Elliott, who with McKee had been present at the proceedings of the council since the deputation had returned from Niagara. At the mouth of the Detroit River the party encamped on Bois Blanc Island; Elliott's farm (where the American commissioners were staying) faced the island on the Canadian side of the river. On July 30, the deputation crossed the river to deliver the message demanding an Ohio River boundary, and on the following day the American commissioners delivered their answer. They told the Indians that an Ohio River boundary was impossible, and that the United States needed approximately the boundary agreed on at Fort Harmar in 1789. They did however now concede that the right of soil to the rest of the land in the Northwest belonged to the Indians, and that the United States had been wrong in the 1780's when she had claimed all the Northwest by right of conquest from Great Britain. Yet the commissioners would not concede the Indian right to all the land beyond the Ohio. On August 1, a Wyandot chief, speaking through interpreter Simon Girty, said that the deputation would lay the reply of the commissioners before the warriors gathered on the Maumee, but to the consternation of Elliott he also added that the commissioners might as well go home and tell the Indian decision to President Washington. The Moravian missionary John Heckewelder recorded in his journal that Elliott immediately exclaimed "*No, No, they was not to have said (the last Words)*," turned to a Shawnee chief, and told him that the last part of the speech was wrong. It would seem that the Wyandot had forgotten his lines, or had at least ad-libbed a little too freely. Simon Girty insisted he had translated the Wyandot's statement correctly, but eventually after some discussion it was announced to the commissioners through Girty that they should wait for an answer while the deputation returned to consult the council on the Maumee.[46]

While the deputation had been away, the council had become even more disunited. On July 28, the day that the message was sent to the commissioners, Brant had written to Simcoe saying that Indian affairs had taken a turn which was not approved by a great part of the Indians. The change had taken place, he argued, while he had been away with the deputation to Niagara. Although the Ottawas, Chippewas, and Potawatomis approved of the deputation's actions, many argued on its return that the group should have insisted on the Ohio River boundary. Brant still expressed the opinion that the Muskingum and not the Ohio would be a just and moderate line, and that the whole question should be discussed at the Sandusky treaty, not definitely resolved beforehand. He expressed the opinion that some of the tribes had not the least inclination for peace, and that the message sent to the commissioners made it almost certain that peace would not be achieved. In this letter, Brant only hinted at the reasons for the attitude of the western tribes. He said that the great change might have occurred owing to advice received from the Creek country. Two weeks before, a British trader had arrived from the South with the news that the Creeks and Cherokees were at war against the Americans. This trader later informed Simcoe that although the Shawnee had been sent by the confederacy last fall to invite the southern Indians to join them, they had not told the southern Indians of the coming treaty, and had in fact assured them that in the event of war the British government would supply them with arms and ammunition.[47] The Shawnee were of course the tribe most closely connected with McKee, Elliott, and the British Indian Department at Detroit.

While Brant was reluctant to blame McKee directly for the failure of the peace negotiations, he became less reticent in the fall and in the years to come. At the end of September, after he had returned disgusted from the council, he gave as a reason for the failure of peace hopes: "the three Nations, Shawonoes, Delawares, & Twightwees [Miamis], being in my opinion too much under the guidance and influence of some white people, who have advised them to adhere to the old boundary line as fixed in the year 1768." Two years later the accusation was made even more explicit. It was reported that it was very difficult to persuade Brant to entertain a favorable opinion of McKee, to whose interference he publicly attributed the failure of peace negotiations with the commissioners. Certainly Simcoe showed no willingness to interfere with McKee's actions in the spring and summer of 1793. To Brant's letter asking for advice on the matter of the split in the council and on the boundary question, Simcoe replied rather vaguely that he could not give an opinion as to the precise boundary, since this was a matter for the Indians.[48] This did not help Brant, whose whole point was that some of the tribes were far too much under the influence of McKee.

The deputation to the commissioners, delayed by contrary winds, did not return to the rapids until August 5. The Brant-McKee rift had become even wider on the previous day. Brant protested that the Six Nations were being left out of the decisions, and that too many private discussions had taken place. "We are not told anything," he asserted, "our opinion and that of

86

three respectable Tribes [Ottawas, Chippewas, and Potawatomis] has not been attended to." When the deputation arrived and gave an account of the meeting, Brant and the Six Nations, who realized that only Elliott had prevented the proposed treaty from ending already, decided to go home. Brant stated that from what had been done it appeared that no treaty was intended. The Shawnee, however, now pressed the Six Nations to stay a few days longer. This was in all probability McKee's desire, as he had been urged to maintain as much unity as possible. The council showed signs of complete disintegration when on August 7 the Creeks made a formal announcement that they were at war with the Americans, were driving them back, and wanted the aid of the confederacy. The Six Nations, and the Seven Nations of Canada who had arrived late for the council, argued that the business for which the council had been called should be completed before the Creek request was considered. The argument continued for several days. On August 9, Captain Johnny again spoke for the Shawnees. Although he acknowledged that the confederacy had been started by the Six Nations, he made it quite evident that in his opinion the Shawnees, Delawares, and Miamis had taken it over since the treaty of Fort Harmar in 1789. He asserted again that although the Indians were willing to meet the commissioners, the Ohio River would still have to be the boundary. Brant opposed him. He acknowledged that the western tribes had led the confederacy since Fort Harmar, but pointed out that the confederacy itself had originally suggested a boundary along the Muskingum River to Lord Dorchester in 1791. On behalf of the Six Nations, Brant urged the tribes to yield land to the Muskingum rather than insist on the Ohio River boundary. The Seven Nations of Canada did not agree with Brant on this, and their spokesman delivered a revealing speech regarding the British attitude: "My opinion when I left home was that we were to defend the Old Boundary which is the Ohio, and in this opinion I was confirmed by the English as I passed their Posts." He announced, however, that the Seven Nations would abide by whatever the council decided.[49]

At this point the attitude of the British Indian agents became even more apparent. The chiefs of the Shawnees, Hurons, Delawares, and Seven Nations of Canada, apparently won over by Brant's arguments, came to see him and told him that they would follow his opinion regarding the boundary, since he knew more about the whites. This idea was soon changed. Brant reported in his journal that at midnight on the same night, McKee held a private meeting with these chiefs, and apparently changed their opinion. There seems no reason to disbelieve Brant on this occasion. Even John Heckewelder, the Moravian missionary at the mouth of the Detroit, had already heard from various Indians that McKee, Elliott, and others had turned the Indians against the deputation which had been to Niagara. In general council on the day after the midnight meeting, Captain Johnny announced that the Ohio River boundary was the final determination, and that this would be told to the commissioners. The Seven Nations of Canada agreed to defend this line, but the Six Nations still insisted that the Muskingum was a more reasonable boundary. Buckongahelas, a Delaware chief, then spoke and Brant wrote in his journal that the Delaware pointed to McKee and said that he had advised them to insist on the Ohio line.[50]

On August 13, the confederacy sent a message to the commissioners and argued that none of the cessions made since 1783 were valid, since they had not been made by the general council. They said that money was of no use to them, and advanced the ingenious idea that the Americans should take the money they were going to give the Indians for the land, and give it to the American settlers on the north of the Ohio as compensation for having to retire beyond that river. The Indians pointed out that these settlers must be poor, otherwise they would never have entered into such a dangerous area. As the message reached its peroration the language befitted this solemn occasion:

> We desire you to consider Brothers, that our only demand, is the peaceable possession of a small part of our once great Country. Look back and view the lands from whence we have been driven to this spot, we can retreat no further, because the country behind hardly affords food for its present inhabitants. And we have therefore

88

resolved, to leave our bones in this small space, to which we are now confined.

A resounding list of tribes affixed their names to this declaration of war – the Wyandots, the Seven Nations of Canada, the Delawares, the Shawnees, the Miamis, the Ottawas, the Chippewas, the Senecas of the Glaize, the Potawatomis, the Conoys, the Munsees, the Nanticokes, the Mahicans, the Missisaugas, the Creeks, and the Cherokees. Conspicuous by their absence were the Six Nations. The Lake Indians and the Seven Nations of Canada had followed the lead of the council, but Brant and his followers would not sign the message. After it was sent, one more council was held. Brant announced that the Six Nations could not assist the confederacy, for they first would have to remove their people from among the Americans.[51] This fact alone goes a long way toward explaining the difference in attitudes. The lands held by the Six Nations were on the American side of the Ohio, and were already surrounded. To them, war was far more serious than the ceding of an extra strip of land on a boundary that had already passed them by. The rest of the Indians looked upon the Ohio as the last great barrier between the Americans and the Northwest – if that barrier fell, then the rest of the Northwest would be unsafe. They thought they could not afford to cede even a small strip to the north of the Ohio, and they were right.

Yet, even if Brant and the Six Nations had carried the council to their point of view, it is difficult to see how peace could have been accomplished. The slight cessions of land that the American commissioners had been authorized to make would not have satisfied even the moderates led by Brant. There would have been a council, but it could well have been a repetition of Fort Harmar, with the Indians pressured into yielding more than they wished, and then revoking the treaty when it was completed. But as it was there was not even a treaty council. The Indian message reached the commissioners on August 16, and they immediately replied that the Ohio boundary was impossible. The negotiation was at an end. On August 17, the commissioners sailed from Elliott's for Fort Erie. Meanwhile, though the Lake Indians (whose main settlements were well-removed from the

Ohio) urged Brant to promote a peace along the Muskingum, a war feast was prepared at the rapids: "the Chiefs of the Shawanoes singing the War Song encouraging the Warriors of all the Nations to be active in defending their Country, saying their Father the English would assist them and Pointed to Col. McKee."[52]

McKee's version of the failure of the council, in a letter to Simcoe, was much different from Brant's. He said that expectations of peace had been disappointed because the Indians insisted on an Ohio River boundary, and that while he had tried to maintain unity the Six Nations had acted alone and had tried to divide the nations by holding private councils. He was pleased that the United States had now acknowledged the Indian right of soil to land not yet sold – "these lands will form an extensive Barrier between the British & American Territory." McKee closed by particularly insisting that he had tried to obtain peace, and had exerted no improper influence to prevent it. He warned Simcoe, however, that he expected to be blamed for the arguments that the Indians had adopted. The part that McKee and Elliott played in all this will never be fully understood – records of midnight councils on the Maumee create few space problems in any library – but it is obvious that the British Indian Department at Detroit used its power, provisions, and influence to strengthen the resolution of the Indians to stand firm against the Americans. They exerted this influence mainly through the medium of the Shawnee, and were to continue to use this tribe for the next twenty years. In spite of McKee's protestations, there seems good reason to believe that he was using his influence on the Maumee in the summer of 1793 to strengthen the Indian will against compromise, and against the concessions advocated by Joseph Brant. Although Simcoe accepted the account of the proceedings given him by McKee, and assured the British Minister in the United States, George Hammond, that McKee had tried to use his influence to persuade the Indians to be content with more moderate demands, even the British Indian agent John Butler was not in agreement with McKee's endeavors at the 1793 council. Some two years later he wrote that he feared he had lost his influence in the Department because of

his disagreeement with McKee at the time of the attempted San-
dusky treaty – "I thought that [the treaty] the most favourable
Opportunity that Perhaps would Ever Occur for them [the
Indians] to make an Advantageous Peace and Save the greatest
Part of their country."[53]

The British Indian Department at Detroit was an exceedingly
capable body with great influence over the Indians, but both
McKee and Elliott were exceedingly pro-Shawnee and had little
love for the Americans. There is considerable reason to doubt
that they carried out the instructions of the British government
in the dispassionate manner that was required. From August
1793, war in the Northwest was inevitable, and the position of
McKee and Elliott was to become even stronger.

Chapter 5

AMERICAN VICTORY

The failure of the American peace effort in 1793 led inevitably to the expedition of General Anthony Wayne. But the hopes that the failure of negotiations could immediately be followed by an expedition in the summer of 1793 were doomed to disappointment. The Indians had taken so long to decide on their messages to the commissioners that it was not until the latter part of August that Wayne received news of the failure. He decided that an expedition in 1793 was now impossible, and contented himself in October with advancing his force some six miles beyond Fort Jefferson and establishing Fort Greenville (the present Greenville, Darke County, Ohio). There he prepared to spend the winter before leading an attack against the Indians in the following spring and summer.[1]

While Wayne pushed cautiously northward, the British Indian Department was engaged in its customary fall task of supplying the Indians.[2] This went on throughout October, being interrupted only by the sudden alarm produced by Wayne's advance to Fort Greenville. Throughout the latter part of October messages reached the foot of the rapids that the Americans were advancing. So pressing did the messages become that at the end of October McKee removed his heavy baggage and papers to Swan Creek, near the mouth of the Maumee. He then returned to the foot of the rapids and sent Simon Girty to report on the progress of the American army. He was able to report that the Americans had encamped six miles north of Fort Jefferson, and at the end of November McKee returned to Detroit.[3] Meanwhile Elliott was busily organizing the shipping of supplies for the Indians. On October 20, he sent McKee ten barrels of powder, twenty cases of shot, and two thousand flints (among other supplies). Elliott also showed a flash of affection either for his wife or for her tribe when he requested that the name of the new boat being used on the Maumee should be "the Shawanoe" rather than the more prosaic, but undoubtedly accurate, name of "Indian Feeder" that had been bestowed on her. In a more practical vein he reported to McKee that little assistance would be available from the region of Detroit, since most of the Indians had left for their winter hunting grounds.[4] At the end of October and the beginning of November, when the fear of the American advance became more acute, Elliott was anxious to join McKee but remained in Detroit to carry out any instructions he might have regarding Indians and supplies. Yet, once it was realized that Wayne had camped for the winter months, the Indian Department settled into its quiet winter routine.[5]

The quiet was to last only a few months, for in February 1794 the British became far more involved in the activities of the Indians. On February 10, the Governor in chief of Canada, Lord Dorchester, delivered a famous speech to the Seven Nations of Canada. The Seven Nations came to Quebec as deputies from the Indian council held on the Maumee during the previous year, and Dorchester greeted them with a rash and ill-advised address. His statements inspired the Indians to believe that British help was inevitable. He said of the United States: "I shall not be surprized if we are at war with them in the course of the present year; and if so, a Line must then be drawn by the Warriors." The close of his speech left little doubt of his opinion. "You are Witness," he stated, "that on our parts we have acted in the most peaceable manner, and borne the Language and Conduct of the People of the United States with Patience; but I believe our Patience is almost exhausted."[6] This rash speech eventually shocked the British government in England almost as much as it did the Americans, but by that time the damage had been done.

Even before Dorchester's speech, McKee and Elliott were actively engaged in preparing the Indians for Wayne's advance. At the end of January both of them hurried to the rapids of the Maumee, owing to rumors of the plundering of British traders by the Indians. This proved untrue, but McKee was still unhappy at what he found. He was most pessimistic about the coming campaign, and feared that the quarrels which had beset the Indians in their council of the previous summer meant that the American army would be able to establish itself in the area in a very short time.[7] While McKee stayed at the rapids, Elliott was sent to the Glaize to investigate the frightening rumors that Indian peace commissions had been sent to Wayne. The Shawnee and Miami chiefs assured Elliott that they had merely agreed with the Delawares that two American prisoners should be exchanged for two Indian women – they also assured him that they had neither sent nor authorized any message to Wayne regarding peace. Even though the Delawares had been communicating with Wayne, the Indians assured Elliott that it was only a small number of that tribe. The keenness with which the Detroit Indian Department pounced on any rumor of possible Indian concession demonstrates quite clearly the interest it had in maintaining Indian resistance. Apart from the Delaware minority, Elliott's news from the Glaize was fairly good. While he was there another party of Delawares came in with an American prisoner and some stolen horses, and Elliott was told that most of the Indians were out observing American troop movements and attacking any parties of troops or convoys that they encountered.[8]

While the Indian Department kept close watch over the Indians, Lieutenant-Governor Simcoe waited for the end of the bitterly cold weather before personally proceeding to Detroit to supervise the defenses of the region. Dorchester had informed him on February 17 that in the interest of British security at Detroit, Great Britain should re-establish the posts on the Maumee that had been abandoned at the peace in 1783.[9] This was an overt advance into American territory, but Dorchester was convinced that it was essential for the safety of Upper Canada. Simcoe finally arrived at Detroit on April 2, stayed there for four days, and after spending a night at Elliott's went to the rapids with Elliott and McKee. Simcoe was able to have private talks with McKee during the week he spent at the rapids. His main task, however, was to provide for the defense of the region. He arranged for the construction and garrisoning of Fort Miami – about a mile below McKee's on the other side of the river –

and placed other troops at strategic points; a corporal's guard at Roche de Bout [on the Maumee near the present Waterville, Lucas County, Ohio], and establishments at Turtle Island near the mouth of the Maumee and at the River Raisin. He also determined the militia that would be available in the Detroit region in the event of an emergency.[10]

In regard to the Indians, Simcoe took a decisive step during his visit to Detroit. On April 14 he delivered Dorchester's inflammatory speech of the previous February to the Indians at the Glaize.[11] The Indians now knew that war was expected between England and the United States, and quite obviously became confident of British aid. During this entire visit in early April, Simcoe acted as though war were only a matter of time, and Lord Dorchester encouraged this belief. In a letter to Simcoe on April 14, Dorchester suggested that the intrigues and influence of France seemed to render hostilities with the United States inevitable.[12]

The effect of all this on the Indians is not hard to imagine. The appearance of British military activity along the Maumee, combined with the already active work of the British Indian Department, could only serve to convince them that the British government was at last ready to provide overt military aid. McKee was able to state on May 8 that the condition of Indian affairs in the area had altered considerably for the better. Dorchester's speech to the Seven Nations, and the arrival on the Maumee of speeches from the Spaniards in Louisiana urging war against the United States, led McKee to think that the situation would result in an extensive union of the Indians.[13] Throughout May, McKee and Elliott were active along the Maumee. At the end of that month, news reached the rapids that the Indians had attacked a party of Americans between Fort Washington and Fort Hamilton and had claimed to have brought away forty scalps with the loss of only one warrior. McKee immediately wrote to the military commander in Detroit, Lieutenant-Colonel Richard England, and directed that Elliott, who had returned to Detroit, should do all he could to hurry the Indians in that neighborhood to the Glaize.[14] The Glaize had become the great gathering place of the Indians preparing to meet Wayne. Now McKee became increasingly optimistic. On May 30 he was able to report that the Lake Indians (Ottawa, Chippewa, and Potawatomi) were at last gathering together, and that several small parties had already gone up from the rapids to the Glaize. By June 3 he was reporting that the Indians were collecting in considerable numbers, and he was hopeful that they would all be gathered at the Glaize within about two weeks. The purpose of their gathering was writ large in McKee's requisition of June 8 for eighty thousand black wampum (for war) and only twenty thousand white wampum (for peace). By June 10 there were five hundred Indians gathered at the rapids waiting to go up to join the Indians at the Glaize, and a large number were expected from Michilimackinac. Simcoe wrote to McKee in the middle of the month, hoping that the Indians would collect in sufficient numbers to resist their opponents.[15] He could rest assured that the Indian Department was doing all within its power to gather the Indian forces.

At the Glaize, all was color and activity as the Indians prepared to make their last great defense of the Old Northwest. By June 15, when the Wyandots came into join the army, there were six hundred warriors there to greet them with a crashing fusillade. Elliott was there, now in his element, helping to organize the warriors; he was accompanied by McKee's son, Thomas, an unknown British officer, and a number of British and French traders of the region. On June 16, any suggestion that these could all be regarded as mere observers came to an end when an Indian council of war resolved that all the whites in the vicinity would have to join the Indian army. In evidence of their determination they handed Elliott a belt of black wampum. On June 18 the whites assumed Indian dress to ensure there would be no mistakes in the heat of battle. By this time provisions were scarce, and Elliott shocked the British officer by wanting to leave some at the Glaize in case of the arrival of McKee. The army was further strengthened by the arrival of Indians from Mackinac and Saginaw. This party, however, had committed depredations and attacked women in the Indian villages through which it had passed, and it was now suggested that the rest of the Indians should be rerouted from the rapids to avoid the Indian villages that were now destitute of men. On June 19, a large number of warriors left to join their advanced party, and the camp was in turmoil. Yet Elliott still found time to send a message saying that he had heard that William Caldwell was "tampering" with his farmer (who supervised Elliott's plantation), and that Elliott was likely to lose him. He wanted Caldwell to desist. As in the Revolution, Indian war was not enough to distract Elliott from all practical considerations. The British officer who was present regretted that five hundred spears had not been procured in time, as he thought spears would be most effective in resisting Wayne's cavalry. He also indicated in his report (intended for McKee) that he had tried to impress upon the Indians that their best strategy would be to starve out the American garrisons by cutting their supply lines and preventing their retreat. The Indians, with the aid of the British Indian Department, had collected an imposing force – by this time it was estimated that the Indians had not less than fifteen hundred warriors in the field.[16]

The remainder of the Indians broke camp on June 20, and Elliott and his compatriots went with them. As the army lacked corn, Elliott bought over three hundred bushels from the traders on the spot. He also pointed out in a letter to McKee that there was a great cry for tobacco, "and ammunition will soon be wanted."[17] In the next three days the main party advanced some sixty miles south of the Glaize. The reason for this comparatively slow progress was that the party was obliged to encamp each day at one or two o'clock in the afternoon in order to give time for the hunters to scour the surrounding country. Even with the help of British provisions, it had not been possible to store enough supplies for this army. The hunters, however, supplied it with an abundance. It is not difficult to understand why the Indians were fighting for this region south of Lake Erie. Even with a large army moving through the country, the hunters brought in as many as two hundred deer and two hundred turkeys in one day. Estimates of the number of warriors advancing south varied from day to day, but the estimates usually ranged from one thousand to fifteen hundred. Part of the difficulty was that fresh parties were joining every day, and some were advancing south by different routes. The Delawares, who said they would journey by another route to avoid the danger of the Americans surprising the Indian villages which were deserted of warriors, did not arrive until after the army had engaged the enemy.

By June 26, the army was over eighty miles from the Glaize, and was now advancing in open files, ten rods between each file, and the hunters were out scouring the flanks and the woods ahead. On the following day it was discovered that Indians were fighting with Wayne as well as against him. A scouting party encountered Chickasaws from the south who were acting as scouts for Wayne – the party killed one and took his scalp. This was immediately sent by courier to the rear to hasten the laggards; the courier also carried the report of the proceedings that was regularly sent to McKee. The British officer with the army urged the Indians to concentrate their efforts on cutting the supply lines between the American forts and the Ohio, but the advice was ignored. The Indians from the Saginaw and Michilimackinac regions persuaded the others that they should make a direct attack upon Fort Recovery, which had been constructed in December 1793 on the site of St. Clair's defeat. The Indian force lacked the artillery for this attempt.

On the night of June 29, the force arrived in the vicinity of Fort Recovery, and the Indian scouts reported that a great number of packhorses had arrived at the fort, and would probably return the next morning. The Indian force, now some fifteen hundred to two thousand strong, overwhelmed the American supply train as it left the fort on the next day. The fort's defenders attempted to relieve the supply train, but they were thrown back into the fort within a few minutes, losing some fifteen killed and four wounded, together with three hundred packhorses. At this point the Indians made a disastrous mistake, and helped to provide for the eventual victory of Anthony Wayne. In their enthusiasm they attacked the fort itself. Though it consisted merely of blockhouses mounted with cannon and connected by wooden pickets, it was too strong for the Indians to capture. The Indians kept up their fire throughout the day and the night following, but achieved nothing. The Indians who had rushed the fort lost sixteen or seventeen killed as well as a good many wounded. For the Indians this was a heavy loss – they seldom suffered severe losses in their engagements with the whites. Elliott and his compatriots were a little more cautious, and their only casualty was a wounded French Canadian. The British officer with the army considered that with two barrels of powder they could have taken the fort by making use of the cannons – grim relics of St. Clair's defeat – that still lay near Fort Recovery. Though only a skirmish, the attack on Fort Recovery was of decisive importance in weakening the Indian resistance to Wayne.

Now short of ammunition and provisions, the Indians resolved to retire. The Delawares, who belatedly joined the army on July 2, agreed to scout the enemy while the remainder returned to the Glaize. Elliott was in considerable difficulty, for the Mackinac and Lake Indians talked of returning home and many left the camp. He tried to organize a council at the Glaize to persuade them to stay, and immediately informed McKee that unless provisions and ammunition were sent, it would be difficult to hold the Indian force together. McKee passed on this warning to Colonel England and to Simcoe, adding that the British posts would be endangered should the Indians disperse. On July 5, several of the Lake Indians arrived at McKee's on their way home. In a letter to Simcoe, McKee bewailed the fact that he was unauthorized to stop them or to forward provisions and ammunition to keep the Indians at the Glaize.[18] This was of course an understatement of his previous powers, but it reflected Indian disgust at the lack of more overt British aid.

Elliott's efforts to keep all the Indians at the Glaize were to no avail. By July 10, many of the Potawatomis and the Indians from Saginaw and Mackinac had passed McKee's, and others were 'daily following their example. McKee did succeed, however, in persuading several of their chiefs to remain at the foot of the rapids in order to send for their warriors at the first alarm of the approach of Wayne's army. McKee was of the opinion that if authorized he could have stopped the Indians departing, but that it would have meant taking an active part in the contest, and becoming at least auxilaries in the war.[19] There was a thin line beyond which McKee would not go. The members of the Indian Department who were still in Detroit did all they could to persuade the Indians who had left Elliott and passed McKee to return to the Glaize.[20]

Simcoe, who was at Niagara, received all this news in the middle of July. He regretted that Elliott had taken part in the action at Fort Recovery, but was pleased that all the traders had been forced to participate. This, he argued, demonstrated that Elliott's participation was the wish of the Indians and not the government. [21] Simcoe also heeded McKee's pleas for provisions. He wrote to Colonel England at Detroit that "I shall most readily agree with you as far as I have authority to relax a rigid adherence to general custom in this hour of necessity, and beg that you will only restrict yourself by the good of the Service and furnish all such supplies as in your judgement Colonel McKee properly requires."[22] This presumably meant that Simcoe wanted England to give McKee what he wanted, within reason, but that he should be careful to avoid any action that would bring higher authority down on either Simcoe or England.

The British government in London was inevitably several months behind concerning events in Upper Canada, and had little way of knowing what Matthew Elliott was saying by his camp fire on the Glaize. On July 4, Secretary of State Henry Dundas wrote to Simcoe and stated "I very much approve of the very prudent and pacific line of Conduct which you have adopted, in consequence of General Wayne's supposed approach to the vicinity of Detroit." The activities of the Indian Department at Detroit in the first half of 1794 could hardly be justly called "very prudent and pacific." Dundas warned Simcoe that "the *immediate* protection of the Post itself" was the only object to be attended to.[23] It is doubtful whether Dundas and Simcoe had the same idea of what was meant by "*immediate* protection," and it is not at all unlikely that the Indian Department would have given it yet another interpretation.

Throughout July the Indian Department worked unceasingly along the Maumee and in Detroit, but it was being placed in an increasingly embarrassing predicament. Although the Department had quite obviously not maintained neutrality in the American-Indian struggle, the Indians themselves were becoming increasingly aware that British assistance was stopping short of direct military aid. The Miami chief Little Turtle – whom

Colonel England called "the most decent, modest, sensible Indian I ever conversed with" – came to Detroit and wanted to know the amount of aid the Indians could expect. More particularly, he asked for twenty men and two pieces of cannon to go to Fort Recovery, and said that if the Indians were not assisted by the British they would not stop the American army. Colonel England could not give him what he wanted, but he talked to him for two or three days and sent him away "seemingly contented." Yet, if Little Turtle was as sensible as England said he was, it seems hardly likely that he was deceived by these tactics.[24]

McKee, however, was able to report to Simcoe on July 26 that the total separation of the Indians had been prevented: "it is a great satisfaction to me, to be able to announce the prospect of their speedily recollecting themselves." He told Simcoe that three hundred of the Indians who lived at a distance had stayed at the rapids, among them several principal chiefs who were now summoning their warriors from their villages.[25] As affairs in the Northwest reached a climax, McKee and Elliott were in hope that they had staved off the complete disintegration of the Indian force. Yet, for all their efforts, the reverse at Fort Recovery and the Indian quarrels of the previous year had severely weakened the Indian position.

General Anthony Wayne had passed the winter of 1793-94 at Fort Greenville waiting for the time when active operations would once again become possible. The only real advance was made in December 1793 when a force was sent to construct Fort Recovery on the site of St. Clair's defeat. Wayne was far more cautious than Harmar or St. Clair, and it was not until the end of July 1794 that he finally decided to move his main force forward from Fort Greenville. His troops were better trained, better equipped, and far more careful of the danger of Indian ambush. As Wayne advanced toward the Glaize, the Indians there retreated to the foot of the rapids with their women and children. McKee immediately wrote to Colonel England (on August 10) and requested provisions. He stated that he would endeavor to keep the Indians together and that he hoped to be able to cooperate with the Indians in defending Fort Miami or Detroit should the Americans, as was feared, attack them.[26]

During the first three weeks in August, the British Indian Department did all that it could to ensure that an effective Indian force would be available to resist the Americans and provide a cover for Fort Miami and Detroit. The letters that were sent by Simcoe during this same period indicate that the Department's actions met with the approbation of the lieutenant-governor. On August 6 he wrote that war (between England and the United States) was inevitable, and in that case "somehow or other Wayne must be driven back." He requested McKee's private opinion on the best way of accomplishing this, and on what could be expected from an autumnal or winter campaign in the Detroit-Maumee region should war be declared around the end of September.[27] On the thirteenth he informed McKee that in the event of Wayne penetrating to the Glaize (which in fact he had already done) the principal British reliance would have to be on the influence which McKee could preserve over the Indian nations. On the seventeenth he wrote to say that he relied on McKee to keep up the resolution of the Indians, and also urged England to use every means to bolster Indian confidence.[28] There are no signs that Simcoe was trying to alter the course of the Indian Department in these last days before the battle.

On August 5, Elliott and Thomas McKee left the rapids for Detroit to bring supplies and any support they could muster. When they returned, they brought not only supplies but also fifty-three militiamen from Detroit under the command of William Caldwell, Elliott's partner of the 1780's. Colonel England and the leaders of the British and French in Detroit had been uncertain whether to call out the milita – the question being whether Wayne's advance to the Glaize constituted an invasion. In the end they compromised by holding the majority of the militia in readiness, while sending a company to fight under Caldwell and over one hundred French Canadians to serve as workmen in strengthening Fort Miami. These arrived on August 12, and during the week following, the Indian Department and Colonel England supplied the Indian force at the rapids with provisions. They also did everything possible to hurry forward to the rapids any Indians from Detroit and from the regions to the north.[29]

Meanwhile, Wayne prepared to advance toward the Indian position. On August 13 he made a last attempt at peace by sending a messenger asking the Indians to come to terms, and requesting them to ignore the advice of the British at the rapids. The Indians, who wanted all possible time to increase their forces, delayed replying until August 17, and then sent a message with the sole object of delaying the encounter for a few more days.[30] This they thought was a vain hope, and they expected an American attack on the following day. To prepare themselves for the coming encounter they began to fast on the night of August 18, and on the following day left Colonel McKee's encampment at the foot of the rapids and took up a position on the other side of the river (the north bank) a little further up the rapids. They positioned themselves in a wood which formed a natural defensework owing to the number of trees scattered on the ground. By this time the Indian force consisted of about thirteen hundred warriors – principally of the Wyandot, Delaware, Shawnee, Miami, and Ottawa tribes. In spite of McKee's hopes, the Lake Indians, apart from the Ottawa of the Maumee, had few men in the engagement, and the Six Nations did not arrive until after the battle.[31]

The Indian force took up its position in the fallen timbers on August 19, but their fast which had started the previous day had to last until the twentieth, when Wayne finally advanced. That day opened wet and stormy, and many of the Indians, unable to fast any longer, went several miles down the river to visit Fort Miami for provisions. This proved disastrous. Before eight o'clock in the morning the left wing of the Indian force encountered the advanced right wing of the American army which was advancing from the direction of the river.

An engagement began immediately, and the Indian force drove the Americans back; for a moment throwing the American right wing into confusion. Yet, the Indian attack lacked reserves, as so many were away collecting provisions, and the Indians were unable to take advantage of a temporary situation that could have changed the course of the whole battle. When the Indians encountered the main body of the American right, they were checked and slowly driven back toward their own position. By this time, many Indians had run from the fort to join in the engagement, but were hardly in the best condition for action. Wayne now threw his left wing in attack against the American right, and here took place the most ferocious fighting of the entire engagement with the Wyandots bearing the brunt of the American attack. The Americans gradually outflanked the Indians and forced them to retreat, taking the whole Indian line with them. While the Indian retreat quickly turned into a rout, a stubborn rearguard action was fought by the Wyandots and by the British militia under Caldwell. Elliott, McKee, and Simon Girty had been in the field but had not taken part in the main action – they observed from near the river. Either they did not wish to implicate the Indian Department any further, or perhaps they were only too well aware of what would happen to them if they were captured in the heat of action. The resistance of the rearguard was to no avail – the Indians were in flight and could not be stopped. They fled downstream hoping to obtain shelter and support from the British fort. In this they were disappointed – the British commander did not wish to implicate himself in the action – and they continued down the river toward the mouth of the Maumee. The Indians were long to remember the British closing of Fort Miami.

The whole action had lasted for some three hours, and when it was over the Americans destroyed the houses of Elliott and McKee, all the storehouses, and the Indian huts in the vicinity. The losses were not great on either side, but they seemed large to the Indians. The actual American losses amounted to forty-four dead (eleven of whom died of wounds), and eighty-nine wounded.[32] The Indians probably lost between forty and fifty warriors with an indeterminate number of wounded. The Wyandots bore the brunt of the losses, and they were particularly disastrous, since among them were a majority of their principal chiefs. The Ottawas were also badly hit, and lost two chiefs. The other Indians suffered less heavily. McKee estimated afterward that not more than four hundred were actually engaged in the battle, and one report asserted that the Shawnee, who had been so warlike, had never actually taken part in the engagement. The militia under Caldwell also suffered losses – four dead and one prisoner. These included Caldwell's second-in-command, Captain Daniel McKillip, and also Charles Smith, who was clerk of the court at Detroit. A later report on Smith by the Secretary of the Province of Upper Canada said that he had been wounded through the knees, captured, and then quartered alive by the American troops. Revenge was speedily taken, for the same source stated that an American officer who was captured shortly afterwards was cut into pound pieces by the Indians. McKee reported that the Americans had scalped and mutilated the Indians killed in the action, and had also opened the Indian graves along the Maumee and driven stakes through the corpses.[33] Reports of barbarities were not all directed at the Indians in this period.

Wayne's victory over the Indians at Fallen Timbers was a death-blow to England's hopes of establishing an Indian preserve northwest of the Ohio. It was now quite apparent that the Indians would have to make peace, and that they would have to concede American ownership of land to the north of the Ohio. The British were now in a position of great weakness in regard to the Indians. Although the Indian Department had worked so desperately to keep the Indians in the field, the only direct military aid had been provided by Caldwell's militia. Fort Miami had been closed to the Indians when they most desired and needed its support. While it did seem for a time that Wayne's force and the garrison of Fort Miami would clash, neither Wayne nor Major William Campbell, who commanded the British fort, wished to provide the spark that would start a British-American war. After an exchange of stiff notes, the American force surprised the British by neither attacking Fort Miami nor advancing on Detroit; instead the Americans retreated on August 22.[34] Wayne had accomplished his basic task – the defeat of the Indians. He went no further.

For McKee and Elliott, the Indian defeat at Fallen Timbers brought immediate and pressing problems. The Indians were now most disgruntled and were proving difficult to control. The Delawares threatened to join the Spanish on the Mississippi, and repeated to Moravian missionary David Zeisberger what they had told the British:

Thou hast always hitherto urged us to go to war against the States. We have followed thee to our great loss .... Thou hast always preached to us and said:

105

"Behold, the States are taking away your land. Be brave, act like men. Let not your land be taken from you. Fight for your land " But now we have got at the truth. The States have struck thee to the ground and overcome thee .... Thou urgest us to war, but sittest still thyself, and mayest not raise thy hand.[35]

Not only were the Indians disgruntled they were also in imminent danger of starvation. Their villages, supplies, and cornfields along the Auglaize and Maumee had been destroyed, and at a time when the use of the Indians was beginning to diminish from the British point of view, their need for supplies was to grow even greater. At the end of August, Elliott and McKee attempted to gather the fleeing Indians at a convenient spot, and it was agreed that Swan Creek, on the north bank of the Maumee near its mouth (near the modern city of Toledo, Ohio), would be the most suitable spot.[36] Here at Swan Creek the Indians gathered, and Elliott, who was left in command when McKee returned to Detroit at the beginning of September, faced a prodigious task, for he was not only attempting to feed the Indians, he was also expected to report on American troop movements. On September 15, Elliott listed 2,556 Indians drawing provisions at Swan Creek – over 2,000 of them Delawares, Shawnees, and Ottawas – and recommended on September 22 that six months provisions for 3,000 Indians should be provided and sent to Turtle Island in Maumee Bay. Eventually McKee decided that this should be a requisition for 3,500 Indians for six months, and his requisition was approved by Simcoe. Only British supplies stood between the Indians and starvation in the winter of 1794-95.[37]

In the early fall, before Simcoe gave his approval to McKee's requisition, Colonel England at Detroit began to show some doubts about the Indian Department. On September 8 he wrote to Simcoe to say that Simcoe would have to judge the propriety of McKee's request for more provisions than were originally intended for the post: "The Consumption for some months past has been prodigious and I see no prospect of its being lessened during the Winter." He went on to say that McKee would no doubt give all the details regarding the Indians, but he cautioned

Simcoe not to give too much credit to reports of unanimity among the Indians, nor to reports of the Indians having a disposition to meet the American army in the near future. Colonel England was careful to say he had a high opinion of McKee – knowing Simcoe's opinions, it would have been injudicious to say otherwise – but mentioned "a little partiality" in McKee natural to a man who has direction of Indian affairs. Colonel England skirted dangerous ground to try to warn Simcoe not to believe any reports from the Indian Department which might speak of the strength of Indian resistance and unity. England was not made any happier when Elliott arrived in Detroit on September 17 with the news of the mass of Indians he was feeding at Swan Creek. He pointed out to Simcoe that supplies at Detroit would rapidly be exhausted unless more were sent, or unless he was given power to buy more in the vicinity.[38]

In this crisis of affairs resulting from Wayne's victory, Simcoe decided to make another visit to Detroit. Not only did he feel that the crisis called for his presence, it also seemed probable that McKee would have to leave Detroit to visit Dorchester in Quebec at a time when Joseph Brant and his Six Nations were at last going to visit the Detroit region. Brant arrived at Detroit in the middle of September with about one hundred followers, and immediately proposed a council with the Wyandots at Brownstown (at the mouth of the Detroit River on its west bank). Simcoe finally left Fort Erie for Detroit on September 23. McKee, who had been on his way to see Dorchester in Quebec, returned with Simcoe rather than proceed on his mission.[39]

The party did not proceed directly to Detroit. On September 26 the governor arrived at Turtle Island in Maumee Bay, and Elliott brought a boat from Swan Creek to pick up the Governor's party and take them up the Maumee. As they rowed into the river they saw that the north bank was thickly covered with Indian huts and tents, and when they reached Swan Creek they were given "a grand salute" by some two or three thousand Indians who had gathered to greet the governor. Elliott, who had a temporary hut at the creek, there provided the governor's party with "a sumptuous dinner." After visiting Fort Miami and the battlefield of Fallen Timbers with Elliott and McKee, the governor met with the Indians at Swan Creek on September 28 in an endeavor to keep them in the British interest. Simcoe spent a few more days at Swan Creek, proceeded to Detroit on October 2, and on the 8th returned to Elliott's farm at the mouth of the Maumee to be ready for Brant's council at Brownstown.[40]

The Brownstown council finally met from October 9 to October 14. Simcoe was in council with representatives of the Six Nations, Wyandots, Delawares, Shawnees, Miamis, Lake Indians, Munsees, and Cherokees. Both the Wyandots and Joseph Brant asked Simcoe when the British promise of assistance would be fulfilled. In answer Simcoe could only make a desperate attempt to bolster the spirit of the Indians; "I am still of the opinion that the Ohio is your right and title. I have given orders to the commandant of Fort Miami to fire on the Americans whenever they make their appearance again. I will go down to Quebec, and lay your grievances before the great man. From thence they will be forwarded to the King, your father." He urged the Indians to unite as one man.[41] Simcoe's promises were of course not enough to convince the Indians, and all that Simcoe said could not disguise the fact that British military forces had not taken up the struggle against the Americans. The council ended on October 14, and after a night at Elliott's, the governor and his party sailed for Fort Erie. The whole visit had helped Elliott's reputation, but had done little to regain the confidence of the Indians. Brant wrote on October 22 that the Indians in the region of Detroit and the Maumee were in considerable confusion owing to their late ill-success, and were in bad temper as they had not received assistance from the British. Brant, with a human overestimation of his powers, said that he thought most of them would have gone to the Mississippi if he had not asked them to remain until the spring for an Indian council.[42]

While Elliott entertained the governor, affairs at Swan Creek were managed by Thomas Smith of the Indian Department. His main problem was the shortage of provisions. Though the Indians had been defeated by Wayne, they were still sending out war parties against the American frontier, and were making few preparations to avoid starvation during the coming winter months. Smith attempted to restrict the consumption of provisions, but his problems were increased by the quantity of rum that private traders were bringing to the Maumee. The British Indian Department made persistent efforts to stop the liquor traffic, but was unsuccessful, and the more liquor that was available, the more constant became the demands on Smith for provisions. There was also pressure on Smith for ammunition, both for hunting, which the Indian Department was anxious to encourage because it lessened the demand for provisions, and for making war on the Americans.[43] Smith reported on October 23: "The Chiefs are sending their young men out to hunt & have been obliged in consequence to give them ammunition, as well as all the parties going to war." He estimated that one hundred pounds of powder and two hundred pounds of lead had been expended since Elliott's departure just over two weeks before.[44]

The attempt to appease the bitter Indians by providing them with food and ammunition continued throughout the winter. The supply problem was constant (it was increased when the coming of winter ended navigation on the Maumee), and it was not until the end of the year that Colonel England was able to inform Simcoe that he had almost completed the approved requisition for the Indian Department.[45] Yet the Indian Department had no real chance of preventing Wayne from reaping the fruits of his victory at Fallen Timbers, and its hopes became even less after November 1794, when by Jay's Treaty Great Britain agreed to cede the northwest posts to the United States. Though it was to be two years before the cession was completed, Jay's Treaty placed the keystone on Wayne's victory and brought an end to British hopes of retaining control over the region south of Lake Erie.

During the winter of 1794-95, representatives of the various tribes visited Fort Greenville to make their submission to Wayne. The Wyandots began their overtures in November 1794 and continued throughout the winter, and in January 1795, Wayne signed preliminary articles of peace with the Chippewa, Potawatomi, Sauk, and Miami. By these preliminary articles it was agreed that the tribes would meet Wayne at Greenville on or around June 15 to establish a permanent peace. Other Indians were quick to follow. On January 24, the Shawnee chief Blue Jacket left Swan Creek with fifty Shawnees and Delawares. They arrived at Greenville on February 7, and on the 11th entered into preliminary articles of peace with Wayne on behalf of the Shawnees, Delawares, and Miamis. They also agreed to come to Fort Greenville on or about June 15. Shortly after this the Wyandots of Sandusky, who had been the first to approach Wayne, also signed preliminary articles. The last remnants of Indian resistance were crumbling.[46]

In January 1795, news reached Detroit from all quarters that the Indians were going in to make peace with Wayne, and once again Elliott and McKee set out for the Maumee. At Swan Creek they discovered that Blue Jacket had already left with his party of Shawnees and Delawares, and they could do little about it.[47] Although McKee reported that there was a strong party at Swan Creek against the proceedings of Blue Jacket, it would seem that his wishes were inflating the strength of the opposition group. The Indian Department was feeding the Indians, but its control over them had been broken by the events of the previous summer. Joseph Brant, who had returned to the Grand River, also sent messages during the winter in the hope of maintaining some unity among the Indians, but he had no effect. Brant, as at the time of the peace efforts in 1793, tended to blame McKee and the British Indian Department for much of what had happened. "It is a pity Colonel McKee should have lost his influence with the Indians," he wrote on February 24, "or that he ever interfered in their councils."[48] In essence, of course, the influence of the British Indian Department had diminished because at the last instant the British had not backed up their encouragement and supplies with active military force, and the Indians had met military defeat. Yet in spite of Brant's attack and the relative impotence of the Indian Department in the winter of 1794-95, McKee was given a promotion in December. He was appointed Deputy Superintendent General and Deputy Inspector General of Indians and their Affairs.[49] This of course also enhanced Elliott's position as McKee's chief aide, and was to lead eventually to Elliott's appointment to the command of the Indian Department in the Detroit region.

McKee was concerned in the early spring of 1795 that the Indians would once again be ignored in British-American negotiations, and that Jay's Treaty, like the treaty of Paris, would leave the Indians – "the poor Indians who have long fought for us and bled fairly for us" – to shift for themselves. He thought such a policy would at a later date prove short-sighted, and though he did not live to witness it, his apprehensions were proved correct after **1807** when the authorities lamented the lack of attention given to the Indians after 1795. At the end of March McKee was incapacitated by a severe illness – "a violent and bilious rheumatic fever" – and after recovering from it in May, he left Detroit to visit Dorchester in Quebec. He did not return until the end of August.[50]

With McKee first incapacitated and then absent, a greater weight fell upon Elliott in the spring of 1795. By the end of March provisions were becoming exceedingly scarce at Swan Creek, but fortunately navigation was now open and Elliott was able to travel there by boat to relieve the situation. His voyage was not a peaceful one. The two sailors who had been sent to assist him on the vessel consumed fourteen days' ration of rum in three, and did not appear on deck throughout the passage. At Swan Creek, Elliott found that while there was still ample pork in the store, there was a need for corn and flour. He requested McKee to send a boatload of supplies, and also reported at the same time that not a grave between the foot of the rapids and the Glaize had avoided desecration by the American army. All had been opened and robbed.[51]

Colonel England immediately took steps to remedy the need for corn at Swan Creek by arranging to purchase some from a farmer on Lake Erie. England also pointed out that the original requisition of the previous fall had been considerably exceeded, particularly in corn and flour, and that as soon as McKee was able to attend to business, he would have to supply a fresh requisition for Simcoe. The spring and summer brought no respite in this matter of provisions. While deputations from the tribes travelled to Greenville to deal with Wayne, large numbers also gathered to receive supplies from the British at Swan Creek. By August, the British shortage of supplies became acute. All the Indian corn in the neighborhood of Detroit had already been purchased, and figures sent from Swan Creek on July 24 gave a total of 5,400 Indians in the neighborhood. The Indian Department faced the problem of economizing on provisions while

reconciling the Indians to the American victory and to the signing of Jay's Treaty.[52]

McKee timed his departure well in May 1795 for he left
Elliott with a hopeless task. The weakening of British control
over the Indians reached a climax as the time approached for
Wayne's treaty at Greenville. The foundations for this treaty
had been well laid during the winter, and by the beginning of
June, Indians began to arrive at Fort Greenville to negotiate
with their American conquerors. Wayne delivered a speech of
welcome on June 16, but owing to the large number of Indians
still expected, he was unable to begin the real business of the
council until July 15.[53]

In the middle of June, Joseph Brant arrived at Detroit from
Grand River. During the previous fall he had suggested a
council in the spring to weld the Indians to a single line of
policy, but this effort now proved hopeless. Not only had many
Indians already left for the council, but the task of Brant and
of the British Indian Department was complicated by the fact
that Detroit had now become a great center for land speculators.
In this period before the treaty of Greenville, prominent Detroit
citizens attempted to make large land purchases from the Indians, in the hope that they could obtain a confirmation of these
purchases by the Americans. These hopes proved illusory, but
to smooth the path of purchase, the speculators dispensed rum
freely at Detroit throughout the spring and early summer.
Elliott was in hopes that the Indian council which Brant planned
to hold at Brownstown would serve as a useful gathering to
reassert British influence, but the whole plan of the council
proved hopeless. Those Indians who were still available were
constantly drunk, and Brant returned from Detroit in disgust
on July 13.[54]

With British influence among the Indians temporarily shat-
tered, Wayne had no difficulty in obtaining the treaty he desired
at Greenville. The real business of the council began on July 15
and the treaty was signed on August 3. There were no negotiations in the real sense of the word, for the American government
had already drafted the treaty it desired. The boundaries were
essentially those of the treaty of Fort Harmar in 1789, but they
included additional land in what is now southeastern Indiana.

The line ran from the mouth of the Cuyahoga on Lake Erie south to the crossing place above Fort Laurens (near the present Bolivar, Ohio), then west to Loramie's store on the west branch of the Great Miami, west to Fort Recovery, and then southwest in a direct line to the mouth of the Kentucky River on the Ohio. What is now the southern half of Ohio and all the state east of the Cuyahoga was open to American settlement. This was not all. The United States also obtained sixteen grants of land on the Indian side of the boundary for the establishment of posts, with freedom of communication between them. These posts ranged from the Sandusky River in the east, to Michilimackinac in the north, and to the mouth of the Illinois River in the west. The Maumee was well-covered by these cessions since the Americans obtained land at Kekionga, at the Glaize, at the Rapids, and at the mouth of the river. The Maumee was no longer to be a British preserve. America not only obtained lands for immediate settlement, but also prepared the way for future cessions throughout the northwest.[55]

British reactions to the treaty were of course bitter. Elliott informed McKee on August 21 that he had heard the Indians were dissatisfied and had only signed under compulsion. McKee finally returned to Detroit on August 26, and was shocked by the terms of the peace. He sent a copy for Lord Dorchester with the comment that he "Doubtless will see the iniquity of it from the beginning to the End." He added that few, if any, of the Indians seemed to know the extent of the cessions they had made, "and probably when they are better informed they will see how Compleatly they have been duped." Presumably the Indian Department, as on so many other occasions in the previous ten years, was willing to act as their informer.[56]

On his return from Quebec, McKee immediately had to join with Elliott in dealing with another problem. It had been decided after Fallen Timbers that arrangements should be made for the settlement in Upper Canada of any Indians who desired to move from the United States. The spot chosen for their settlement was an area twelve miles square just north of Lake St. Clair, where the Chenail Ecarte' River ran into the River St. Clair from the east. Simcoe recommended this location to Dorchester in December 1794, and in July 1795, McKee was ordered to discover how many Indians might want to settle there. He was also to purchase the area from the Indians who claimed it. McKee travelled north of the Thames River in September to find out whether the Chippewas would cede the area at Chenail Ecarte.´ McKee had little difficulty. The Chippewas, who were the only claimants of the lands, readily agreed to the sale in exchange for goods to the value of £800 Quebec currency. The sale would be consummated when the goods arrived for distribution. McKee estimated in October 1795 that perhaps two or three thousand Indians might want to take advantage of the British offer to give them land on which to settle. He hoped that the greatest part of the Indians who had been at Swan Creek, together with the Ottawas from the River Raisin, would take part in the move. Some of the Ottawas had gone with McKee when he went to arrange the purchase, and they were very pleased with the area, which was suitable for hunting as well as for cornfields and villages. They wanted the sale to be completed in time for them to move there and plant in the spring. Although this settlement never flourished as hoped, Great Britain had thus taken steps to maintain her influence over the western Indians in spite of Wayne's victory and the agreement to withdraw from the posts.[57]

For the time being, however, the main problem was still the large number of refugee Indians gathered around Swan Creek. While McKee was away negotiating with the Chippewas, Elliott had been exceedingly busy distributing presents and supplies to the Indians from the Maumee. As usual, supplies were short. Cold weather had set in early, and the Indians had flocked to the British. The position was complicated by the fact that Elliott had no winter hunting supplies to hand out, and the Indians stayed and consumed provisions as they waited for the arrival of goods from the east. Throughout the fall, Elliott arranged for the winter comfort of the Indians at Swan Creek, and was able to report in November that they had a sufficient supply of pork, peas, rice, and butter for the winter. As usual, however, they were short of flour and Indian corn. Elliott's liberality was in accord with government policy, for on December 5 the Duke of Portland wrote to tell Simcoe that it was not to be a matter for concern if the distribution of presents was a little above normal. He hoped, however, that once affairs had settled down, Simcoe would effect a system of economy.[58]

In the winter of 1795-96 the British authorities at Detroit clung to the frail hope that British influence had not been weakened by the events of the previous two years. At the beginning of September 1795, Colonel England expressed the opinion that the attachment of the Indians to England had not been lessened, and McKee in the same month argued that the attachment of most of the Indians to the British had been increased by "the duplicity" of the American commissioners. Some Indians undoubtedly were unhappy that they had been obliged to concede defeat at Greenville, but others were actually appeased because for the time being they believed that, as stated in the treaty, this was a permanent line to separate the Indians and the Americans. The British Indian Department naturally had more contact with those who were dissatisfied. In January 1796, Elliott received a report from Swan Creek that the Shawnee had sent one of their chiefs to call in all their people who wished to remain in the British interest. They had also sent to the Creeks to take up the hatchet, and proposed to ask the Chippewas to come to their assistance. Captain Johnny, McKee and Elliott's main Shawnee contact, had sent this message. McKee wrote that while the Indians were very quiet, they did not seem satisfied with the Treaty of Greenville. He also reported that many of the chiefs who had attended the treaty had died since returning, and that it was generally believed among the Indians that they had been poisoned at Greenville. McKee himself said that it was more probable that they were poisoned by some of their own people who disapproved of the treaty.[59] Yet, it would seem that the members of the Indian Department were clutching at straws, for the Indians showed little inclination to renew the struggle against the Americans.

The removal of those Indians who wanted to leave the United States was a slow process. Although Dorchester approved the idea of the purchase of Chenail Ecarte in January 1796, he could not send the necessary supplies until the opening of navigation, and even then they were delayed. The Indian Department fretted at the delay, since it meant that they could not relocate the Indians in time for early spring planting. The Department maintained that this would have enabled them to reduce the consumption of provisions, and also to open communication with the nations westward to the Mississippi. By the time the Indian Department was able to complete preparations for the removal to Chenail Ecarte, the Indians themselves delayed the operation. They had planted corn at the foot of the rapids, and they did not want to move until they had harvested it. Eventually, rather than the thousands of Indians forecast by McKee in the previous fall, it appears that only hundreds moved to British territory. Some of the Shawnee under Blackbeard and Captain Johnny moved to Bois Blanc, opposite to Elliott's, in July, and there were scattered bands of other tribes, but it was not until 1797 that the Indians actually moved to Chenail Ecarte. [60] There was no great exodus from American territory, in spite of the preparations of the Indian Department.

The removal of friendly Indians to Chenail Ecarte was only a minor part of the end of an era in the Detroit region, because from the fall of 1795, the British authorities were also preparing for the evacuation of Detroit in accordance with the terms of Jay's Treaty. Evacuation did not mean abandonment of the whole area, since the British resolved to establish another post to take the place of Detroit – a post on the Canadian side of the Detroit River. They decided that the ideal spot was the land opposite to the isle of Bois Blanc at the mouth of the Detroit River, but had to compromise with land a little further from the mouth because Elliott and his friends of the Revolution already had their farms opposite to Bois Blanc. Here, eighteen miles south of Detroit on the opposite side of the river, the British were to build Fort Malden and the adjacent town of Amherstburg. Throughout the winter of 1795 - 96 and the following spring and summer, plans went ahead for the removal from Detroit, until on July 11, 1796, American forces landed to assume control of that old stronghold.[61]

It was perhaps fitting that as Britain yielded Detroit, Lieutenant-Governor Simcoe, who had so firmly attempted to uphold British rights in the Old Northwest, should also leave his post. He had been ill throughout the fall of 1795, and had requested leave of absence. This was granted in the spring of 1796, and at the beginning of August, Simcoe sailed for England. Lord

Dorchester had also returned to England in the previous month. The new era was to start with a new administration. Lieutenant-General Robert Prescott arrived to succeed Dorchester, and following Simcoe's advice, the British government appointed Peter Russell to administer the province of Upper Canada. Russell was an Irishman who had served with the British army in America during the Revolution. After returning to England he had been appointed Receiver-General of Upper Canada in 1792.[62]

The month of July 1796 was also a significant one for Matthew Elliott. At the request of Dorchester in June, Alexander McKee submitted a plan for the future government of the Indian Department. He recommended that in the future, superintendents of Indian affairs should be appointed for the three posts of Niagara, Detroit, and Michilimackinac, or for the places to which these posts were removed. There should also be three men to act as storekeepers and clerks. McKee recommended men for these various positions, and as a result William Claus, a grandson of Sir William Johnson, took over at Niagara, McKee's son Thomas at St. Joseph's (to which the British moved from Mackinac), and Matthew Elliott at Amherstburg. Dorchester announced these appointments in July, and Elliott advanced higher in the British Indian Department. He was now Superintendent of Indian Affairs at Amherstburg – by far the most important post of the British Indian Department in Upper Canada.[63]

Elliott's appointment came at an unfortunate time. His experience in the Indian Department had been gained solely in times of crisis, when great freedom was given to the members of the Department, and results were considered more important than a strict accounting of provisions. For a decade after 1796, the Detroit River was to be a comparatively peaceful outpost of the British Empire, and Elliott was to clash with the more rigid peacetime routine. Moreover, in 1796, a new complication was given to the general administration of the Indian Department in Upper Canada. Simcoe, irked by the control of Dorchester, had long suggested a change in the chain of control of Indian affairs. This change came about in a modified form in 1796. Instructions were sent to Robert Prescott and Peter Russell in

117

December 1796 informing them that for the time being the Indian Department in Upper Canada would be under the control of the man heading the government of that province, subject only to the special orders of the commander in chief. However, the expenses of the Department were still to be defrayed from the army budget, and this created a definite cause for future friction.[64] As he assumed his new position of responsibility, Elliott was to discover that the laxity of the previous twenty years was to come to a sudden end.

Chapter 6

A QUICK DOWNFALL

Elliott's first major task as Superintendent of Indian Affairs was the purchase of land as a home for Joseph Brant. It was the land on which Elliott later was to die. Simcoe had informed McKee in the spring of 1795 that it was necessary to purchase land for Brant to satisfy his claims for military services. The land in which Brant was interested was at the head of Lake Ontario, on Burlington Bay. The area was claimed by the Missisaugas, and the first steps to purchase it had been taken by Colonel John Butler in the fall of 1795. But Butler, who died in 1796, had not gone through the formal procedure as required by official regulations, and it became necessary in 1796 to go through the whole proceeding again. William Claus had not yet taken up his position at Niagara, and it was decided that Elliott would travel east from Amherstburg to arrange the purchase. In spite of a severe illness he sailed from the mouth on the Detroit River on September 2, and proceeded to Niagara. There, on September 12, Elliott signed an agreement with the Missisaugas. For Indian goods to the value of three hundred dollars they agreed to cede some 3,450 acres on Burlington Bay for Joseph Brant. The formal deed of conveyance was to be given as soon as the goods were in the hands of the Indians. There was no difficulty in this purchase. The chiefs had gathered before Elliott arrived, and he had only to stay for three days. The Missisaugas were pleased to cede the land for Brant, and the British government, though at times irritated with him, was anxious that he should stay in the British interest until his death.[1]

The settlement to which Elliott returned in the fall of 1796 was more placid than any he had known since he fled to Canada

119

in 1778. For a time there was peace in the Old Northwest as American settlers flooded into the lands ceded by the Indians at Greenville. The British acknowledged the cessions they had made in Jay's Treaty, and set up only a small establishment at the mouth of the Detroit River to replace the old stronghold of Detroit. The military establishment in the whole of Upper Canada was reduced, and the new fort being built at Malden was garrisoned by just over one hundred men under the command of twenty-year-old Captain William Mayne.[2]

The complexion of the Indian Department had also altered with the withdrawal from Detroit. Elliott now had direct control of Indian affairs in the region, and used his farm opposite Bois Blanc as his Indian agency. His chief assistant was his storekeeper and clerk, George Ironside. Ironside had been educated at King's College, Aberdeen, before coming to America. In the years after the Revolution he had traded along the Maumee, and like Elliott and McKee, had lived with a Shawnee woman. He now settled at Amherstburg, and proved a most useful aide to the illiterate Elliott. Alexander McKee was retiring from the center of activity. He now made his home not on the Detroit River but on the nearby Thames, and from there exercised a general supervision over Indian affairs in Upper Canada.[3]

For all its new placidity the Indian establishment on the Detroit River was a colorful spot in the fall of 1796. Irish traveller Isaac Weld arrived at a most opportune time to describe the scene in October. Weld arrived on the vessel which brought the presents for the fall distribution to the Indians. Sailing into the mouth of the Detroit, it anchored at Elliott's home opposite Bois Blanc, and Elliott invited Weld to live on his farm during his stay in the area. Although Weld later mentioned that there were a number of respectable houses, with considerable land, in this district of Malden, he saved his greatest enthusiasm for Elliott's farm. He estimated its size at two thousand acres, a very large part of which was cleared, and he thought it was "cultivated in a style which would not be thought meanly of even in England." The house itself, Weld stated, was the best in the whole district; situated some two hundred yards from the river, the parlor windows afforded a view of the Indian canoes passing and repassing before the island of Bois Blanc. Running down from the house to the water was "a neat little lawn, paled in, and ornamented with clumps of trees." At the end of the lawn, not far from the water, stood the "council house." This was a large wigwam used for Elliott's transactions with the Indians.

The island of Bois Blanc teemed with activity during Weld's stay. Not only did it hold those Indians who had been on Bois Blanc throughout the summer waiting to go to Chenail Ecarté, but it was also a temporary home for Indians from the whole region who had come in for their annual presents. Some five hundred families were now encamped on Bois Blanc, and large numbers came daily to visit Elliott's. Weld was well-received, for Elliott told the Indians that he had crossed the Atlantic especially to see them. Weld saw part of the annual distribution of presents, and later described it for his European readers. The chiefs had previously visited Elliott, and each had given him a bundle of small cedar sticks to the amount of the number in each tribe that expected the King's bounty. The sticks were of three lengths, ranging from the longest for the men to the shortest for children. Elliott then gave the sticks to his clerks for entering on the books. On the day of the distribution (on this occasion to over four hundred Indians) Elliott had a number of large stakes fixed into different parts of the lawn. To each stake was attached the name of a tribe, and the number of its members who expected presents. The presents were then brought out from the storehouses adjoining Elliott's house; "several bales of thick blankets, of blue, scarlet, and brown cloth, and of coarse figured cottons, together with large rolls of tobacco, guns, flints, powder, balls, shot, case-knives, ivory and horn combs, looking-glasses, pipe-tomahawks, hatchets, scissors, needles, vermilion in bags, copper and iron pots and kettles, the whole valued at about £500 sterling." The bales were opened, and the blankets, cloths, and cottons cut up into small pieces, each sufficient to make for one person "a wrapper, a shirt, a pair of leggings, or whatever else it was intended for." When this was completed, the presents for each tribe were heaped around the stake that bore its name. Weld asserted that no liquor was ever given by the government to the Indians, except to favorite chiefs in private.

While Elliott's assistants arranged the presents, the warriors loitered about the farm beyond the edge of the lawn. When all was ready the chiefs assembled their men, and they all gathered in a large circle to hear Elliott deliver a speech. He asked them to remember their father's bounty, and to use their weapons for hunting, not war. Elliott spoke in English, and at the end of each paragraph, interpreters repeated it to the different tribes. At each pause the Indians showed their approval by a loud shout of "Hoah! Hoah!" When the speech was finished, Elliott called the chiefs forward and showed them their heaps of presents. They thanked him, and summoned some of their young men who darted forward to gather the goods. Within three minutes they had cleared the lawn, and piled the goods into canoes on the waterfront. They then swiftly bore them away to Bois Blanc and to their villages.[4]

Apart from the formal annual delivery of presents, Elliott was also still engaged in the task of feeding those Indians on Bois Blanc who had lost their villages and fields to the American advance. Elliott had ordered a large storehouse built on Bois Blanc, and twice a week clerks in the Indian Department went across from Elliott's to distribute supplies. On each trip the Indians normally received three barrels of salted pork or beef, the same of flour, beans or peas, Indian corn, and about two carcasses of fresh beef. Weld commented that these Indians received their provisions "not in thankful manner" but as a matter of right. Late in October the Irish visitor took his leave, bestowing profuse thanks on his fellow countryman, who sent him on his way with a silver inlaid pipe-tomahawk. The illiterate immigrant from County Donegal always enjoyed entertaining his guests in style at the mouth of the Detroit.[5]

While Elliott kept up the customary liberality toward the Indians, the movement toward economy was gaining ground. Even McKee sent official word to Elliott at the end of the year that he should cooperate with Captain Mayne in husbanding supplies. Yet, for the most part, relations between the Indian Department and the military were strained at Amherstburg. The Indian Department thought Mayne foolish to lend fifty barrels of pork to the Americans at Detroit (as he did in the fall of 1796) at a time when it was in short supply for the Indians. The Indian Department was less willing than the professional soldier to forget and forgive, and thought first of the Indians, not of friendly relations with the Americans.[6]

The clash with Mayne became overt in January 1797, and it began a year of turmoil for Elliott. The turmoil began quite simply on January 10. Captain Mayne posted a notice asking for applications for supplying teams, horses, and oxen, complete with carts and trucks, for the use of the post in the coming year. Bids were to be entered by January 14. Elliott presented a formal protest on January 31, claiming that even though he had furnished a proposal on January 14, as required by the advertisement, William Caldwell had applied on January 21 and had received the contract.[7]

That this was only the outward sign of deeper problems became apparent in Captain Mayne's letters of early February. On February 1, Mayne wrote to James Green, the Military Secretary of the Indian Department, to say that he did not approve of the Indian stores for the post being desposited in the house of Captain Elliott. He considered that both the storehouse and the storekeeper should be within the military garrison. Moreover, he added that the Indian Department was very jealous of his power, and claimed that McKee "acts and does independently of me." It is hardly surprising that those old campaigners Elliott and McKee should have paid little attention to the twenty-year-old Mayne, nor is it surprising that Mayne, who had only been promoted from ensign in 1795, should have been jealous of his prerogatives. On the following day, February 2, Mayne again wrote to Green, this time enclosing Elliott's formal protest. Now he turned fully to the attack on Elliott, saying that he had "conducted himself indecorously" relating to the contract for teams for the post, and that Elliott "was not qualified in my opinion for this situation." This first clash of Elliott with Mayne was eventually to end in success for the Indian Department, for in June 1797, Mayne, after pressure from above, gave the contract for teams to Elliott.[8] Yet before that time, dispute had arisen on two other questions between Elliott and Mayne; one regarding the machinations of the French and Spanish among the Indians, and another on the ever-present problem of the distribution of presents to the Indians.

The idea that the Spanish west of the Mississippi were likely to tamper with the Indians was not new in this period and, along with the idea that France might try to regain influence on the continent, it was to persist until the War of 1812. Mayne, in his letter of February 1, had expressed the view that there was little to be feared from Spanish intrigue among the Indians – Spanish influence was not great. This was a typical attitude in the military department during the following year. The Indian Department, however, gave much credence to the idea that there was a danger of Spanish or French intervention. The military thought that the Indian Department was stressing this to try to increase its own influence at a time when the end of hostilities with the Americans had diminished its importance. Throughout the spring and early summer of 1797, the Indian Department paid close attention to this supposed danger. On May 10, Elliott reported that two men had arrived with a story, reputed to be from Captain Brant, that Quebec would be attacked by the French and Spanish during the spring. On June 23, Elliott amplified this information in letters to Sir John Johnson and to Peter Russell. He said that it appeared that the French and Spanish had for some time past been tampering with the Indians in his area in an attempt to alienate their affections from Great Britain and lure them into the Spanish possessions. For this purpose they had sent "one Lorimier" among the Indians. Elliott also reported that "beyond doubt" the Spanish had a number of troops moving up the Mississippi, that it was said they had blocked up its entrance, and that the objects of the expedition were Michilimackinac, Detroit, and Niagara – no doubt to provide a diversion should they attack Lower Canada. Although Elliott's information regarding the invasion was incorrect, there was no doubt that Louis Lorimier had been engaged in the task of persuading some of the northwestern Indians to emigrate beyond the Mississippi. Certainly the British authorities in Canada treated Elliott's reports with much more attention than the military department at Amherstburg. On July 22, Governor in chief Robert Prescott forwarded a copy of Elliott's letter to Lord Grenville in London, with the information that he had also transmitted it to the British representative in the United States so that he could inform the Americans if he desired. These fears of Spanish or French intervention were to continue, and were to increase friction between the military and the Indian department at Amherstburg.[9]

The problem of the distribution of supplies to the Indians was acute now that peace had come to the Old Northwest. The basis of the problem was that the military department held the purse-strings and the Indian department the power in regard to the Indians. The military always endeavored to ensure that officers were present when Indian agents distributed presents to the Indians, and favored the distribution of presents at a regular time and place. The Indian Department on the other hand claimed that small parties of Indians were constantly resorting to the agents, and required small gifts – thus making it impossible to arrange for the military officers to be present on every occasion. Often the practice had been for the Indian agents to issue orders to the storekeeper for such small articles as were needed from day to day, and then at the end of the quarter to present them to the commanding officer at the post for approval. The emergency conditions of the years before Wayne's victory had enabled the Indian Department to win most of its arguments with the army officers, but with the coming of peace the balance of power began to change. As far back as the summer of 1795 there had been a minor clash with Colonel England on this question, but it was not until the spring of 1797 that the problem became of major importance.[10]

With the coming of spring in 1797, Indians began to flock to Elliott's at the mouth of the Detroit. On May 6, Elliott wrote to Mayne (who was at the fort, about one and a half miles from Elliott's) to tell him that although he would begin to give out goods on that day, the distribution would probably spread over several days. As this was not the formal, annual delivery of presents, it would be impossible, Elliott wrote, to give all the presents at the same time. By the beginning of June, Mayne's annoyance at the desultory handing out of provisions was increasing. Mayne asked Elliott to appoint the day of the week most convenient for the Indians residing in the vicinity of the garrison to receive their provisions. They would have to appear on that day to receive their provisions in the presence of the officers of the garrison, who would certify them for quality and quantity. This was a slap at Elliott's honesty, and Mayne also informed Elliott that during the absence of McKee (who was visiting St. Joseph's) he should send a weekly return of the families to be victualled so that the Assistant Commissary, Thomas Reynolds, could make the necessary arrangements before the Indians appeared in the garrison. In future, Mayne said, he would not approve any private deliveries of major stores to the Indians. When any Indians came in who wanted the King's bounty, they would have to be sent to the garrison to receive their presents. If any minor items were delivered to straggling parties of Indians, Elliott's clerk would have to produce an account of expenditures for approval in the following week.[11]

Elliott reacted typically to this pressure. On June 30, Mayne met in council with four Shawnee chiefs – the Blackbeard, Captain Johnny, the Bonner, and the Buffalo – and they brought various complaints. Captain Johnny said that Colonel McKee, who for so many years had been their friend, now took no notice of them, and that they knew that most of the presents sent by the King for the Indians were kept by McKee for his own use. They then went on to speak of Elliott, who they said had told them last summer that he was to take care of them:

> We do not know what to make of this Capt. Elliot – he gives us but very few presents. When first Colonel McKee left us He took pity on us and used us well of late Capt. Elliot does not take much pity of us as formerly he did, he told us the other day that he had nothing to do with us that we were to go to our Father in the Garrison and get our provisions there.

Captain Johnny then asked Mayne to give out provisions twice a week rather than once, as he had suggested earlier. Mayne granted this request.[12]

This group of Shawnee was of course the group which had been most strongly under the influence of Elliott and McKee, and it would seem that a scheme of Elliott's had somewhat misfired at this conference. He had obviously told the Indians of the new regulations in the hope of forcing Mayne's hand, but it would hardly seem likely that he had told them to say that McKee was keeping back a good part of the King's stores. Either this was an interpolation of Captain Johnny's, or it is not impossible that Mayne had merely interpreted the Shawnee's statements in the worst possible manner. However, what seems obvious is that the disgruntled Elliott was now telling the Indians that he could do nothing for them, and that if they wanted provisions they should go and see Mayne.

The pressure on the Indian Department was also reflected in the actions of George Ironside, Elliott's clerk and storekeeper. On July 4, he wrote to John Lees, the Storekeeper General of the Indian Department, to say that although he thought he was to receive his orders from his superiors in the Indian Department, Mayne was now asserting that Ironside was under the control of the officer commanding at Amherstburg. Ironside stated that until he received specific orders on the subject he would not believe this assertion, and that he had not accepted Mayne's requisitions to the store. Ironside thought the latter was one great reason for Mayne's antipathy toward the Indian Department in general: "Without doubt private pique influences his public conduct & his overbearing vindictive temper has greatly disquieted most of the Servants of Government." Lees himself was unwilling to answer this tricky problem, though he clearly showed where his sympathies lay. On August 7, he transmitted Ironside's letter to the Military Secretary of the Governor in chief. He stated that in his opinion, the problem was that Mayne had given or proposed to give orders for the delivery of goods from the store without consulting Elliott, and that Ironside had refused or hesitated to comply with the orders. Lees wanted to point out to Governor in Chief Robert Prescott that the general practice had been for the Indian agent to make out a list of such goods as he thought proper to give the Indians on any occasion, and that this had then been shown to the commanding officer for approval. If approved, the goods had then been delivered in the presence of one or more officers of the garrison.[13]

Before any decision was taken, the situation at Amherstburg had changed. Mayne had reached his majority in April, and had requested permission to go to England to settle his affairs. Permission was granted, and Mayne left Fort Malden in July 1797. Though it might seem that the change could only be for the better for Elliott, it turned out in fact to be worse. The new commanding officer at Malden, Captain Hector McLean, showed no hesitation in continuing his predecessor's quarrel. Within a month of assuming command he wrote to the Military Secretary to complain not only on the matter of Indian stores, but also on the whole question of the reliability of the Indian Department. His main objection was that the Department issued far too many provisions in private, and also that the Department was guided by custom, rather than by official instructions. In this first month in command he turned down all requisitions for "Casual or Incidental issues." Like Mayne, he argued that small parties should be sent with an interpreter to the commanding officer to receive their supplies. He also threw doubts, as had Mayne, on the information supplied by the Indian Department. He stated that the Indian Department was eager to seize on every idle tale and exaggerate it to suit its own private views. Any intelligence coming from the Department merited little attention, wrote McLean, unless corroborated by more substantial evidence. McLean reached these conclusions with great haste, for he had only commanded at Fort Malden for a month.[14]

September brought a crisis in the situation at Amherstburg – a crisis which at times reached comic opera proportions. McLean raised the ire of the Indian Department by having its members conform exactly to official instructions, even when the custom had been quite different. The arrival of a quantity of Indian stores brought the first clash, this time involving McLean and Ironside. Whenever a new supply of stores would arrive, the established procedure would be for the storekeeper to request the commanding officer to assemble a Board of Survey to view their condition. Ironside made such an application early in September, and McLean wrote back to say that the storekeeper had not conformed with the general order of December 1, 1791 (this required the listing of the probable cause of damage to the stores), and should resubmit his request. Ironside replied that he had never heard of the general order, and that it had never been done that way before. He refused to obey McLean's command, and once again submitted the whole matter to the Storekeeper General. A storm was beginning to rage over the tiny community at the mouth of the Detroit.[15]

The quarrel went a stage further on September 13. A few

128

days before, McLean had sent a subaltern to ask Elliott when a certain requisition was to be delivered to the Indians (McLean had signed the requisition). The subaltern was told that the delivery would be made when the Indian Department and the Indians were ready. Elliott was ready to give battle. When Ironside brought a requisition on September 13, McLean not only signed it, but also, unbeknownst to Ironside, wrote on it that the supplies were to be distributed in the presence of the officers of the garrison at twelve o'clock. Ironside noticed this when he got back to Elliott's, and immediately wrote a letter to McLean for Elliott, saying that the Indians who were there were impatient to leave, and that supplies would have to be distributed immediately. The "P.S." threw down the gauntlet: "If the Officers cannot attend when presents are ready I am directed to tell you from Capt. Elliott that the service is not to be delayed on that Acct." McLean wrote back a surprisingly mild letter, saying he did not mind Elliott setting the time, but the time should be clearly specified, otherwise the officers could not know when to attend. In future Elliott should give timely warning, so that the officers could be told. McLean, however, immediately sent three officers to Elliott's to attend the distribution. When they arrived they were told by one of Elliott's Indians that he was not in, and that the presents had already been distributed. The same afternoon another message arrived for McLean with a requisition for him to sign – the message arrived for him at 4:00 o'clock saying that the Indians were to get the presents at 4:00 or 4:30. McLean signed it, but later told the Military Secretary that he could not send his officers at such short notice.[16]

The events of the thirteenth brought an all-out attack from McLean. On the 14th he wrote two long letters to Captain Green, the Military Secretary. These letters went much further than before; instead of merely accusing the Indian Department of lack of formality and carelessness, they amounted to an accusation of peculation against Elliott. He first attacked the general insubordination of the Indian Department, and argued that it had previously had things far too much its own way – "as is evident from their wealth (particularly Mr. Elliott) which renders them insolent and Independent even of the Government itself." McLean said he was astonished at the consumption of provisions since he had been at Amherstburg, even though he had rejected all requests for casual issues (where no particular Indians were specified). McLean, who had only been commandant for two months, argued that what was needed was a gradual diminishing of the issuing of provisions to the Indians, and that their visits to the post should be made less frequently – "I have reason to believe that their coming in so often is incouraged [sic] by Mr. Elliott." As he was unable to obtain exact numbers of the Indians, McLean argued, there was far too much room for abuse; a few score Indians would pick up a requisition for several hundred, saying they were taking supplies to their families and absent friends. McLean wanted reform, but said he had not had enough experience to know exactly what the reform should be. He had not talked to McKee, for McKee lived on the River Thames and had not been to Amherstburg since McLean had arrived at the post. McLean could not hide his obvious dislike, and it might seem to be jealousy of Elliott. He objected bitterly, and with a good deal of justification, that the stores were not kept in the garrison but on Elliott's farm (the government paid Elliott £60 per year storage). As this was over a mile away, it was inconvenient for the officers to attend at every delivery, particularly since the Department gave such short notice and generally gave the notice at the dinner hour. Moreover, argued McLean, this distance "renders peculation the more easy, & detection the less so." Finally McLean delivered a full blast against Elliott:

> He lives as I'm inform'd in the greatest affluence at an expence of above a Thousand a year. He possesses an extensive Farm not far from the Garrison Stock'd with about six or seven hundred head of Cattle, & I'm told employs fifty or sixty persons constantly about His House and Farm, Chiefly Slaves. If the Question shou'd be askd, How these people are fed and Cloathd or How this wealth has been accumulated, I shall not undertake to give a positive answer but the General opinion of people better acquainted with these matters is well known.[17]

For the rest of the month McLean increased his attacks as tension mounted at the mouth of the Detroit. Elliott did nothing to calm him, for while Elliott gave notice of the issue of presents to the Indians he gave it only at the last moment, with the result that the officers could hardly ever reach his farm in time. In these last weeks of September, the peaceful settlement witnessed officers scrambling into their equipment and rushing to reach Elliott's before the provisions were handed out to the Indians. Elliott's attitude reflects not only his own character, but also the confidence the Indian Department had gained during the early years of the 1790's. McLean, however, was determined to curb its power.

A week after the explosion regarding provisions, McLean turned to the attack on another aspect of Elliott's activities – the supposed peculation of bread. The normal practice in securing bread for the Indians had been for Elliott to send a requisition to the commanding officer for a certain amount, and when the commanding officer signed it, Elliott's servants or slaves obtained the bread from the garrison bakery. After McLean arrived, he refused to sign these general requisitions on the grounds that they gave neither the name of the tribe involved nor the number to be served. He did, however, direct the baker to issue bread to Indians who came for it themselves. This went on for some time, until McLean noticed that Elliott's servants were picking up some twenty or twenty-five loaves per day (Elliott had both Indian and Negro slaves). McLean then issued an order to the commissary that no bread should be charged to the government unless delivered to the Indians for their own use. McLean wrote about this affair not only to the Military Secretary but also to Peter Russell, the Lieutenant-Governor of Upper Canada. To Russell he said of his new arrangements regarding the bakery "that whatever inconvenience this mode may put Mr. Elliotts family to it can be attended with none to the Indians the intention being only to prevent abuse."[18]

Now in full cry, McLean added yet another item to the list of Elliott's crimes. He reported to the Military Secretary that he had been informed that the Indian Department was bartering items from the Indian store with private merchants. This of course could lead to serious abuse, although the Indian Department could maintain that this had been necessary in the past when the store had run out of vital items.[19]

131

By the close of September, Elliott's position became more precarious. At the end of the month, the former commander of Fort Malden, Captain Mayne, was at Quebec on his way home. He took the opportunity to be more specific regarding the sins of the Indian Department than he had ever been at Fort Malden. In doing so, he backed up the assertions of Captain McLean. It was next to impossible to prevent completely the peculation of the officers of the Indian Department at Amherstburg, argued Mayne, although the practice could be greatly checked. He advocated a strict adherence to regulations, and a close supervision by the commanding officer at the post. If this did not work, the reform might be accomplished by appointing a new storekeeper who was not subservient to the Indian Department, and having him reside in the garrison. He should issue supplies there only when a voucher recommended by the Superintendent of Indian Affairs and signed by the commanding officer had been delivered to him. Also, the office of storekeeper should be separated from that of clerk. Mayne singled out the power of the Indian Department to barter stores as his main point of attack, saying that under this cloak the Indian Department filled the stores of the merchants.[20]

As if all this were not enough, the problem of the machinations of the Spanish once again arose to plague the relations of the Indian Department and the military at Amherstburg. At the end of September, the interpreter who had been sent by Elliott several months before to investigate Spanish activities to the westward returned to Amherstburg. He brought the news that the Spaniards were still trying to persuade the Indians to settle in their territory. He also informed Elliott that General James Wilkinson, who had become commander in chief of the American army after Wayne's death in December 1796 had offered him $2.00 per day and two rations for life to go with him to Fort Wayne. He also reported that Wilkinson had offered the Shawnee chief Berry $150 to go with him. As Wilkinson's offers had not been accepted, Wilkinson then made a formal request to Captain McLean, arguing that reasons of state that were of interest to both countries made it essential that the interpreter, James Day, should accompany him to Fort Wayne. McLean thought this was a reasonable request, and communicated it to Elliott. Elliott declined to send Day. McLean's explanation of Wilkinson's request was that it was supposed that Day had spread false reports while in the Fort Wayne region, and that Wilkinson wanted to confront him with the Indians to undeceive them. This is possible, although not all would have said with McLean that "I have no reason to doubt Mr. Wilkinson's sincerity." Wilkinson eventually caused practically everyone to doubt his sincerity.

This incident served to feed the flames that were already raging at Amherstburg, and in reporting it to the Military Secretary, McLean made another attack on the Indian Department: "What Intelligence this man [Day] may have brought or if any I am totally ignorant of, these people making a mystery of everything relating to their Department so much that their Interpreters are sworn to secrecy, consequently cannot disclose anything so that no information of what relates to the Department can be obtain'd from them being mere creatures and dependents of their Superior in that Line." It would appear that the military did have a genuine grievance regarding the excessive secrecy in which the Indian Department cloaked its affairs. It made it exceedingly difficult to control the actions of members of the Department.[21]

The feuding at Amherstburg obviously could not continue to be ignored by those in authority, and eventually action was taken at the very top, by Governor Robert Prescott. On October 9, he sent his opinion to Peter Russell in Upper Canada. It is perhaps not surprising that as an army man he should have come out on the side of the military at Amherstburg. He first repeated the injunctions regarding economy in the Indian Department which he said had guided his conduct of affairs, and he reminded Russell of the orders of the Duke of Portland in this regard. Next he argued that the conduct of the Indian officers at Amherstburg had been actuated by different motives – in some instances of late their attitude toward the commanding officer had been highly improper, "and even Insolent and Impertinent," when he had insisted on compliance with orders and regulations. To put an end to this, Prescott told Russell that he should order McKee to instruct the Indian officers at the different posts that they were under the orders of the commanding officer in the same manner as the members of other departments. Their independent conduct should cease immediately. The Superintendent should notify the commanding officer on the spot before handing out presents, and that officer would approve the quantities and set the time of delivery. Presents were only to be given to Indians actually present, and in the presence of such officers of the garrison as the commanding officer should send. Moreover, no bartering with the merchants was to take place; if some goods ran out others should be substituted. If any gifts were given by the Indians, they should be given into the charge of the commissary at the post. Above all, no goods whatever should be issued without requisitions. Prescott also administered sharp reprimands to the members of the Indian Department. He first dealt with Colonel McKee, saying that officers who held positions of trust should personally carry out their duties, "and not delegate the performance of them to persons who abuse their trust." If McKee had resided at Amherstburg instead of on the River Thames, Prescott argued, all this improper conduct would not have happened. Finally, Prescott dealt with Elliott and Ironside: "I request you will cause the Superintendent Mr. Elliot, and the Storekeeper Ironside to be informed, that unless they make forthwith suitable apologies to Captain McLean Commanding at Amherstburg, I will dismiss them from their situations in the Indian Department." Prescott emphasized that he had given these regulations to frustrate improper speculations, and he wanted to be liberal with the Indians.[22]

The Governor in chief had thus firmly backed McLean, but his decision took several months to reach Upper Canada. By that time the breach at Amherstburg was irreparable. The last skirmish really started on October 12, 1797, when Prideaux Selby wrote to Elliott on behalf of McKee, and sent him a list of such Indians as had signified their intention to remain during the winter at Chenail Ecarte. The plans to make Chenail Ecarte a refuge for several thousand Indians from the United States had proved somewhat disappointing, but the Indian Department still hoped it would become the gathering place for a considerable number. The list of Indians given to Elliott by Selby amounted to 423, and he mentioned that Elliott should add to this number the two bands that were at the moment in his vicinity. At a later date McKee explained what inspired this request. Apparently during most of 1797 only a small quantity of provisions was sent to Chenail Ecarté as the few Indians who were there were able to be supplied from provisions left over from the treaty with the Chippewa for the cession of that area. However, in the fall of 1797 the Indians from Chenail Ecarté requested provisions for the winter so that they could live in the neighborhood of their towns and make an early planting in the spring. They also gave their numbers, and McKee sent this list to Selby for transmission to Elliott. Selby thus sent his letter of October 12, and on October 13 McKee himself wrote to ask Elliott to send in the necessary requisition. He explained that many had already gone hunting, and that the requisition was only for those who proposed to remain at Chenail Ecarté through the winter.[23]

On October 14 Elliott followed McKee's orders and wrote a requisition for goods to supply the Indians at Chenail Ecarté during the winter months. It was a requisition for 543 Indians. This was 120 more than on Selby's list; presumably this 120 was the number of Indians in the two bands that Selby had asked him to include. The same day Elliott wrote to McKee, telling him that he had heard that an officer was to proceed to Chenail Ecarté, no doubt to check the number of Indians. However, McLean had signed the requisition for 543 Indians "and no questions asked." The danger became apparent on October 18. On that date Captain McLean wrote to the Military Secretary. He enclosed a return of Indians at Chenail Ecarté to the number of 160, and said he had obtained this number from the principal chief at that spot, Chief Bowl. He also mentioned that the Indian Department had requested supplies for 543 Indians, and that he had sent Lieutenant Fraser to check the actual number.[24]

Fraser did not present his report until October 26, and in the meantime relations between Elliott and the commanding officer worsened. On October 16 Elliott reported to McKee that McLean had on his own authority held a council with the Indians, had given them a barrel of rum, and that after the meeting the Indians had come and abused Elliott for having cheated them. On October 20, McLean wrote to Elliott to complain once again of the shortness of notice given for the delivery of provisions –

Elliott did not reply. On the following day McLean wrote again, and asked Elliott henceforth to put in writing everything concerning the Indian Department. On October 23, he wrote to tell Elliott that he intended to recommend a reduction in the number of interpreters to the commander in chief. He also told Elliott that the Indians were staying around the post drinking rum after receiving their provisions – the Indian Department should attempt to get them away as quickly as possible.

To this last letter McLean did get a verbal answer – Elliott sent word by Ironside that when McLean was at the head of the Indian Department Elliott would attend to his orders. Elliott was under considerable provocation, but this last comment was made without the knowledge that Governor Prescott had already decided against him. Elliott defended himself in a letter to McKee on October 24. He blamed McLean for the presence of Indians around the post as the Indians were obtaining rum from the canteens in his garrison. He also bitterly resented the accusation that he was using government provisions for his own family, asked for an inquiry into his conduct, and stated: "I will assert also that my house is and from the nature of my employment must be open to all Indians, who make no ceremony in seating themselves at my table or that of my servants daily in numbers, and the calumminator from that circumstance no doubt may have judged of me by himself and what he would have done in the same case."[25]

On October 26, the noose around Elliott's neck drew a little tighter when Lieutenant Fraser reported after his trip to Chenail Ecarte' that the total number of Indians there amounted to 167. On October 28, McLean wrote to McKee, asking him to send a requisition for the Indians at Chenail Ecarte' – possibly he was trying to trap McKee, or more likely hoping to trap Elliott by finding a discrepancy between the requisitions of Elliott and McKee. McKee replied on November 5, requisitioning not for a specific number of Indians but for certain quantities of provisions. On the 8th, Selby transmitted information to Elliott from McKee. He said he had received a new requisition from McKee for provisions for the Chenail Ecarte' settlement. This was the same requisition as McKee had sent to McLean on the fifth, and Selby explained that since many of the Indians who had intended to remain had now decided to go hunting, less provisions would be needed. Elliott was to present the new requisition to McLean for approval. McKee was obviously retreating, and on the following day he was in full flight. Selby sent another letter to Elliott stating that McKee had now heard that all the Ottawas had left Chenail Ecarte' to hunt, because they supposed they would not be allowed any provisions for the winter. Thus McKee thought it would be unnecessary to present the requisition sent on the previous day. All this, however, was too late, for on November 10 McLean wrote to the Military Secretary pointing out the discrepancy between Elliott's original requisition and the figures McLean had obtained from Chief Bowl and from Lieutenant Fraser. On November 11, McLean informed Governor in chief Robert Prescott that "Mr. Elliott has of late convicted himself by giving in a false Return of the Indians at Chenail Ecarte' settlement he makes them 543 which exceeds by about 360 the number that any other can make them." He then added that since writing the above he had received a letter written by Selby at the request of McKee telling him that as the Indians at Chenail Ecarte' were all going out hunting, it would not be necessary to send provisions there – even the last requisition could be dispensed with. McLean was now determined to overthrow Elliott, and on November 18 he reiterated, in a letter to the Military Secretary, the discrepancy between Elliott's figures and those of Chief Bowl and Lieutenant Fraser. On the following day, another letter (McLean deluged the Military Secretary with letters in the fall of 1797) suggested that McKee's sudden change of mind was owing to McLean's production of accurate figures. He also added to the list of Elliott's sins, accusing Elliott of keeping a considerable quantity of sugar he had received from the Indians during the previous summer, and also of using the government schooner *Miamis* for his personal needs during most of the summer – bringing grindstones and bark for his tannery from distant parts of the lake, and carrying wood for individuals in the Indian Department.[26]

Meanwhile Governor in chief Prescott became increasingly angry at the news which was reaching him from Upper Canada, and on December 8 he informed Russell that as long as McLean was attempting to enforce regulations, he had Prescott's full support. Russell in this quarrel showed a definite tendency to side with the Indian Department, while Prescott had no hesitation in believing the reports of Captain McLean. Prescott told Russell that it was his job to put an immediate stop to the irregular proceedings of the Indian Department at Amherstburg. The Governor in chief stated ominously: "I am well convinced that the Duties of the Indian Department in Upper Canada would be carried on with more Honor and Justice to the Kings Interest, if some of the Present Officers were dismissed from their situations." Finally, on December 15, 1797, Prescott took the step which had seemed likely for some time. He wrote to President Russell to tell him that his confidence in Elliott had ended, and that Elliott was therefore removed from his position as Superintendent of Indian Affairs at Amherstburg. Prescott intended to recommend a successor to the Duke of Portland. For the time being Alexander McKee should take up his residence at Amherstburg. The occasion of Elliott's dismissal was the Chenail Ecarte' affair, but this was compounded by the whole controversy with Captains Mayne and McLean during the previous year. In explaining the dismissal to the Duke of Portland, Prescott pointed out that the order to place control of Indian affairs under the head of the government in Upper Canada had no sooner been made than the greatest irregularities were committed by the members of the Indian Department, particularly Mr. Elliott. It would seem more accurate to say not that the officers of the Indian Department had noticeably changed their practices, but that the army, and particularly the officers at Amherstburg, were now assuming a different attitude.[27]

Elliott had two months grace, for it took that long for the news of his dismissal to reach Upper Canada. During that period the Indian Department devoted considerable effort trying to save a situation that was already lost. In January 1798, affidavits were obtained from the leading trading establishments in the area to the effect that they had not engaged in trade for Indian Department goods with members of the Indian Department. Alexander McKee did his best to save his old associate. On January 23, he reported to President Russell that an enquiry into the Indian Department at Amherstburg had shown that only in one or two minor instances had there been any irregularities in the proceedings of the Department. He also tried to take responsibility for the Chenail Ecarte' affair. He explained in a letter to Russell on February 7 that he had sent the numbers on which Elliott had based his requisition, and that he had subsequently discovered that since many Indians had gone hunting, fewer provisions would be required. Yet, at the same time that the Department tried to show it had been mistaken, it also tried to show that its original estimate for the Chenail Ecarte' settlement had been a reasonable one. On February 6, Frederick Fisher, who had been an interpreter in the Indian Department and who had resided at Chenail Ecarte' during the past two years, swore that the number of Indians who normally drew provisions during that period was generally from four to eight hundred, and sometimes as many as eleven hundred. McKee sent this affidavit to Russell on February 7, along with his own account of the Chenail Ecarte' affair.[28]

Elliott meanwhile acknowledged his defeat, though he did not know he was too late. On February 2, McLean reported to the Military Secretary that the Indian stores had been removed from Elliott's farm into the garrison, and that Elliott and Ironside had carried out the wishes of the Governor in chief, and had come to McLean to make the required apologies for their conduct of the previous summer. That must have been a bitter pill for Elliott to swallow, and it must have seemed even more bitter when he discovered the apology had been in vain. On February 6, Russell was at last able to transmit Elliott's dismissal notice to Amherstburg. The reason given for the dismissal was that Elliott had not conformed to instructions, and had given an incorrect return of the number of Indians at Chenail Ecarte' Russell later expressed regret (March 7) that he had not received McKee's explanations in time to send them to Prescott before the Governor in chief decided to remove Elliott from office. Russell was obviously in sympathy with Elliott and McKee, and he regretted that an inquiry had not been instituted into Elliott's conduct before he was dismissed. He mentioned that the last command of the Governor in chief had left nothing to his discretion.[29]

There seems little reason to doubt that Elliott was guilty of some of the practices of which he was accused in this controversy of 1797. Undoubtedly the Indian Department was careless in its methods, was not loath to use government facilities and supplies on its own account, and was inclined to practice excessive secrecy in its affairs. If he had not been guilty of some of these practices, Elliott would have risen not only above the Department but also above the century. Yet, it would also seem that he was unfortunate to be dismissed from office. Elliott was dismissed purely on the reports of the two army captains at Amherstburg, in spite of the fact that he denied the charges, and in spite of the fact that Alexander McKee, his superior and the second-in-command of the Indian Department in Canada, came to his defense. Whatever the justice of the complaints of Mayne and McLean, there seems no reason why their unsubstantiated word should have been accepted, when their accusations were denied by both Elliott and McKee. Moreover, in the Chenail Ecarté affair, the guilt, if there was any, clearly rested on McKee more than it did on Elliott. McKee admitted that he had ordered Elliott to submit the first, and decisive, requisition.

The real difficulty, however, stemmed from the changed conditions following Wayne's victory and Jay's treaty. Before 1795 the Indian Department had been given great latitude and general support by Lieutenant-Governor Simcoe. When Elliott and McKee were on the Maumee they had only to indicate the supplies they needed, and the numbers of those to be fed, and their demands were met. If on those occasions they took out a little for their own profit, no one appeared to be particularly perturbed. Lieutenant-Colonel England, though at times worried by the expenditure of provisions, did not essentially interfere in what was looked upon as the business of the Indian Department. Because the Northwest was in a state of emergency, regulations were waived and general orders were modified. The Indian Department was looked upon as essential to the control of the Indians, and the Indians were looked upon as essential to the protection of the posts and Canada against Wayne. With the coming of peace all this changed, and unfortunately for Elliott it changed just as he assumed command at Amherstburg. The practices he indulged in seem to have been little different from those indulged in during the early 1790's, and in the affair of Chenail Ecarté he was acting under the orders of his superior.

The military officers in command at Amherstburg began in 1797 to establish the order and regulation so beloved by the peace-time army, and they carried out the change in a manner well-designed to provoke resentment. Neither Mayne nor McLean excelled in tact, and they clashed head on with Elliott. Undoubtedly Elliott did not realize the changed situation soon enough – he was too confident of his power, and of the support of McKee. Governor in chief Prescott arbitrarily dismissed Elliott without benefit of investigation, and Elliott became in effect the scapegoat for the Indian Department in Upper Canada, and in particular for McKee. If Elliott was guilty, so was McKee. But McKee escaped unscathed, and Elliott suddenly found himself out of the Indian Department, just at the moment when he seemed about to reap the reward of twenty years hard work on behalf of the British among the Indians. He was to spend nearly the next ten years of his life in attempting to clear himself, and to obtain reinstatement.

Chapter 7

PEACE AND PROSPERITY

In the three years following his dismissal from office, Elliott devoted most of his time and energy to an attempt to obtain a hearing for his case. His efforts were hampered by persistent attacks on his character by Captain McLean, who carried on a personal vendetta against Elliott. Throughout 1798 he gloated on the good effect of Elliott's dismissal, and lost no opportunity of pointing out further crimes of which Elliott was guilty. He said Elliott had lived at the rate of £2,000 or £3,000 a year, which was certainly an exaggeration, and asserted that in the summer he had paid out no less than £100 a month in wages to his helpers – mostly in tobacco, blankets, and other items from the Indian Department stores. Elliott discovered that his difficulties did not end with dismissal. As if McLean's attacks were not enough, the garrison baker successfully prosecuted Elliott for the cost of the bread delivered to his servants. As McLean had refused to sign the requisitions, the government had refused to pay the baker for the bread.[1]

By the fall of 1798, Elliott decided to take steps to end the persecution he was suffering from the seemingly relentless Captain McLean. He retained the Attorney-General of Upper Canada, John White, for the purpose of instituting an action against McLean for defamation of character. Though this case apparently was never brought to trial, it at least partially put McLean on the defensive and caused him considerable worry. The proposed action dragged along for several years, and as late as 1800 McLean was unhappy to learn that Elliott proposed to sue him for damages of £20,000 New York currency. McLean was obliged to retain two lawyers in case Elliott should go ahead with his action.[2]

While he was skirmishing with McLean, Elliott was also making a direct effort to secure an inquiry into the whole Amherstburg affair. His task was made infinitely more difficult when on June 8, 1798, the Duke of Portland approved Prescott's action, and stated that it appeared that Elliott's dismissal was highly necessary. Elliott really began his campaign in July, after waiting for several months in the hope that some inquiry would be instituted by the government, "notwithstanding the trifling mistake which was committed by my condemnation preceding my trial." As there were no signs of governmental action, Elliott appealed to President Russell for a public inquiry, and asked Russell to intercede with His Majesty's ministers.[3] This effort by Elliott consumed the whole summer, and ran up against a brick wall in the person of Governor in chief Robert Prescott. Russell immediately transmitted Elliott's request to Prescott, but was told by the Governor in chief "that His Grace the Duke of Portland has signified to him. His Majesty's approbation of the Dismissal of Mr. Elliott and that the King would name a successor to the Office he lately held in the Indian Department."[4] Lieutenant-General Prescott was not the most flexible administrator ever to journey to the British Provinces in North America, nor it would appear the most just.

Undaunted, Elliott decided to go a step higher. In December 1798, he transmitted a memorial to the Secretary of State for Home Affairs, the Duke of Portland. This listed Elliott's many services since 1776, and pointed out that authoritative documents existed which showed that Elliott was acting under "*positive written orders*" from Alexander McKee. McKee himself had very little else to say on this matter, for on January 14, 1799, the old campaigner died suddenly of "a fever" at his home on the Thames. Elliott continued his pressure. Within two weeks he made another appeal to the apparently immovable Governor in chief Robert Prescott, and requested aid from that old friend of the Indian Department, John Graves Simcoe, who was now in England. Joseph Brant also wrote to Simcoe in support of Elliott. Brant pointed out that Elliott had been dismissed without trial, and stated that Elliott "for a series of years has been & continues to be to this day high in our confidence, in our esteem & in our love nor can anything but a public trial convince us

143

that he has ever rendered himself undeserving of these sentiments." To round out his appeals, Elliott sent a memorial in
April to the head of the Indian Department, Sir John Johnson,
asking him to use his influence to secure justice. Elliott certainly
had no fear of a public inquiry – either he thought he had done
little wrong, or he thought that what he had done could not be
proved.[5]

As he did not receive a favorable reply, Elliott set out for
Montreal early in August 1799 to present his case in person
to the head of the Indian Department. The trip served another
purpose in that he also took his eight-year-old son Alexander to
begin his education in Montreal. Elliott's family life was like that
of so many of the Indian agents and traders of this period. His
wife rarely appears in the letters of either Elliott or his friends.
Like McKee, he lived with a Shawnee woman as his wife, and
in the early 1790's she bore him two sons – Alexander (presumably named after McKee), who was born in November
1790, and Matthew Elliott Jr., who was born a few years later.
Elliott treated his sons well, and in the case of Alexander gave
him an excellent education. Most surprising about Elliott's
family is that the only children of whom there is any record are
those born after 1789, when Elliott was already over fifty. There
is no doubt that he had lived with Indian women before he
lived with the mother of his sons – he had been among the
Shawnee since the 1760's – and his two sons of the 1790's as
well as the two who were given him by his white wife when he
was over seventy bear evidence to his virility. If children were
born to him before, as one would expect, they must either have
died in infancy or stayed among the Shawnees.[6]

Elliott quite obviously intended to give his eldest son the
education he himself had never received. Though Matthew Elliott
was sadly unable to write (except to sign his name), his eldest
son was trained as a lawyer. In August 1799, little Alexander
was taken on the long journey across Lakes Erie and Ontario
and down the St. Lawrence to Montreal. Here in September he
was placed as a pupil under the care of Alexander Skakel. He
was to stay with him until 1806. From 1799 to 1811 Alexander
came home only for visits. The younger son, Matthew Jr., lived
more the life of his father, and became well-known among the
Shawnees.[7]

144

The placing of his son under the care of a schoolmaster was only one of Elliott's tasks in Montreal during the summer of 1799. His major concern was the attempt to secure an inquiry into his conduct, which was complicated by further attacks from McLean.

The early months of 1799 had been a period of additional alarms and fears in regard to the province of Upper Canada. At the beginning of the year, Joseph Brant informed the authorities in Upper Canada that the French were engaged in machinations among the western Indians, and that the British dominions could expect an invasion in the spring. It was rumored that an army was advancing up the Mississippi to give support to the Indians. President Russell wrote to Prideaux Selby at Amherstburg and asked him to investigate the truth of these assertions. He also told Selby that Elliott thought the army would cross from the Upper Mississippi to Lake Superior, to reach the posts of Upper Canada and avoid the American posts, particularly that of Mackinac. The attitude toward Elliott at this time is revealing. Even though he had only recently been disgraced and dismissed, Elliott was called upon by President Russell for advice in this supposed crisis. As McKee was dead, Elliott was the most experienced agent to whom the authorities could turn. On February 1, the Legislative Council of Upper Canada suggested that Russell should arrange for a messenger to be dispatched from the Detroit region as soon as anything worthy of notice occurred, and also spoke significantly of Elliott: "The great influence which Capt. Elliott possesses with the Indians and the infinite importance which a person of that description is of at this critical moment forces us to obtrude upon your Honor a Suggestion that it might be highly proper to give to that gentleman a prospect of the Enquiry into his Conduct which we understand he is anxious to have." Should war again threaten Upper Canada, Elliott was in a position of great strength.[8]

The fear of French invasion proved unfounded, but by July rumors had again disturbed the peace of Amherstburg. The Shawnee chief "the Bonner" (Keckanathucko) brought news that a large body of Chickasaws had crossed the Ohio to attack all the Indian nations who had been concerned in the attack on Fort Recovery five years before; prior to that attack the Chicka-

saws who were with Wayne had suffered losses, including one
of their principal chiefs. Thomas McKee, the son of Alexander,
transmitted the news to McLean, but McLean treated it as he
had treated Elliott's suggestions and reports. McLean's original
reply to McKee was quite reasonable – he said it appeared
rather improbable but that McKee should check into the truth
of it – but in writing to the Military Secretary he entered into
one of his usual diatribes against the Indian Department. He
had no doubt, he said, that McKee had been imposed upon,
for the Bonner was "a Shawanae Chief who lives with Mr.
Elliott and is entirely under his influence, from which it may be
easily conjectured how the report originated and the motives
which gave rise to it." Elliott in fact was just leaving for his
visit to Montreal with the Bonner and the Berry (another Shawnee chief), and with Frederick Fisher, the interpreter. Toward
the end of August, McLean repeated his charges against Elliott,
saying that there had been frequent attempts at creating alarm,
and that there were strong reasons to believe that many of these
had originated with Elliott and "his principal advisor and
strenuous supporter Mr. Selby" with the object of showing that
Elliott was too important to be disposed of. Though McLean
was making all these charges without proof, he did make an
interesting and begrudging acknowledgment of Elliott's influence
with the Shawnee:

> Any influence that this man had was of no consequence
> excepting wt that contemptible tribe calld the Shawanese,
> with whom he is connected & who are the only people
> that were particularly distinguished by his Liberality
> while he had the disposal of the Stores. The whole of
> the Officers of the Department are indeed in some way
> connected with this tribe either by Marriage or Con-
> cubinage which occasions that partiality so manifest in
> their favor, & which has been evidently the cause of that
> nation having been always more insolent and trouble-
> some than any other.

As McLean was keen to show that Elliott was completely useless
in his position, and had no influence whatever, it is a measure

of Elliott's influence with the Shawnee that McLean was obliged to acknowledge it.[9]

Thus when Elliott travelled eastward to Montreal in the summer of 1799, he was still unable to get away from McLean's accusations. At Montreal he went to see Sir John Johnson, who at last appeared to be giving some slight support to his old subordinate in the Indian Department. At the end of September, Johnson wrote to the new lieutenant-governor, Lieutenant-General Peter Hunter, to say that he was glad that the Indians continued quiet, "which I would flatter myself is more owing to the judicious management of the Gentlemen of the Department, than to any other Interference." He also added that Thomas McKee had acted very properly in sending McLean information concerning the Chickasaws who were supposedly coming to attack the northwestern Indians. This of course was quite true. The Indian Department had the task of giving intelligence concerning the Indians on the borders; it would soon have been in trouble if it had not passed on reports merely because they might subsequently prove to be untrue. Johnson furthermore added that he had asked Elliott what he thought of the reports, and Elliott had expressed the opinion that it was probably a report spread by the Americans to drive from their frontiers the straggling parties of Indians who were often there for the purpose of stealing horses. Elliott also said that from the beginning he had cast doubts on the truth of the report to those with whom he spoke on the subject. On September 26, Elliott had sworn before the Storekeeper General, John Lees, who was acting in his capacity of Justice of the Peace, that he had neither spread nor believed this report concerning the Chickasaws.[10]

On this visit to Montreal, Elliott impressed Sir John Johnson with the strength of his case for an inquiry into his conduct. In his letter to Hunter, Johnson stated that he had documents in his possession which acquitted Elliott of the charge of making a false return of the Indians at Chenail Ecarte:

> I could not but think it cruel that after having been deprived of his Office, the very person who had been the cause of it, should still endeavour to injure him more by private Insinuations, that appear to me now, to be more the result of private resentment, than with

147

a View to the Public good, and that are as Ill founded
as they are unjust and ungenerous.

Elliott had won another convert to his case, and Johnson said
he was taking steps to discover the origin of the frequent rumors
coming from the region of Amherstburg. Johnson said that although the Shawnee who had come with Elliott had set out on
their return "pretty well satisfied," this was by no means the
case with Elliott "who considers himself an Injured Man."[11]

The only problem with all this is that even if one concedes
that McLean was biased and vindictive, and he certainly was, it
is difficult to understand who had inspired the Bonner to his
tale if it was not Elliott. The Bonner lived on Elliott's farm
during at least part of the year, and was certainly in his interest.
The Bonner eventually died in about 1806, still under the care
of Elliott at the mouth of the Detroit.[12] It had also been clearly
shown during the previous winter, at the time of the French invasion scare, that even the Legislative Council of Upper Canada
was prepared to come out in Elliott's behalf in time of crisis,
and any danger on the frontier made Elliott's case for inquiry
and reinstatement a far stronger one. Although, as in so much
that concerns the Indian Department, proof is lacking, it is not
possible to exonerate Elliott of complicity in the reports that were
causing concern on the Upper Canadian frontier in 1799. He
was desperately keen to be reinstated, and there seems no reason
to suppose that he would have been loath either to spread reports, if they were in his interest, or to deny that he had spread
them, if that was also in his interest.

Yet, the journey to Montreal produced no real success for
Elliott, and he returned disappointed to Amherstburg in the late
fall. Sir John Johnson was clearly won to his side, but Elliott
obtained no concession from the new lieutenant-governor and
commander of the forces, Peter Hunter. Johnson pointed out in
a letter to William Claus that "private letters had paved the
way to prejudice the General against him."[13] McLean was a
major stumbling block to Elliott in these last years of the eighteenth century.

Matthew Elliott was remarkably persistent. He had appealed,
without success, to all the relevant authorities in Canada, and
to the Duke of Portland and Colonel Simcoe in England. His

148

hope of gaining support from Simcoe in London came to an end in the spring of 1800, when Simcoe referred him to Lieutenant-Governor Hunter as the proper person to consider an appeal.[14] Elliott had of course already appealed to Hunter without success. Yet, Elliott, who had spent the summer of 1799 in the several-hundred mile round trip to Montreal, now determined that he would spend the summer of 1800 in the several-thousand-mile round trip to Halifax, Nova Scotia. The reason for this ambitious plan was that a dignitary higher than any other to whom Elliott had yet appealed was now stationed in Nova Scotia. George the third's soldier son, Edward, Duke of Kent, had established himself in Nova Scotia, with his entourage and mistress, as commander in chief of the British armies in North America. In the summer of 1800, Elliott crossed the British settlements to carry his case to the man who was to achieve a modicum of fame as the father of Queen Victoria.

As usual in his appeals, Elliott listed the many services he had performed for the British government, and pointed out that the late commander in chief, Robert Prescott, had dismissed him and refused an inquiry in spite of the application of President Russell and Sir John Johnson. Elliott's long trip to Halifax seemed at first to have been worthwhile, for on July 26 the Military Secretary to the Duke of Kent wrote to Lieutenant-General Hunter on behalf of Elliott, and he allowed Elliott to carry this letter from Halifax to Montreal. "On a very minute examination of the several documents in Mr. Elliots possession and a careful enquiry into the general tenor of his conduct," wrote the Military Secretary, "the Commander in Chief is fully persuaded of the injustice which this gentleman labours under." He therefore asked Hunter, who had the direction of Indian Affairs in Upper Canada, to give this case his careful consideration.[15] With this letter from a son of George III in his pouch, Elliott must have felt some confidence in his ability to obtain a rehearing and reinstatement, but once again he was disappointed. In spite of all the pressure, Hunter did not feel justified in reversing the decision of his predecessor. Many might well have given up at this point – that Elliott did not bears witness to a remarkable tenacity of purpose. Elliott again petitioned the Duke of Portland in 1801, and in the following years eased the pain of his dismissal by gaining increased stature and prosperity in Upper Canada.[16]

That Elliott retained considerable support in Upper Canada was shown quite clearly in 1800 when he was elected to serve for the county of Essex in the Legislative Assembly of Upper Canada. Although its actual powers were limited, the assembly did serve to express provincial discontent and it obviously also gave prestige to those who were elected to it. Not all in the Detroit River region were behind Elliott. One correspondent of merchant John Askin spoke of Elliott and two others "whom in justice to myself I set my face against, as Representatives, altho' perhaps worthy persons in any other situation."[17] There were those who looked with doubt on being represented by a man who could neither read nor write, but this was not enough to defeat him. In fact, the Indian Department gained complete representation when Thomas McKee, Alexander McKee's son, was elected with Elliott. Thomas McKee, who was eventually appointed to the Superintendency at Amherstburg to succeed Elliott, was the son of McKee and a Shawnee married Therese, the daughter of John Askin, in 1797. It seemed that he had started a promising career, but gradually after 1800 he developed a greater and greater liking for liquor. His career and life were ruined, and he eventually died in Lower Canada in the last stages of alcoholism in 1815. Elliott and McKee were elected for a four year term in the third Upper Canadian Parliament – Elliott was to be re-elected until the start of the War of 1812.[18]

The first session of the third Parliament met in York (now Toronto) from May 28 to July 9, 1801. The House of Assembly was a small provincial body, and had only nineteen members. Elliott was in attendance for practically the entire session. He seems to have fallen quite easily into the role of member of Parliament, and showed none of the reticence traditionally associated with a member's first session. He was also treated with respect by the other members. When on June 1 the House resolved to go into a committee of the whole to take into consideration the question of disputed elections, it was Elliott who replaced the speaker; only three days after the opening of his first session in the Assembly. Elliott usually voted in the majority in this session, and on occasion was sent as one of the three who took bills to the Legislative Council for their approval. He served on a conference committee with the Legislative Council to discuss amendments to a bill that was to stop sales of liquor to Elliott's old acquaintances, the Moravian Indians, and he seconded various bills in the Assembly. On June 20, he seconded a bill to prevent the sale of strong liquor to the Indians, and to prevent traders and others buying the provisions and presents given to the Indians by the government. He also, as befitted one of the most prosperous farmers in Upper Canada, seconded a bill to provide for more ample means of recovering debts. All in all, Elliott in this first session conducted himself as an exemplary and respected member of the Assembly. He was no wild frontiersman.[19]

This pattern continued in the next three sessions of this third Parliament which gathered early every summer in the little settlement of York. He attended with great regularity, took an active part in all the proceedings, and seems in every way to have been a conscientious member. If anything can be told from his voting record, it might be said that he voted in the conservative ranks, and on the side of substance and property. He voted against a bill for the relief of the Methodists, and apparently possessed far more reluctance to support education in general than education for his own son, for in February 1804 he voted against a bill to establish schools in every district of the province. In view of the careful manner in which he carried out his duties he was given nothing more than his due when in 1804 he was elected for another four year term.[20]

While Elliott increased his standing in the community, he also showed his usual care in building his own prosperity during these first years of the nineteenth century. He increased the acreage of his lands by government grant in 1801, and the productivity of his farm maintained it as one of the most prosperous in the district of Amherstburg.[21] Strangely enough, Elliott was once again on good terms with the military garrison of Fort Malden. In 1802, Captain McLean had been replaced by Lieutenant-Colonel John Vincent, and this meant that friendly relations were once again possible. After the bitter argument about provisions, and Elliott's use of them, it would have been a considerable blow for McLean to have known in December 1802 that Vincent wrote Military Secretary Green to tell him that as he was running out of flour he had been obliged to purchase ten thousand pounds from Captain Elliott. Elliott was going to deliver the whole ten thousand pounds by January 1, 1803. Moreover, Elliott had also offered to furnish another twenty thousand pounds on February 10 at whatever the market price might be on that day. Vincent received orders to take advantage of this offer, and Elliott supplied Fort Malden with flour in the winter of 1802-3. This produced good relations between Vincent and Elliott, and in March 1803, Vincent reported to Green that Elliott had "fulfilled the last contract, fully to my satisfaction." After this success, Elliott was given other contracts to furnish the Fort Malden garrison both with flour and with beef.[22]

As at the time of his bankruptcy in the 1780's, Elliott's setback in 1799 seemed to spur him to increase rather than accept a diminishment of his prestige. By the summer of 1804, with good relations restored at Amherstburg and solid service in the Assembly, Elliott was in a strong position. In June of that year he served as land agent for twenty-two settlers in the Amherstburg region before the Land Board in York. Settlers were supposed to appear in person to obtain their two hundred acres, but on this occasion the Board was induced to recommend them for two hundred acres each, because of its conviction that Elliott would not recommend persons who were unworthy of the favor of government. Elliott was no longer the rogue and peculator depicted by McLean and endorsed by Governor in chief Prescott.[23]

Yet, for all this, Elliott had not forgotten that he had been ignominiously dismissed, and in the summer of 1804, after the conclusion of the Assembly session, Elliott took his most ambitious step to regain his office – he visited England. It was over forty years since Elliott had crossed the Atlantic from Ireland to America. He was now to visit London in an attempt to seek redress. He finally left for England in mid-summer 1804, and Sir John Johnson sent him a recommendation (which missed him in Canada and finally reached him in England) to aid him in his quest. Johnson not only listed Elliott's many services to the government, but also expressed the opinion that Elliott would not have been dismissed "had he had an opportunity of producing the Orders under which he Acted." At Southampton, Elliott received another recommendation, this time from David William Smith, who had been Surveyor-General of Upper Canada from 1792 to 1804 and who had also served as speaker of the Upper Canadian Assembly. Smith, like many others before him, told in his letter of Elliott's many services, and he also stressed Elliott's loyal service in the Assembly in spite of his dismissal. Smith also mentioned the prodigious journeys taken by Elliott in his attempt to obtain a hearing, and the fact that at the time of the supposed crisis in Upper Canada (1799) the civil government had wanted to employ him.[24]

Elliott travelled up from Southampton to London bearing Smith's letter, and the frontiersman was thrown into the greatest city in the world. Once again this man of remarkable persistence went through the now long-established form of submitting a memorial – this time to Earl Camden, who was now in charge of colonial affairs. He listed his services, pointed out the impossibility of obtaining a hearing in Canada, and asked for a court martial or some other form of inquiry. The matter dragged on into the fall, and Elliott received a damning blow in the intractability of the ex-Governor in chief Robert Prescott. Prescott, who was now in England, wrote that he "should be sorry to shrink from any enquiry, as it will lead to prove Mr. Elliot's conduct was highly blameable, to give it the gentlest epithet in my power," and he came into Downing Street to discuss the case at the beginning of October. The discussion, Elliott's journey, and his array of impressive support all came to naught – no one was prepared to re-open the case. Robert Prescott, who had dismissed him, still stood firm, and no one cared to reverse either his decision or that of the Duke of Portland who had supported him. Thus Elliott once again had to acknowledge defeat, and late in the season he took his passage for Canada. For the next four years he had to acknowledge that there was nowhere else to appeal.[25]

Elliott now returned to his steady round of farming and service in the Assembly, and for the next three years lived a quiet existence. Only occasionally did glimpses of the great events occurring elsewhere in the world come through to the tiny Assembly in Upper Canada. In February 1806, Elliott was one of the four appointed to draft the reply to the President's speech on the opening of the session. We may be sure that Elliott did not write it, but he reported it from committee and spoke to the Assembly. He concluded: "We feel more than ordinary pleasure in your communication of His Majesty's late Naval Victory, and though we may much regret the fall of the illustrious Nelson in that action, we cannot refrain from expressing our sensations of joy. May our Navy be permanent, and its successes perpetual." Thus was the news of Trafalgar and the death of Nelson officially received in Upper Canada.[26]

Elliott's prestige and prosperity continued to increase after his return from England. In February 1806, he again acted as land agent for a group of Upper Canadian settlers – this time twenty-eight – who did not want to come in person to the seat of government. He presented a petition on their behalf to President Alexander Grant and his council, and Grant left it to the Executive Council to decide. The council stated that the rule of personal application was a sound one, but suggested that Grant should give them discretionary power to dispense with the rule "whenever the Agent is of such known Respectability and Honor that it can safely place a confidence in his Recommendation, and the distant Residence of the Petitioners may be judged to be a sufficient Reason for their not appearing in Person." As Elliott was of sufficient respectability and honor, the petitioners obtained their desired land patent.[27]

In this same year of 1806, Elliott also made further arrange0 ments for the education of his son Alexander, who since 1799 had been at school in Montreal. Alexander was now fifteen, and old enough to take another step forward in his studies. His father now set him on his career as a lawyer. In June 1806, an agreement was drawn up with James Stuart, the Solicitor-General of Lower Canada, for the future training of Alexander. It was arranged that Alexander would enter into a regular clerkship under Stuart to qualify him for admission to the bar of Lower Canada. He would be a clerk for five years from June 20, 1806, and during this period his father would allow him board, lodging, apparel, "and all other necessaries requisite and needful for him." In addition, Elliott was to pay one hundred guineas to Stuart, who on his part agreed to instruct Alexander, and who agreed that at the end of the clerkship he would do his best to have the boy admitted as "Attorney at Law, Advocate, and Proctor in His Majesty's Courts" in Lower Canada. It was a proud moment for the old frontiersman.[28]

By 1806 Matthew Elliott, now approaching seventy, was apparently quietly ending a long and moderately successful career. The fur trader and frontier captain had become the distinguished farmer and public servant of Upper Canada; his eldest son training to be a lawyer with the Solicitor-General in Montreal. Yet, the most notable part of Elliott's frontier career was still to come.

Since the treaty of Greenville, Great Britain and the United States had enjoyed remarkably good relations along the border of the Great Lakes. The British government, proceeding on the assumption that the Indians were no longer needed, had neglected them. In August 1804, Thomas McKee stated in a letter from Amherstburg that the object of government, as he saw it, was "to have as few Indians to come to the Post as possible in order to lessen the expenditure of Provisions."[29] This of course did not mean that the Indians were as contented as the British and the Americans. In the years after 1795 American settlers rapidly poured into the lands obtained at the treaty of Greenville, and by the beginning of the nineteenth century they were hungry for more. After 1800 the Governor of Indiana Territory, William Henry Harrison, acting under instructions from Thomas Jefferson, negotiated with the Indians for lands beyond the "permanent" Greenville line. By 1805, the Indians of the Northwest were becoming increasingly discontented at American pressure, and in that year at Greenville, a Shawnee prophet arose to proclaim an Indian religious revival. Under the leadership of the prophet's brother Tecumseh, this rapidly became an anti-American movement. Yet, in this period immediately after 1800, the British attitude toward the American frontier was one of peace, and they did not wish to interfere in American-Indian quarrels. In council at Amherstburg in June 1805, McKee told a group of Sac and Fox, Ottawas, and Potawatomis that war was a scourge that should be avoided by all possible means. He also told them that the commander in chief in Canada had strenuously recommended peace and good relations between the Indians and the Americans.[30]

Yet, even while the Canadian frontier was still quiet, relations between Great Britain and the United States after 1803 were rapidly deteriorating. With the renewal of the war in Europe in that year, and with the great threat presented to England by Napoleon, the British government began a policy of increased severity toward the shipping of neutral nations. Sailors were impressed from American ships in increasing numbers, and the trade of the United States with the continent of Europe labored under more and more restrictions. Tension between the two nations increased, although this did not at first affect relations on the Canadian-American frontier. When it did, in 1807, Matthew Elliott was given the opportunity for which he had waited since 1799. Britain again needed experienced Indian agents.

Chapter 8

FRONTIER CRISIS

The event that finally disturbed the calm of the Canadian-American frontier was the British attack upon the American ship *Chesapeake* in June 1807. This event in the Atlantic had great significance for Upper Canada, because it released a storm of protest against Great Britain in the United States which for a time seemed likely to produce war. The bellicose American reaction immediately produced a fear of invasion in Canada, and the placid life of Upper Canada was transformed. Throughout the summer the authorities in both Lower and Upper Canada became increasingly apprehensive of war and invasion, and attempted to strengthen the defenses that had suffered neglect in the previous ten years. An important element in these defenses was the Indians of the Northwest, and there was a sudden desire to remedy the neglect of the previous ten years.[1]

The Indians who had gathered at Amherstburg in the fall of 1807 for their customary distribution of supplies were told before they left that they might hear from the British in the following months. Thomas McKee took this step on his own responsibility, presuming that the threat of war would soon bring him new instructions. He was proved correct, for on October 7, William Claus, who had succeeded Alexander McKee as Deputy Superintendent in Upper Canada, wrote to tell Thomas McKee that he should assemble the western Indians as soon as possible because the Lieutenant-Governor of Upper Canada, Francis Gore, wanted to communicate with them. McKee was ordered to send messages to Saginaw, to St. Joseph's on Lake Michigan, and to L'Arbre Croche (near Mackinac), requesting the Indians to assemble at Amherstburg. The Indians at Chenail Ecarté and those on the River St. Clair were to be assembled immediately, and were to await the arrival of those from the west. In fact, McKee was to gather as many Indians as possible at the British post. Claus specifically stated, however, that it was Gore's positive order that McKee should restrain the Indians from committing any act of aggression agains the subjects of the United States. McKee replied to Claus that he would lose no time in carrying out these orders, but also mentioned that as he had just dismissed the Indians prior to receiving Claus's order, those who had gone would probably be dilatory in returning to the post, as they had hastened to their different villages and hunting grounds. McKee also mentioned that his health was necessitating a constant confinement in bed; the common opinion was that this sickness was occasioned by an excessive use of rum. Thus, in ,the fall of 1807, under the apprehension of war with the United States, the British Indian Department began the task of collecting together the Indians, and communicated with those as far away as the west of Lake Michigan.[2]

While the machinery of the Indian Department once again began to accelerate, Matthew Elliott was beset with legal problems. These partially stemmed from the war crisis. His difficulties began in the winter and spring of 1806-7, when eight of his Indian and mulatto slaves, six men and two women, fled across the river into the territory of the United States. When the threat of war developed in the summer of 1807 Elliott's male slaves, together with other slaves who had crossed to Detroit, were enrolled in a Detroit militia company of thirty-six men. Those on the Canadian side of the Detroit River were obviously not happy to see their slaves drilling in the Detroit militia which might be used for the invasion of Canada. Elliott and another slaveowner, Richard Pattinson, brought suit before the Supreme Court of Michigan Territory for the recovery of their slaves. This whole case has a certain irony, for within half a century the flow of escaped slaves the other way across the river was to grow to large proportions, and Elliott's old home was to become a northern terminal of the underground railroad from the south. The question of slavery was somewhat confused in both Michigan Territory and in Upper Canada. In Upper Canada an act providing for the gradual emancipation of slaves had been passed on July 9, 1793, but the slavery of existing

158

slaves was continued. In Michigan Territory slavery was prohibited by the provisions of the Northwest Ordinance of July 1787, but those who held slaves before the Americans took over Detroit in 1796 had successfully maintained their legal right to keep them.[3]

As tension increased on the Detroit-Amherstburg border Elliott not only had a suit pending for the recovery of his slaves, but was also defendant in the Michigan Supreme Court in a case brought against him by merchant John Askin. Askin had sued Elliott for an old debt of $327.39 which he claimed had been advanced to Elliott in money and goods, and he also was claiming $2,000 damages. The case began in September 1807, and the lot and house which Elliott still owned in Detroit were attached by order of the court. Elliott appeared in court in September and October of 1807, and Elliott's lawyer argued that since the debt was over five years old, it could not be recovered and there was no case to answer. Askin's lawyer, Solomon Sibley, protested this point, and Judge Augustus T. Woodward decided for Sibley. The case eventually dragged on for a year before the jury found in favor of Askin. They gave him $225 for the debt, ten cents for damages, and made Elliott pay the costs of $31.[4]

But, in the fall of 1807, Elliott faced great difficulty in both his legal cases. Anti-British feeling was intense in Detroit, and this feeling was even more intense toward anyone who had been a member of the British Indian Department. The triumvirate of Elliott, McKee, and Girty, who had fled from Pittsburgh in 1778, had become ogres to the American frontiersmen. Even though Elliott at first managed to visit Detroit for his debt case without serious incident, his visits in the fall of 1807 gradually produced considerable popular opposition. On October 15, when he was in court in Detroit, plans developed, apparently under the leadership of tavern-keeper and hatter Richard Smyth, to catch Elliott and tar and feather him. Elliott got wind of this, did not go through the town, and by taking a devious route, managed to reach the house of his lawyer, Elijah Brush, without incident. Elliott had lived too long on the frontier to be caught by a tavern-keeper and his friends. A group then wanted to go to the lawyer's house to get Elliott, but was dissuaded by Smyth. On the following day Smyth told lawyer Brush, who doubted that the group would go to the length of tarring and feathering Elliott, "oh yes by God they will, and if he comes over again, he will get it, and it is no matter at what hour of the day or night they can catch him." Smyth also observed that if the judge decided in Elliott's favor in the slave case, he would be served in the same manner.[5]

That the group meant what they said was clearly shown on October 19. On that afternoon, James Heward came across from the British side of the river to testify on behalf of Elliott in the case of the slaves. Heward drank steadily during the afternoon, and although drunk, decided to go out to visit a friend. On passing the tavern of Richard Smyth he decided to go in for a drink, which was as ill-advised a move as Heward could have made, but in spite of the efforts of his companion to stop him, in he went. He ordered half a pint of brandy, and immediately got into a row with William Daily, a carpenter, who eventually called Heward "a British rascal," and threatened to pull his wig off. Daily was removed before the fight started, but Heward had by now ordered another half-pint of brandy and had only begun to fight. Shortly after Daily left, another man removed his coat and threatened to fight Heward, who by now was ready to fight the whole of Detroit. Heward got up to fight, but was pushed down again by his friend. He then tried to go out the back door, but his friend stopped him, thinking he was too drunk to go out "as he could scarcely stand." Heward then began to swear and called all the people in the room "a damned rascally Set of beggars." Heward, who was again called "a damned British rascal," now left by the back door in spite of his friend's efforts to stop him. A group in the room, including the nucleus who had already threatened Elliott, now followed Heward, "and assaulted and beat him, and Covered the Side of his face with tar, and part of his hat with tar and feathers, and deprived him of His Wig, Contrary to the laws and treaties of the United States." It was not specified which particular law or treaty covered removing wigs from British subjects. On the next day the wig was hanging from a nail on a public corner in Detroit, but Heward did not recover it. His friend had eventually extricated Heward, and that night at his lodgings they not only

160

locked the door but also nailed up the windows. It was later testified that it was probably a preconcerted plan to get Heward into a fight, though it might be said that Richard Smyth's tavern was not the best place for an Elliott sympathizer to go for a drink.[6]

In the meantime Elliott was safely back in Amherstburg, having dodged his tar and feathers, but he had been threatened with sudden action if he dared show his face again. On October 20, Elijah Brush, Elliott's lawyer, wrote to Elliott and asked him to come and show himself in Detroit with the object of proving that the group which had made the threats did not dare flout the law by tarring and feathering him. This idea was better for Brush than for Elliott, but Elliott came. On October 22, he crossed to Detroit, and at Brush's request appeared in different streets of the town throughout the day. He was not attacked, and Brush's theory was proven – along with Elliott's courage. Smyth later stated that the reason for the threats against Elliott "was that he had formerly taken an active part with the Indians against the United States."[7]

Elliott's claim for the recovery of his slaves was finally decided upon by Judge Woodward on October 24, 1807. By that time the verdict was a foregone conclusion for on the previous day the judge had decided against Richard Pattinson in a similar suit. Woodward pointed out that England herself had not provided for the restoration of American slaves that might go into Canada, and in fact there was no system of reciprocity. Elliott thus lost his case – it was certainly a most unfortunate time for him to bring it before the Supreme Court of Michigan. The question of the attack on James Heward and the threats against Elliott were not resolved for another year. Indictments were eventually levelled against some of the participants for contempt of court and for assault and battery, but in October 1808 the attorney-general declared that he was not going to prosecute, and the defendants were discharged.[8]

The feeling against Elliott and the British Indian Department could not have been more clearly shown than by the events in Detroit in the fall of 1807, and it was reflected in the information passed on to Thomas McKee by Adam Brown, the Wyandot chief of Brownstown at the mouth of the Detroit River, at the end of November 1807. Brown supposedly reported what had been said to him by Colonel Hull, the son of Governor William Hull of Michigan Territory. Hull, according to Brown, had said that if war came, ten thousand men from Kentucky would take Amherstburg, and Elliott, McKee, Caldwell and all the members of the Indian Department would be put to death.[9] By December 1807, Elliott and the members of the Indian Department at Amherstburg had ample reason to organize the Indians with efficiency and ensure that the Americans would not be victorious in any struggle in the Old Northwest. The Americans in Detroit had demonstrated quite clearly what they thought of those ex-Americans and British who had devoted their lives to the cause of the Indians.

Although preliminary measures had been taken in the early fall of 1807, the creation of a general policy to meet the new situation in the Northwest became the task of the new Governor in chief of Canada, Sir James Craig. Craig arrived in Canada in late October 1807, and between December 1807 and May 1808 issued the instructions that were to guide the Indian Department until the spring of 1811. His philosophy was clearly expressed in his letter to Lieutenant-Governor Gore on December 6, 1807: "If a war takes place, they [the Indians] will not be idle. If we do not employ them, there cannot exist a moment's doubt that they will be employed against us." The latter part of this statement was open to question, as the Americans had normally urged the Indians to keep a neutrality in the event of war with England, on the theory that if they went to war at all their interests would lead them to the English. Craig went on to say that in the event of war he had "no hesitation in saying that we must employ them if they can be brought to act with us." His final advice regarding the Indians left great responsibility with the Department on the Detroit frontier: "I would avoid coming to any explanation with them as long as possible, at least to any public explanation, yet whenever the subject is adverted to, I think it would be advisable always to insinuate, that as a matter of course we shall look for the assistance of our Brothers. It should be done with delicacy, but still in a way not to be misunderstood." Craig also suggested that he would be happy to receive some information regarding the Prophet. If his influence were great, and if some of the Indian Department could enter into intercourse with him, it might be worthwhile to purchase his goodwill.[10]

On December 28, Craig went still further in a letter to Gore. He pointed out that England and the Indians had long-lasting ties, and that the British could supply the Indians with provisions to enable them to protect themselves against the Americans who obviously desired to take their country. If these facts were properly insisted on, they should act as powerful motives to keep the Indians bound to Great Britain:

> but then the officers of the Indian Department must be diligent and active, the communication must be constant, these topics must be held up to them not merely in Great Councils and public Assemblies, they should be privately urged to some of their leading men, with whom endeavours should be used to lead them to a confidence in us, two or three gained over to us will be of more avail than all that can be said in a Council.

This statement gave a tremendous amount of power to the Indian Department; it gave them wide discretion to confer in secret with the Indians and convince them of the iniquities of the Americans.[11]

When Lieutenant-Governor Gore replied to Craig on January 5, 1808, he stressed that in addressing the Indians "we must take care in this matter not to be too passive," for there had been reports that some of the Indians had discovered "a degree of coldness" in the British cause. He also pointed out that Amherstburg was the key post. By far the greatest body of Indians assembled there, Gore pointed out, and England needed an excellent man to head the Indian Department at that spot. The name Gore suggested to Craig was that of Matthew Elliott – he pointed out that Elliott had served with the Indians during the whole of the Revolution. He also pointed out that Elliott was personally acquainted with the Prophet, and that as Elliott was expected at York in the near future he would enquire whether the Prophet was worth buying.[12]

The move to reinstate Elliott, which had apparently collapsed after Elliott's abortive visit to England in 1804, took on new life in the fall of 1807. Thomas McKee, although the son of the famous Alexander, was considered to have too little experience and to be too much addicted to the bottle to hold such a key post as the Amherstburg Superintendency at a time of crisis. Sir John Johnson, who still headed the Indian Department, expressed the opinion to William Claus early in December 1807 that

> Capt. Elliott who was hastily dismissed from the service, and who I know Governor Gore wishes you to bring into the Service if possible, has great weight among the Delawares, – Shawenoes, and Wyandots and is beloved by the Inhabitants would be of great benefit to the service in aid of Mr. McKee.

On January 8, Gore went still further in an attempt to influence Craig. He pointed out that Thomas McKee's influence over the Indians was nearly lost, and that he had habits of great intemperance. He again urged the employment of Matthew Elliott.[13]

Gore had the opportunity of consulting with Elliott soon after he had written to Craig, for in January 1808, Elliott arrived in York for the session of the Upper Canadian Assembly. Elliott's abilities impressed Gore so much that he decided to use him even though Craig had not yet agreed to his reinstatement. On January 29 Gore wrote a secret dispatch to William Claus which was personally delivered by Matthew Elliott. In it Gore told Claus that he was enclosing instructions to guide his conduct while he was with the Indians at Amherstburg. He added that Captain Elliott had been prevailed upon to accompany and assist Claus, and that as Elliott was well aware of the motives behind Claus being sent to Amherstburg, Gore relied with some degree of confidence upon the success of the mission. But Claus was told "you will on no account whatever, let it be known to a third person, that this Gentleman is so employed." Claus was also told that as it was supposed that the Shawnee chiefs would not come in at the invitation of Thomas McKee, Elliott was to send for them. Claus was particularly enjoined to discover what the Americans were saying to the Indians, as it was important to obtain such information as would allow the British to speak to the Indians in plain terms. Goods for presents to the Indians would have to be obtained by purchase or loan from the merchants since the Indian stores in Upper Canada were empty.[14]

Elliott's fortunes had turned once again. He was now to proceed to Amherstburg on a secret mission for the lieutenant-governor of Upper Canada, in spite of the fact that his status was still that of a dismissed member of the Indian Department. On January 30, it was moved in the Assembly (no reason being given) that Elliott should be given leave of absence for the rest of the session. This was granted.[15]

The secret instructions enclosed in the dispatch which Elliott carried to Claus presumably were drafted by Gore with Elliott's aid; at least Gore stated that Elliott was "a perfect master" of the motives for which Claus was being sent to Amherstburg. They went a long way toward carrying into practical application the general instructions that had been handed down by Craig to govern the conduct of the Indian Department. They were divided into fifteen separate points and were designed to give Claus perfect guidance. He was to proceed to Amherstburg and find out what measures the American government had taken in regard to the Indians, and was to call together the principal chiefs of the Shawnee and the other Indian nations "to consult Privately, on the critical situation of Affairs." Those chiefs that were presumed to have the greatest influence were to be kept about Claus, treated with respect, and entertained; he was to use his discretion to avoid jealousy among the other chiefs. In all communications with the chiefs he was to impress upon their minds that in the event of war between England and the United States, England, as a matter of course, expected the assistance of the Indians: "this is to be done, with Caution and Delicacy, but in such a manner as not to be misunderstood by them." The friendship of Great Britain for the Indians was to be stressed, and

> The Chiefs must be reminded, when proper occasions offer, of the Artful and Clandistine manner, in which the Americans have obtain'd possession of their Lands, and of their obvious intention, of ultimately possessing themselves of the whole, and driving the Indians out of the Country.

One cannot escape the conclusion that the Americans had justification in fearing British influence among the Indians at this period.

The remainder of the instructions continued in a like vein. Gore said he had been told (obviously by Elliott) that the Shawnee chief Captain Johnny was the person to be used in communicating with the other chiefs. When Claus had satisfied himself that Captain Johnny could be confided in, he was to prepare him, with frequent repetitions, for what might have to be communicated confidentially to the chiefs. Claus was to be particularly cautious and reserved in all conversations with the interpreters, and if possible was only to confide in one. Moreover, if it was necessary to make a speech in public council, he was to make only general comments about the wish of the Great Father to remain in peace and harmony with the Indians. Finally, if possible, the Prophet was to be conciliated, and Claus was to distribute corn and fresh beef to the Indians.[16]

The need for all the secrecy was quite obvious, since public knowledge of these instructions would certainly bring down the wrath of the American government upon the British authorities in Canada. The whole emphasis was on weighty communication with the Indians in secret and on innocuous speeches in public, and it is quite obvious that to cite speeches made in public council does no more to explain the entire British policy toward the Indians in this period than does the citing of the general comments made by the British ministers in their letters to Canada. When it came down to the actual implementation of policy, the vital steps were taken by loyalists who had ample sympathy for the Indians and a corresponding dislike for their old brethren in the United States.

As Elliott set out for Amherstburg with Claus, Governor in chief Craig wrote to Gore and indicated that it would hardly be suitable for him to reappoint Elliott, a man dismissed by one of his predecessors and denied reinstatement in England. Craig would have been surprised to learn that his lieutenant-governor had already employed Elliott to aid in the carrying out of the whole British policy along the Detroit frontier. Craig also in this letter referred to American attacks on British Indian policy, and said that though this did not change his wishes, Gore should be as careful as possible to avoid irritating the public mind in the United States, and should abstain as far as possible from any

166

"public communication" with the Indians.[17]

Claus and Elliott arrived at Amherstburg on February 8, and found to their disappointment only some six hundred and thirty Indians; only about two hundred of these were warriors. The tribes represented were Chippewa, Ottawa, Potawatomi, Munsee, Nanticoke, Delaware, and Wyandot. The Shawnee had not come in, and the British agents at first could find no chief they could trust. Claus eventually did find two chiefs at Amherstburg with whom he was able to speak in private – a Chippewa and an Ottawa. From their information he concluded that, with the exception of the Wyandots, the Indians were decidedly opposed to the Americans. Claus, however, turned to Elliott for word of the Shawnee. He sent a messenger recommended by Elliott to the principal village of the Shawnee at the Auglaize to request the attendance of the Shawnee chiefs and the Prophet at Amherstburg. The message was verbal to avoid accidents. The Auglaize was of course well within American territory.[18]

Meanwhile the campaign to remove McKee and install Elliott continued. Claus wrote to Prideaux Selby on February 16 to say that he did not see what could be done "unless Elliott is placed here for it is impossible for the service to be carried on in the same way it has been for some time past." He suggested on the following day that McKee should be allowed to retire, and a proper person appointed to succeed him, "for unless some fit person is appointed to this post, I see no end to the very great abuse from inattention." Claus was disgusted with the whole state of affairs at Amherstburg. He thought not only McKee but also the interpreters were incompetent. Claus reported to Selby that "S. Girty is incapable of doing anything," although Elliott had strongly recommended Simon's brother, James.[19]

The Shawnee chiefs sent for by Elliott did not arrive at the mouth of the Detroit until the latter part of March, and even then the Prophet did not come with them, owing to some jealousy between him and the chiefs. On March 25, Claus met in private council with Captain Johnny, Blackbeard, and the Buffalo, in the presence of Elliott, and with James Girty as interpreter. Claus told them that the King was trying to obtain peace with the Americans, but that if he failed they could expect to hear from the British. If they did so they should open their ears, for not only would they help England, they would also probably regain the country taken from them by the Americans. He pointed out to them that the little land they had left was now fast disappearing. In the event of any disturbance between the British and the Americans, Claus stated, "your friend Captain Elliott will send word to you." In reporting this meeting to Craig, Gore stated regarding the role of Elliott: "This has no doubt been done with a view to gratify the Indians, whose attachment to that Gentleman is very great." Gore was still working hard for the reappointment of Elliott, but on March 10 Craig had once again expressed the view that Elliott would not be suitable for appointment to the Amherstburg post.[20]

Throughout April, Claus and Elliott continued their work at Amherstburg. On April 20, Claus estimated that the warriors in the area probably amounted to fifteen hundred men, but he feared that the Indians would be backward if their assistance were required, owing to the defenceless nature of Amherstburg. If the British had an adequate force at the post, they might obtain sufficient Indian support to hold their ground until the Indians from the west of Lake Michigan arrived. Though messages had been sent to the nations west of Lake Michigan in the previous October, they had still not come, and Claus told Gore that he was immediately sending another messenger. He added the usual praises for Elliott's work, and was emphatic about the faith which the Indians placed in him – he attributed this to Elliott's long and active service with the Indians during the Revolution.[21]

At the beginning of May, Elliott's old underling, Frederick Fisher, who had stood by him in the Chenail Ecarte' days, arrived with a message from the Prophet. Fisher had been sent for in February when the messenger had gone to the Auglaize, as, probably on the advice of Elliott, he had been reappointed as an interpreter in January. Fisher had been in contact with the Prophet for a number of years, and was established at Greenville as a trader in 1806. Elliott had presumably been able to watch the progress of the Prophet's work through this means. Fisher brought the news (which was already known) that the Americans were advising the Indians to keep quiet in the event of hostilities, and he also reported that the Prophet had moved to the Wabash with nearly eighty men. He was expecting a visit from some thirty nations. The Prophet sent a message through Fisher assuring the British of his friendship, and saying that he would come into the post whenever the British sent for him.[22]

The constant pressure for the reappointment of Elliott finally caused Craig to change his mind. His decision was based on fear of the French rather than of the Americans. In a letter to Gore on May 11, he first informed the lieutenant-governor that there seemed, at least at present, no probability of the American government declaring war, but that there was a possibility of the appearance of the French on some part or other of the continent. With this in mind, he was prepared to waive his objections to the reappointment of Elliott. Moreover, because whenever the French appeared, great efforts would be made to detach the Indians from the British, Craig asserted he was even more convinced of the importance of the Indians and the Indian Department than when he first arrived in North America. The British would have to make even greater efforts to win the support of the Indians, and in particular he suggested that some means might be employed for opening an intercourse "with the nations situated to the Southward." Craig suggested that Gore might inform Claus and Elliott of these new endeavors, but he should be cautious about extending it lower.[23]

Craig did not want to incite the Indians to war against the United States, but he did want the Indians firmly in the British interest, and prepared to fight for Great Britain if the British possessions in North America were attacked by either the Americans or the French. To insure this support, he was prepared to give his subordinates permission to contact Indians within American territory. Although Craig insisted that he neither wanted war with the United States nor incitement of the Indians, his subordinates were allowed to win Indian allegiance by pointing out that American expansion would eventually lead to the total expulsion of the Indians from the country. The object of the policy was not the immediate incitement of the Indians, but the methods used inevitably helped to stir up Indian resentment against the Americans.

169

At Amherstburg, Claus and Elliott went about their task of winning Indian allegiance. Claus sent word to the Prophet in the middle of May that he would like to see him and the chiefs of any of the other nations who were with him. Claus asked him, however, to keep his young men from "doing any mischief" to settlers and their cattle as they travelled through the country. Though the Prophet did not come in to the post at the invitation of the British, his famous brother Tecumseh arrived at Amherstburg on June 8 with a party of five Shawnee. Up to this point in their correspondence, the British had always referred to the activities of the Prophet, but never to the activities of his brother. But the role of Tecumseh was becoming of increasing importance, and the British discovered that rather than negotiating with the Prophet they were obliged to negotiate with his brother. On June 13, Claus had three hours private conversation with Tecumseh and four members of his band, and on the following day delivered "a handsome Present" to the Shawnees.[24]

In the middle of June, news arrived from York that Lieutenant-Governor Gore had decided to visit Amherstburg to meet the Indians in council. It was not until June 4 that Gore had received Craig's letter permitting him to reappoint Elliott, and enjoining him to be even more energetic in winning the allegiance of the Indians. He immediately took steps to carry out Craig's orders. On June 6, he announced that Elliott had been reappointed Superintendent at Amherstburg, and also repeated much of Craig's letter in a secret letter to Claus. He told Claus that he should increase his exertions to attain influence with the Indians to the south and west, and should also find a means to open an intercourse with them. For the present, Claus was to avoid mentioning the possibility of war with the United States.[25]

When Claus heard that Gore was to visit Amherstburg, he indicated in a letter to the lieutenant-governor that he would wait until Gore arrived before taking steps to contact the Indians to the south and west. He said he was fearful to act on his own judgement in sending confidential envoys into a foreign country.[26] Claus and Elliott had, however, already sent agents to visit the Shawnee at the Glaize, the Prophet on the Wabash, and the nations west of Lake Michigan, without feeling such compunction.

Elliott was in a position to rejoice in these days before the

Governor's arrival. He had received news of his reappointment, and in June he was one of the two members re-elected to the Assembly without opposition. The arrangements for the visit of the lieutenant-governor were left to Elliott, who decided to go and meet him. Claus told Selby that Elliott wished to pay every respect to Gore. On June 21 Elliott set out from Amherstburg to meet Gore, who eventually arrived at the post on June 29. There was little wonder that Elliott looked with friendship upon Gore, since he had not only reappointed him, but had also issued an order on July 16 that George Ironside, the Indian store-keeper, could reside at Elliott's farm until further notice. The earlier victory of Captain McLean was thus overthrown.[27]

In the first weeks of July, a thousand Indian warriors with some one hundred chiefs gathered at Amherstburg for the visit of the lieutenant-governor. Among them was Tecumseh, who had agreed to stay for Gore's visit. There were few women and children, since they were for the most part at work planting their corn fields. Through the first ten days of the month, Elliott and Claus spoke in private with various groups of Indians, urging them to join the British and ignore the Americans, and warning them that it was possible that they might be visited by the French. On July 11, Gore spoke in public council to the Indians. As he had promised Craig, he was most guarded in what he said. He presented Elliott to them as their new Superintendent, and told them that he had not come to invite them to take up the hatchet, but to be on their guard. He hoped that the present state of peace would be preserved. The Wyandots replied for the Indians on July 13. They expressed their great pleasure that Elliott had been restored to them – "we can place confidence in, and rely upon him as a man of experience." Of Thomas McKee they were less complimentary – he "was too young and inexperienced, he loved to frolick too much and neglected our Affairs, therefor we did not like him." The rest of the Indian reply was couched in general terms. They like the lieutenant-governor's speech, and they would send it to the nations to the south who had not yet heard his words.[28]

As usual, the public council had been innocuous, and Gore left for York soon after its conclusion. More interesting is the confidential information which Gore brought back for transmission to Craig: "The Superintendents private communications with confidential Chiefs, afford ... hopes, of a cordial assistance if we shew ourselves in any force to join them; but without that encouragement it is to be feared they will not be induced, at least generally, to become active friends." Conversations with Tecumseh had made it evident that the British were having difficulty owing to the lack of military support they had given the Indians at the time of Wayne's advance in 1794. Gore told Craig that he had learned that the "Prophets Brother" (Tecumseh was the Prophet's principal support, and observed that Tecumseh appeared to be "a very shrewd intelligent man." Tecumseh had told Claus and Elliott that they were endeavoring to collect the different nations on the Wabash in order to preserve their country from any encroachment. They did not at present wish to take part in the quarrels of the white people, but they were resolved to strike should the Americans encroach upon them. Tecumseh added that if the British were in earnest, and appeared in sufficient force, the Indians would support them. Tecumseh, however, spoke a great deal about the fact that at Fallen Timbers the British fort had been shut against the Indians, and he reminded Elliott how many chiefs fell because of that event. The Prophet and Tecumseh were certainly hostile to the Americans, but Gore seemed to think that they would have to see actual signs of British military strength before they would act firmly on the British side. The other important confidential news that Gore brought back from Amherstburg was that Blackbeard, "a Principal Shawenoes Chief, and a very confidential man," was shortly to set out for the Cherokee country "to feel the Pulse, and renew the friendship with Those People and the Indians to the Southwest."[29] By July 1808, though little had been said in public council, the British were actively engaged in winning the support of the Indians within American territory. Elliott, who for so long had met with failure in his attempts to obtain reinstatement, was back in the favor of government because the time had come when his particular accomplishments and long acquaintance with the Indian tribes were desperately needed by Great Britain.

Although the agitation of 1807-8 had once again set the machinery of the British Indian Department into motion, the actual fear of war diminished in the summer of 1808, and the flurry of orders and instructions for the direction of the Indian Department at Amherstburg gradually died away. This reflected the lessening of anxiety, but it also reflected the fact that the firm hands of Matthew Elliott had taken the helm along the American frontier. In the next two years, he brought all his old abilities into play to win back the allegiance of the Indians.

The activities of 1808 proved very satisfactory to Elliott. In the fall of that year some five thousand Indians (men, women, and children) visited the post to receive the King's bounty, and Elliott once again became very confident of his hold over the tribes. By the beginning of 1809 he was convinced that with one regular regiment, Detroit and the country to the Ohio would soon be in British possession, and the Indians actively in support. Gore thought Elliott too sanguine in his hopes of Indian assistance, since in his opinion there would have to be a considerable increase of the regular forces in Upper Canada before England could safely depend on the cooperation of the Indians. Yet, Elliott was in the key position, and it would seem that his confidential communications with the Indians in 1808 had led him to believe he could expect their assistance against the Americans if it were needed.[30]

The events of 1807-9, in the same manner as those before 1795, clearly show that at the moments of crisis on the Canadian-American frontier, immense power was wielded by the Indian Department in Upper Canada. Communication with the Indians was not by formal notes, which could be placed under the careful scrutiny of the British government. Policy was carried out by Elliott speaking in confidence with various chiefs in the council house at the end of his lawn, or by Claus confidentially visiting the different bands of Indians gathered at Amherstburg. General injunctions by Craig to win the support of the Indians for use in the event of war often became far more specific by the time they reached the end of the chain of command. The British government in England was even further detached from the control of affairs. It had far too many problems in Europe to work out the details of British policy toward the Indians on the American frontier, even if it could have sent the instructions to Canada in time to be of any use. Thus, in April 1809,

Secretary of War Castlereagh approved the reappointment of Elliott, just as the Duke of Portland had earlier approved his dismissal. He also agreed with Craig's principle that in the event of war, if the British did not use the Indians, the Americans would. He was ready therefore to support any temporary arrangements that Craig might make.[31]

Castlereagh certainly did not want to give any overt offense to the United States if it possibly could be avoided, but he also wanted Canada defended if the United States should go to war either over British maritime policy or for any other reason. He was obliged to leave the details of this defense, and of the nature of Indian support, to the officials in Canada. To a lesser extent, Craig was obliged to leave certain details to Gore, and Gore was obliged to leave details to Claus and Elliott. The problem with this was that in Indian relations it was frequently the details that were most important. This was particularly the case when the general policy ordered was one which necessitated walking a tightrope between being too bellicose and offending the Americans, and being too non-committal and offending the Indians. Relations with the Indians along the frontier were conducted almost exclusively from Amherstburg, and from 1808 on, Indian policy at that post depended once again on Matthew Elliott, a man who had devoted a good part of his life to strengthening Indian resistance against the advance of the American frontier. It is not surprising that the Americans constantly objected to British influence among the Indians in the years before the War of 1812.

For the time being the fear of war had decreased, but the authorities in Canada ordered no reversal of the policy that had been laid down between December 1807 and July 1808. In 1809 and 1810, Elliott was once again engaged in the task of winning and keeping the allegiance of the Indians. On his visit to Amherstburg in July 1808, Lieutenant-Governor Gore had handed the Indians a belt composed of 11,550 grains of wampum, and had asked them to send it to all the western nations as a belt of amity and friendship. Since the British had treated Tecumseh so well at Amherstburg, the Wyandots had entrusted the belt to him, supposing he was in the confidence of the British government. In actual fact, while the British were anxious to obtain support from any influential Indian, they were not at all in close alliance with Tecumseh in these early days of the confederacy. Tecumseh somewhat distrusted the British after the events of the 1790's, and the British were unsure of Tecumseh's power. Yet, he took Gore's belt of wampum to the Wabash and, according to Elliott's report, showed it to forty nations. By May 1809, when Elliott reported all this to Gore's headquarters, the belt was back at Brownstown at the mouth of the Detroit. Elliott was still doubtful whether the Prophet could retain his influence, as one hundred and sixty Ottawas and Chippewas had died while with him, whereas in the same period the Shawnees [the Prophet's tribe] only lost five. In the period before 1810 there is little indication that the British were particularly concerned in the Tecumseh confederacy, although they were of course actively working to win the allegiance of all the Indians in the region.[32]

In June 1809, Elliott reported bad news from the Cherokee country. The messenger Blackbeard who had been sent the previous summer had returned in a poor state of health, and Elliott believed that he had since died. What was worse from the British point of view was that the Cherokee had sent a pro-American speech in reply to the message sent by the British. Elliott pointed out to Claus that he believed there were two groups among the Cherokees – one of which was staunch Republican and the other British. Elliott was so incensed at this incident that he went so far as to say he could wish to hear that everything had been amicably settled between the British and the Americans – the Indians would then see the effect of their ingratitude toward the British. The British message had been sent on to the Creeks and the Choctaws, but Elliott warned Claus that they too could be divided into pro-British and pro-American factions.[33]

Yet, despite the disappointments occasioned by the cool reception given to the British message by the southern Indians, and in spite of the doubts entertained by the British of the influence and efficacy of the work of the Prophet and his brother, there seems little doubt that in the years from 1807 to 1810, the British Indian Department entered willingly and to a great extent successfully into the task of winning the allegiance of the Indians.

What is more, it is reasonable to assume that the British policy of telling the Indians that the Americans were stealing their land contributed to the rise of Indian discontent against the Americans in these years. By 1810, Indian anger at violations of the treaty of Greenville, and the cessions of land in Indiana Territory, were both reaching a peak. The Americans had practically digested the land ceded by the Indians at Greenville, and were busily engaged in taking the next series of bites from the land of the Northwest. The Indians would have fought had there been no British in Canada. The British did not create Indian discontent but took advantage of it to win the Indians for the defense of Canada in the event of war. But in winning Indian allegiance, they had helped to increase the already existing Indian discontent. Matthew Elliott had been a key figure in this policy, and was to become even more important in the period from 1810 to 1812.

Chapter 9

PRELUDE TO WAR

The winter of 1809-10 brought a problem that was all too familiar to Elliott and the Indian Department. At the distant British post of St. Joseph's (just east of Mackinac) a clash occurred between the Indian Department storekeeper (who also had to act as superintendent) and the military commandant. The whole affair was a remarkably familiar one. John Askin Jr. was accused of having issued short weights and of committing other misdemeanors. The officer commanding at the post suspended him from his position, and eventually the news reached Amherstburg and York. The ensuing events clearly showed the difference between Governor in chief Robert Prescott and Lieutenant-Governor Francis Gore, and between the situation on the frontier in 1798 and in 1810. Gore referred the matter to Elliott for a report on how far this dispute might affect the British interest among the Indians. Elliott replied on February 23 that the suspension of Askin might well make an unfavorable impression upon the Indians, and would strengthen the efforts of the Americans to detach the Indians from the British interest. Elliott lamented that Askin should have been suspended without an appeal to Gore at a time when every exertion of the Indian officers was needed. Gore immediately issued an order reinstating Askin, and sent another officer to take command at the post. An Indian officer was sent with him to investigate the stores, and to replace Askin should they be found deficient. Eventually Askin was cleared, and it would appear that by 1810 the Indian Department had won back the influence that it had last held under Simcoe before Fallen Timbers.[1]

At the time the decision was taken to send a mission to St. Joseph's, Elliott was in York for a session of the Upper Canadian Assembly. Elliott was late in arriving, but was excused from paying the usual fine because of the poor state of his health. This was also given as the reason why Elliott did not personally go to St. Joseph's to settle the dispute. It is not surprising that Elliott should not have been in perfect health, for by this time he was at least seventy years of age. Apart from an occasional illness, he was still in remarkably good condition. Indeed it was probably early in 1810 that for the first time he contracted a legal marriage. His choice was a fascinating one – the young Sarah Donovan, daughter of Irishman Matthew Donovan. Matthew Donovan, an excellent Latin scholar who apparently on occasion had too great a liking for the bottle, had been a schoolmaster in Detroit in the 1790's and stayed there until the great fire of 1805. Sometime after that event he took his family across the river to Amherstburg where he died by July 1809. Whether the family fortunes now needed reviving is not recorded, but it was shortly after her father's death that Sarah married the prosperous Matthew Elliott. She could not have been very old, for she was to live until 1869. The marriage between the young schoolteacher's daughter and the old, unlettered Indian agent produced two sons: Francis Gore Elliott, born in January 1812, and Robert Herriot Barclay Elliott (named for the British naval commander on Lake Erie), born in December 1813.[2]

In the spring and summer of 1810, the tempo of Indian affairs was once again moving more swiftly. Indian dissatisfaction at American encroachment on their lands was reaching a peak, and the British were now beginning to face a different problem from that of 1807-8. At the earlier period the British had feared that they had lost their influence over the Indians, and that the Indians were not sufficiently embittered against the Americans. By 1810 it was becoming obvious that the Indians were ready to fight the Americans, and the British now faced the problem of keeping the Indians in check until they were needed and yet still retaining their friendship. The British had tried to convince the Indians that they should dislike the Americans, but they did not want the Indians to go to war until the moment that England needed them. By 1810 this policy was proving increasingly difficult to maintain.

At the beginning of July 1810 a party of one hundred and twenty-five Sac and Fox arrived at Amherstburg and demanded a council. They pleaded great poverty and requested some clothing, kettles, and other necessities. They also begged some guns and ammunition for their young men. Elliott spoke to them and advised them "to observe a Peaceable conduct towards all Nations & to each other and told them that if their Father wanted them, they should have the token [a pipe] they left with me presented to them." Although the words were of peace, they contained the possibility of future action; Elliott also reported in a letter to Claus that these Indians were "handsomely supplied" with most of the articles that they demanded.[3] On July 18, Governor William Henry Harrison of Indiana Territory reported to the War Department that a Miami chief who had just returned from Amherstburg had been told by Elliott: "My son, keep your eyes fixed on me; my tomahawk is now up; be you ready, but do not strike until I give the signal."[4] There seems little reason to doubt this report, as its sentiments were clearly in line with British policy, though perhaps expressed more ferociously than some in Canada would have liked.

The Americans themselves were afraid that Indian war was imminent, and Governor Harrison was constantly warning the War Department of the danger in the Northwest. In September 1810, Governor William Hull attended a large gathering of Indians at Brownstown, across the Detroit River from Elliott's farm, in the hope of influencing them against the Prophet and his young warriors. Elliott thought that the council had failed to win the Indians to the American point of view:

> I sincerely believe that the Indian Nations are now more ripe than ever for War, and would be more hearty in the cause than formerly should such a Calamity again assail this Country; because they now see that their Interests are trampled upon by our Neighbours – they publickly say so.
>
> I dread indeed that they will of themselves soon commence hostilities, & our Government will (indeed already is) blamed for encouraging them, as may be seen in their Public Prints particularly in some documents published in Vincennes by Governor Harrison.[5]

The British authorities in Canada were now in a precarious position, for since 1808 the Indian Department had been pointing out to the Indians that Indian interests were being trampled on by the Americans. It was now difficult to find arguments to keep the Indians at peace until they were needed.

The problem reached its peak in November 1810. In that month Tecumseh visited the British post at Amherstburg and met in council with Elliott. He came with one hundred and sixtynine Potawatomis, Ottawas, Winnebagoes, and Sacs. On November 14, Elliott distributed supplies, and on the fifteenth Tecumseh spoke in formal council. He told the British that he and the warriors had taken from the chiefs a belt given to them when the British had defeated the French (in the French and Indian War), and had forced all the chiefs to turn their eyes away from the Americans and toward the British:

> You Father have nourished us, and raised us up from Childhood we are now Men, and think ourselves capable of defending our Country, in which cause you have given us active assistance and always advice – We are now determined to defend it ourselves, and after raising you on your feet leave you behind, but expecting you will push forwards towards us what may be necessary to supply our wants.

He went on to say that he intended to proceed toward the "Mid Day," and that he expected before next autumn and before he visited Amherstburg again, the business would be done. He explained to Elliott later in private that he had meant that the confederacy would be complete by that time. He also explained that at first the Indians had intended to keep their plan a secret even from the British until everything was fully agreed on among themselves, but that Governor Harrison had pushed them into an open avowal of their intentions. Tecumseh concluded his council speech by thanking Elliott for the ample presents that the Indians had received.[6]

On November 18, Elliott sent Tecumseh's speech to Claus. Elliott stated that the speech "fully convinces me that Our Neighbours are on the eve of an Indian War, and I have no doubt that the Confederacy is almost general, particularly towards the quarter in which the Prophet resides." Elliott was now well aware that his position was a delicate one, and he asked for ample and explicit instructions to regulate his future conduct toward the Prophet and his followers: "I am well aware that I cannot, and might not, during the present circumstance of affairs do any thing overtly but whether it would not be proper to keep up among them the present Spirit of resistance I wish to be Informed." Though Elliott wrote for explicit instructions in the middle of November, he did not receive them until some four months later. It does not seem unreasonable to conclude that during the interim period, and earlier in the fall of 1810 (he had already supplied six thousand Indians with their annual presents when he wrote to Claus) he had in fact done what he suggested in his letter to Claus – kept up the "Spirit of resistance."[7]

Colonel Isaac Brock, the military commander in Upper Canada, wrote to Governor in chief Craig in February 1811 on the subject of the November council. His letter was an attack on the Indian Department, and on the extent to which Elliott had committed the British to the support of the Indians:

> I lament to think that the Indians retired from the council, in which they declared their resolution of going to war, with a full conviction that, although they could not look for active cooperation on our part, yet they might rely with confidence upon receiving from us every requisite of war.
>
> Our cold attempt to dissuade that much-injured people from engaging in such a rash enterprise could scarcely be expected to prevail, particularly after giving such manifest indications of a contrary sentiment by the liberal quantity of military stores with which they were dismissed.

Brock then had no doubt that the British Indian Department at Amherstburg had given the wrong impression at the November council, and as the November council saw Elliott do nothing more than in the previous two years, presumably this can be taken as a condemnation of earlier actions as well. Brock came down to the root of the matter in his comments upon Elliott. They seem a very fair summary of Elliott's position:

> Mr. Elliot, who has the management of the Indian department at Amherstburg is an exceedingly good man,

and highly respected by the Indians; but, having in his youth lived a great deal with them, he has naturally imbibed their feelings and prejudices, and partaking in the wrongs they continually suffer, this sympathy made him neglect the considerations of prudence, which ought to have regulated his conduct. If he had delayed the issue of presents until he reported their mission to Lieut.-Gov. Gore, they would have returned to their companions, carrying with them the positive sentiments of government.[8]

Brock was just in his estimate of the result of Elliott's conduct, but less than just in placing the whole responsibility upon Elliott rather than also considering the instructions that had been issued for his guidance. The Indian Department had been given considerable discretion, and had been given orders to win the allegiance of the Indians and to turn the Indians away from the Americans. It would have taken a magician to accomplish this without also making the Indians wish to fight.

Governor in chief Craig was in a difficult and embarrassing position by the close of 1810. He had accomplished the task of winning the allegiance of the Indians, but the Indians were obviously ripe for war. If they went to war, it would obviously increase the tension between the British and the Americans, and perhaps help to create the war which Craig's home government did not want. Craig therefore now became vitally interested in restraining the Indians, and in avoiding blame for creating an Indian war. Even before Elliott's request for specific instructions had reached him, Craig had taken steps to extricate himself from any guilt in regard to the coming Indian war. He had written to John Philip Morier, the British *charge d'affaires* in Washington, and had asked him to warn the Americans of the danger of Indian war in the Northwest.[9]

Yet, to this point, no new instructions had been sent to Elliott. On December 29, 1810, Gore transmitted Elliott's request for detailed instructions to Craig and said: "As I do not conceive His Majestys Interests will suffer by my waiting for your Instructions, I shall not give any directions to Captain Elliott to alter his conduct, or depart from the existing Orders which guide him in his Intercourse with the Indian Nations."[10] As

Gore took no action in response to Elliott's request, it was not until Craig replied to Gore's letter on February 2, 1811, that new orders began the long journey back toward Amherstburg. Craig now made desperate attempts to avoid Indian war. He told Gore that he was decidedly of the opinion that they should strive to avoid a war between the Indians and the United States. Gore was to instruct the officers of the Indian Department to use all their influence to dissuade the Indians from their projected plan of hostility, giving them clearly to understand that they could expect no assistance from Great Britain. These instructions were above reproach, but they were too late. Two days after Craig had sent the new instructions to Gore, he also sent a confidential letter to Colonel Brock. He said that though intercourse with the Indians was vested in the civil authorities and not in the military, army officers could be present at the various councils without interfering. He now wanted Brock to instruct the army officers at the different posts, particularly Amherstburg, to report confidentially to Brock on what happened at these councils, as well as on any other transactions regarding the Indians that might come to their knowledge.[11] Craig was obviously suspicious of the activities of the Indian Department.

It was not until February 26 that Gore was able to transmit to William Claus the instructions for Matthew Elliott. Claus was to instruct Elliott "to be more than usually circumspect in his communications with the Indians, so as to leave no possible suspicion of favouring their projected hostilities against the United States." He even spoke of the possibility of completely withholding arms and ammunition from such tribes as decided upon war, and compensating them with a proportionate supply of other articles.[12]

A week later Colonel Brock transmitted Craig's instructions regarding the necessity of reporting confidentially on Indian affairs at the post to Major Taylor, the military commander at Fort Malden. Craig added a warning to Taylor:

I wish you to comprehend clearly the sentiments of Sir James upon this essential point; because although I entertain great respect for the personal character of Mr. Elliott, yet I should be unwilling to place entire dependence, in an affair of such manifest importance, upon a judgement biassed and prejudiced, as his is known to be, in every thing that regards the Indians. To act with due prudence, he participates in and feels too keenly the grievous wrongs they have suffered.

If Taylor observed the slightest inclination on the part of the Indian officers to depart from the policy laid down by Craig, he was to offer friendly advice, and even use a written protest, to deter them from persevering in any act which might have a tendency to irritate relations between England and the United States.[13]

For a time in 1811, as they strove to prevent an Indian war, the policy of the British authorities in Canada was above reproach. The problem was that the instructions did not reach the vital spot in time to be of use. By March 1811, when the instructions reached Amherstburg, the pattern of Indian events for 1811 had been established by the activities of the previous fall. If, as Brock argued, Elliott had given the wrong attitude to the Indians in the council of 1810, little could be done about it in the spring of 1811, when the Indians were widely dispersed at their villages. By the end of the year, as war between England and the United States became more likely, the British policy returned to that of 1807-8. One can sympathize with Governor William Henry Harrison's comment to the War Department in February 1811 that "If the intentions of the British Government are pacific, the Indian department of Upper Canada have not yet been made acquainted with them: for they have lately said everything to the Indians, who visited them, to excite them against us."[14]

While the instructions for the absolute restraint of the Indians were at last reaching Amherstburg, Elliott had journeyed east to York for the session of the Upper Canadian Assembly. He stayed there throughout February and during much of March, as usual playing an active role. Elliott showed no signs of relaxing in these years of his seventies, though apparently he was beginning to show the signs of age. A Moravian missionary stopped to see him at the mouth of the Detroit in the spring of 1811. In his autobiography he recorded how Elliott had mistreated the Moravians of Sandusky in 1781, but commented of him in 1811: "He was now an old man and sought to help the mission wherever he could." Old man or not, Elliott was still exceedingly active, and he was now reaching the age at which his half-Indian sons could be an aid to him. In June 1811, his son Matthew Jr. was appointed interpreter in the Indian Department at Amherstburg in the place of Frederick Fisher who had died in the previous November. His eldest son, Alexander, was reaching the end of his clerkship in Montreal, and in February 1812 was to be admitted to the bar of Lower Canada. Both were to serve with Elliott in the War of 1812.[15]

By the summer of 1811 the fear of war with the United States was once again increasing. American disillusionment at British policy was reaching a peak, and in the elections of 1810 the young War Hawks, led by Henry Clay, gained a sizeable representation in the American House of Representatives. They were not to take their seats until November 1811, but it was quite obvious that a new war-feeling was spreading in the United States. While the government in England refused to believe to the very end that the Americans would declare war, it was increasingly obvious to the authorities in Canada that they would have to build their defenses to resist American attack. From the summer of 1811, the British authorities in Canada energetically prepared for a war they now thought inevitable.[16] These preparations were to bring another change in the instructions to the Indian Department.

The government in England as usual agreed with the measures pursued by the authorities in Canada. On July 28, 1811, Lord Liverpool approved the steps taken by Craig to restrain the Indians and said that the same policy should be continued.[17] But by the time this agreement with Craig's actions had reached Canada, the fear of war was already producing another change in policy. At this time of crisis along the Canadian frontier, leadership once again changed hands. Sir James Craig, who had given his resignation in November 1810, finally left for England in June 1811. In October his position as Governor in chief and commander of the forces was taken by Sir George Prevost. There was also a change in Upper Canada. Isaac Brock, who was promoted to Major-General in June 1811, took over civil as well as military authority in Upper Canada in October when Francis Gore went on leave of absence to England.

185

Thus in the fall of 1811 the combination of Craig and Gore gave way to Prevost and Brock. This affected Elliott and the Indian Department, for in fear of war the new commanders reverted to the Craig-Gore policy of 1807-8 rather than that of 1810-11.

At the beginning of December 1811 Brock wrote an urgent letter to the new governor, Sir George Prevost. Brock argued that Madison's warlike message to the recently assembled Twelfth Congress justified the taking of every precaution, and he submitted his views on the state of Upper Canada. Brock attached primary importance to the Amherstburg district, and he believed that the military force there would have to be increased. In the event of war he thought it would be necessary for the British to take Detroit and Michilimackinac in order to convince the Indians that the war was being waged in earnest, and to erase the memory of the British desertion in 1794.[18]

Prevost's reply to Brock is significant in showing the extent to which he immediately returned to the Indian policy adopted by Craig in a similar crisis at the end of 1807. His instructions copied, at times word for word, the instructions issued by Craig on his arrival in Canada. Prevost wished the Indians to be attached to the British cause, but urged that if possible all "direct explanation" should be delayed until hostilities were more certain. Yet, whenever the subject of hostilities was mentioned, it was to be intimated that, as a matter of course, the British would expect the aid of their Indian allies. "I am sensible this requires delicacy," wrote Prevost, "still it should be done so as not to be misunderstood."[19] Craig's policy of early 1811 had proved short-lived.

From the point of view of American-Indian relations, Craig's 1811 policy had never really taken effect. Tecumseh had left the November 1810 council liberally supplied with British goods, and he was not to return until after the outbreak of open hostilities between the Indians and the Americans. After leaving Elliott at Amherstburg, Tecumseh had striven to complete the network of his confederacy, and eventually departed for the south in the summer of 1811 to win the support of the southern tribes. While there, he was apparently liberal in promising British supplies to the Indians. During his absence Governor William Henry Harrison of Indiana decided to take action against the Prophet's

186

village on the Tippecanoe, a tributary of the Wabash. In the fall of 1811 he advanced his troops northward from Vincennes, and on the night of November 6 halted his army close to Prophet's Town. On the next morning the Indians attacked Harrison, but were beaten off. Although it was not by any means a decisive victory for the Governor, it dispersed the Indian settlement, and when Tecumseh returned from the south he found that his carefully-laid plans had collapsed in this premature engagement.[20]

On January 12, 1812, Elliott reported to Brock that he had just heard of the battle of Tippecanoe from a Kickapoo chief who had been in the battle. The Kickapoo estimated Indian losses at twenty-five (they were probably nearer fifty), and American losses at not less than one hundred (they actually lost about sixty with over one hundred and twenty wounded). He also reported that the Americans had burned Prophet's Town. Elliott told Brock that from this man's report, it did not appear that the Prophet and his people were vanquished. The Kickapoo stated that it was the determination of the chiefs of the various tribes to come into Amherstburg in the spring to demand arms and ammunition.[21]

The combination of land appropriation by the Americans, and the work of the British Indian Department since 1808 had ensured that in the event of war the Indians would be in the British camp. The difficulty during 1812, however, was that the British wanted to avoid war with the United States if they possibly could. Prevost, who had begun as though his policy was going to be a copy of that of Craig in 1807-8, actually became more cautious early in 1812. In January he received instructions from London, sent the previous July, informing him that the British in Canada should do all they could to prevent the Indians from making war upon the United States.[22] Prevost now tried to carry out this policy. Yet Brock, who had been worried in late 1810 and early 1811 that Elliott was being too liberal with the Indians, now chafed under the restraints imposed by Prevost. Brock warned Prevost in February that if Great Britain continued her inert and neutral proceedings toward the Indians, she ran the risk of losing their allegiance. Each time the officers of the Indian Department were prevented from interfering in the concerns of the Indians, each time they advised peace and withheld "the accustomed supply" of ammunition, argued Brock, their influence was diminished, and eventually they might lose it altogether. If this occurred, Brock feared for the safety of Upper Canada.[23] Brock's policy in 1812 was governed by the expectation of war. If war came, his task was to defend Upper Canada. He could only envision the success of that task with Indian support, and in 1812 he moved away from the position of Prevost and toward that of the Indian Department. Throughout the early months of 1812, Brock's concern for defense competed with Prevost's fear of being accused of causing a war with the United States by instigating the Indians.[24] In spite of the caution of Prevost, the Indian Department succeeded in maintaining its influence.

At the end of January 1812, Elliott was confident enough to leave Amherstburg and travel east to the session of the Upper Canadian Assembly. This journey was not completely wasted for the Indian Department, for it enabled Elliott to see Brock and present his views. After Elliott's visit to York, Brock was even more ardent in his assertions to Prevost that control over the Indians was essential to the success of British arms on the Detroit frontier. The Upper Canadian Parliament was opened by Brock's message to the Legislature on February 3, 1812. He told the assembled members that "We wish and hope for peace, but it is nevertheless our duty to be prepared for war." Elliott was one of the three appointed to draft the reply to the message. The fact that he was so lacking in education apparently did not harm his participation in the various committees to which he was appointed during his parliamentary career. In February 1812, while the Indians and the Americans were already skirmishing on the frontier, and while the American House of Representatives were trying to pass the bills to make war possible, the Upper Canadian Assembly settled into its usual round of domestic business. Apart from Brock's speech and the loyal reply, there was little sign in these activities of the Upper Canadian Parliament that Upper Canada was on the verge of war. Elliott stayed in York until the end of the parliamentary session on March 6.[25]

As soon as the session ended, Elliott returned to Amherstburg to take up his duties with the Indian Department. Prevost was still mainly concerned that the activities of the British in Canada might increase the tension between the United States and Great Britain, and eventually lead to war. At the end of March he warned Brock that whatever temptations might be held out, he should not depart from a strictly defensive system, even should a declaration of war be laid on the table of Congress because of Madison's influence. The apparent American neglect at Detroit, warned Prevost, might be a bait to tempt the British into an act of aggression which would enable the American government to obtain support for a declaration of war. As late as the end of April, Prevost was urging Brock to use every effort to prevent any collision between the Americans and the British.[26]

At this point, however, and in spite of Brock's dire warnings, the pressure to avoid irritating the Americans could not really affect the control of Elliott over the Indians in his area. That support had been built during the period from 1808, and after the Americans and Indians had clashed at Tippecanoe, it was quite obvious that the British would gain considerable Indian support in the event of war. The Indians had little choice. Although many of them knew that the British were using them for their own ends, they had more to gain from the British than from the Americans, who were intent on appropriating the land of the Northwest. The British were only taking advantage of a situation which was made inevitable by the rapid American expansion across the continent.

British endeavors were not even restricted to the Indians south of the Great Lakes. Since the fall of 1807, when Thomas McKee had sent messages to the nations west of Lake Michigan, the British had been cultivating the support of the Indians in that area. As it was obviously impracticable to depend on agents in that vast region, the British looked to the support of the fur trading interests. Robert Dickson, the foremost British trader on the Upper Mississippi, acted for the British, and in the winter of 1810-11 tried to keep the support of the Indians by a liberal distribution of supplies.[27] In February, a list of confidential questions was drawn up by the British and sent to Dickson. They wanted to know the number of Indians he could muster in the event of war, and the quantity of supplies they would need. The letter took four months to reach him. It was eventually sent from Amherstburg by Elliott in the middle of April. The man who took it, Jean Francois Reheaum, was detained by the Americans at Chicago on May 1, but the Indians with him escaped with the message. It eventually reached Dickson early in June at the Fox-Wisconsin portage. Fortunately for the British, he had already obtained Indian support. He said he had two hundred and fifty or three hundred Indians ready to march when necessary, and that they would be ready at St. Joseph's by the end of the month.[28]

As the American government slowly pushed its cumbersome war machine into motion in May and June the Indians of the Northwest converged on the British posts of St. Joseph's and Amherstburg. At Amherstburg, Elliott was in his element as the Indians gathered for the coming struggle. On June 14, Claus arrived at Amherstburg to join him, and was able to inform Brock that word had been received from Tecumseh. At the time that the Indian message was sent, Tecumseh had collected some six hundred men and was at a spot roughly sixty miles west of Fort Wayne. The messenger also reported that Tecumseh had left another three hundred men at his village. They had been constantly employed in making bows and arrows, since they had no ammunition. Claus pointed out that owing to the restrictions placed on the Indian Department in the last few months, little ammunition had been issued to the Indians. In his message, Tecumseh regretted that his brother had engaged the enemy in the previous fall before his plans were complete. But now Tecumseh was ready to fight, and seemed anxious for the British to commit themselves openly. Tecumseh had in fact visited the American post of Fort Wayne on June 17, and had told the American agent that he was going to Amherstburg for powder and lead.[29]

When, on June 18, 1812, the American government at last declared war on Great Britain, the Indian Department in Upper Canada was well-prepared for the event. Although the policy of the Canadian authorities had vacillated in the previous five years, Elliott had made a determined attempt to spread British influence during that period. The preparations were now over, and Elliott was ready to lead the Indians into battle. McKee was dead, and Girty was incapable of the effort, but one of the triumvirate who had fled from Pittsburgh thirty-four years before was once again ready to use his knowledge in an attempt to bring about the defeat of the Americans.

Chapter 10

AMERICAN DEFEAT

When the United States declared war on England, it was assumed that the primary American means of waging the war would be the invasion of Canada. It was also assumed that the United States would stand little chance against the mighty British navy, although it was hoped and expected that on land England would pay for her policies by the loss of Canada. One wing of the American attack upon Canada was to proceed by way of Detroit; in this way the United States could thwart the threat of British-supported Indians ravaging the American frontier from Amherstburg. William Hull, the Governor of Michigan Territory and a revolutionary veteran, was given command of the army on the Detroit frontier. In June, as Congress was taking America into war, Hull was marching an army of militia and regulars northward out of Ohio to Detroit. Hull received warning on June 26 that war was likely, but he did not receive definite news of the conflict until July 2, when he was at the River Raisin some forty miles from Detroit. Unfortunately for Hull, the British at Malden had definite news of the war on June 30. This enabled the British to seize a schooner which Hull had loaded with his personal effects, including his official correspondence, as it passed Amherstburg. This was not the most satisfactory start to a campaign. Hull reached Detroit on July 5, and by that time his army consisted of over two thousand men.[1]

Since mid-June, the British at Amherstburg had prepared desperately for the coming hostilities, but as yet were not in a strong position. Every effort was made to call out the militia to reinforce the small regular force (about three hundred men) under the command of Lieutenant-Colonel Thomas B. St. George at Fort Malden. Yet it was feared that the British were not strong enough to resist the American force, and when on July 11 the Americans were observed moving northeastward out of Detroit, the British militia retreated from Sandwich (now Windsor) to Fort Malden. On July 12 the Americans crossed the river without a shot being fired, and in the next few days established themselves at Sandwich. Hull had hopes that the Canadians might voluntarily join the Americans, and issued a proclamation, offering full protection for the property and lives of those who remained at home. Elliott reported to Claus on July 15 that this had exerted a powerful influence on the British militia. Although this was only two days after the issue of the proclamation, many of the militia had gone home. In two or three days he expected that very few of them would be at Fort Malden. Elliott reported, however, that he had at Amherstburg between three and four hundred Indians, who showed no signs of listening to American blandishments: "Tech-kum-thai had kept them faithful – he has shown himself to be a determined character and a great friend to our Government." Tecumseh repeatedly won the respect of the British while fighting with them in the War of 1812. Elliott himself showed some of his old impatience. He thought that delay in attacking the enemy had been detrimental to British interests, and had greatly cooled the spirits of the militia. The people at Amherstburg were also much dejected, and were moving all their property out of the area. Elliott's main problem was that he had no ball left in the Indian store, and did not know how he could supply the Indians if any more of them came.[2] In spite of this, the Indians proved their worth and seriously harassed the Americans in the early days of August.

Although Indians were scouting on the American side of the river from the beginning of the war, they struck their first real blow on August 5, at the battle of Brownstown. The American line of supply to Detroit was a tenuous one – it ran along the west bank of the Detroit River, and was exceedingly vulnerable to attack from the British forces across the river at Amherstburg. Elliott's Indians presented a constant threat to American communications. On August 5, Elliott's lawyer son Alexander, Tecumseh, and twenty-four warriors ambushed a party of some one hundred and fifty Ohio militiamen who were coming out of Detroit with American mail, and to help escort American supplies from the River Raisin. As the militiamen rode into the Indian ambush north of Brownstown, they fled in terror, with the loss of seventeen men. Some of them were massacred after the engagement, much to the disgust of young Elliott.[3]

This incident served well to show Hull that his lines of communication were in imminent danger of being severed. The danger was again revealed four days later, on August 9, at the battle of Monguagon. This was another ambush on the American supply line; this time the British attacked between Brownstown and Detroit. Hull knew that he had to clear the road south to the River Raisin and to Ohio in order to enable supplies to reach him, and the British knew equally well that they had a chance to sever Hull's life-line. Following the Brownstown ambush, a regular British force crossed the river from Amherstburg and joined the Indians to wait for the American attempt to clear the line of communication from Detroit. On August 9, an American force of some six hundred men proceeded south toward Brownstown, and was ambushed by the British. The Americans fought back with such tenacity that the British and Indians were forced to retreat. They took to their boats and canoes and returned to Amherstburg. American losses totaled eighteen killed and fifty-seven wounded, while British losses totaled only six killed and twenty-one wounded (including two Indians killed and six wounded). The American force had successfully repulsed the British, but Hull had been made particularly aware of the thin thread upon which his communications depended. They could be threatened at any time by Indians, or even regulars, from Amherstburg.[4]

Although Hull had crossed the Detroit River, he had considerable doubt as to the ability of his force to take Fort Malden by assault. He decided to prepare for a siege. His invasion plans were put in jeopardy both by his failure to attack, and by the British capture of the American post at Michilimackinac on July 17. The British preparations among the Indians west of Lake Michigan had reaped their first reward. With the threat of hostile Indians from the west, and with an apparently interminable march through Upper Canada ahead of him even if he took Amherstburg, Hull's confidence began to wane. Eventually, he decided to retreat to protect his lines of supply, and on the night of August 8 the American army recrossed to Detroit. Hull would have liked to retreat even further, beyond the Maumee, but his officers would not agree to this suggestion. Hull thus stayed in Detroit while the initiative moved to the British.[5]

Major-General Isaac Brock, who was perhaps the most distinguished soldier of this whole war on the Canadian frontier, had acted with great energy while Hull and his force tried to decide on the correct policy to pursue. On August 5 he left York on his way west, and arrived at Amherstburg on the night of August 13 with three hundred militia and forty regulars. The party was greeted by the Indians encamped near Elliott's farm. On the day after his arrival, Brock issued a general order praising the work of Elliott and the Indian Department, and the gallantry of the Indians in the face of the enemy.[6]

Brock decided that immediate attack was the best policy. On August 14 and 15, the British force proceeded north toward Sandwich with the intention of attacking across the Detroit River. By this time the British had a force of some six hundred Indians under the command of Elliott, and on the fifteenth he was ordered to place the Indians in a position to take the Americans in the flank and rear, should they be disposed to oppose the crossing of the Detroit River. Also on August 15 Brock added psychological warfare to his onslaught on Hull. He sent a message to Hull demanding the immediate surrender of Detroit, and arguing that should a battle commence "the numerous body of Indians who have attached themselves to my troops, will be beyond control." The phrase "who have attached themselves" seems somewhat less than the truth when one considers that the Indian Department had been working for five years to ensure that at this moment the Indians would be alongside the British.[7]

Hull rejected the demand for surrender, and the attack began. During the night of August 15-16, some six hundred Indians under the command of Elliott crossed the Detroit River. The British crossed early the next morning. Although the Indians did no harm to the citizens on the Detroit side, the first British troops across found that houses had been plundered, and that the Indians were stealing all the horses that they could find – about three hundred on the sixteenth and seventeenth. Yet, as the Indians advanced, they acted with remarkable restraint.

195

Brock later reported that "nothing could exceed their order & steadiness." The few prisoners they took were treated with humanity, and Brock happily reported that such was the forbearance of the Indians that the only losses suffered by the Americans were occasioned by the fire of the British batteries. The Indians under Elliott were able to advance within about one mile of the fort at Detroit, finding little or no precaution had been taken, and Brock intended that the Indians would penetrate the American lines while he led an assault with the rest of the troops. It was not necessary. With the Indians entering the outskirts of the town, and reminding Hull of Brock's warning of the previous day, Hull decided to surrender Detroit and its army to the British. Michilimackinac had already gone, the garrison from Fort Dearborn had been massacred on the previous day, and now Detroit was ceded without resistance. The energy of Brock, and British control over the Indians, had brought about a striking victory in the Northwest. It is doubtful whether Hull could have successfully defended Detroit – by the time of the British assault his force was numerically inferior – but the surrender without a battle was a crushing blow to American prestige. A major factor in Hull's decision to surrender was his fear of a massacre by the British Indian forces.[8]

The Indians had committed no atrocities, but their plundering of houses caused Elliott considerable trouble in the days following the surrender of Detroit. On August 20, Elliott, who was at the River Raisin with his son Alexander, showed marked reluctance when asked to come and stop some Indians who were plundering a house. He was finally persuaded to make the attempt, but was unsuccessful in curbing the Wyandots who were pillaging. Charles Askin, who reported the incident, gave as a possible excuse for Elliott's reluctance that he was unwell. Yet, all in all, it seems unlikely that anyone could have stopped the Indians from at least plundering the houses and stealing horses. Even Tecumseh, whom Askin had praised for his efforts, was unable to prevent Indian depredations along the Raisin.[9]

While Matthew Elliott returned from the Raisin to Amherstburg, his son Alexander went with Major Peter Chambers to the old Elliott stamping grounds along the Maumee. Chambers was sent to accept the surrender of the American garrison at the rapids. The Indians under Alexander went ahead of the British party, and when Chambers arrived he found that the Indians were already plundering, although here they took little except horses. Tecumseh had set fire to the American blockhouse, but the only Americans still at the rapids were a few sick.[10]

The Chambers party arrived back at Amherstburg on August 23 and had breakfast at Elliott's. The cordiality was shortlived, for when Major Chambers went into town he discovered that his horse had been stolen by the Indians. Moreover, a great many other horses had been taken by the Indians on the Canadian as well as the American side of the Detroit River. Before Major Chambers left Amherstburg, it was reported that "he had a very serious quarrel with Col. Elliott." Elliott must have found it like old times as he came under the attack of the army at Amherstburg. On August 24, Major Chambers wrote to Colonel Henry Procter, who had taken command of Fort Malden at the end of July, to complain of the Indians. He attacked the pillaging of the Indians at the River Raisin, and said it could have been prevented if the proper officers had exerted the necessary control: "it was with the Utmost difficulty I could prevail on any of them to interfere, and when they did it was with so little Interest it was of no avail." He went on, however, to praise the efforts that Thomas McKee and Tecumseh had made to prevent "these disgusting scenes." Elliott was not attacked by name, but he was now under fire by process of elimination. Edward Dewar, the Deputy Assistant Quarter Master General, also wrote to Procter on August 28 to complain of the conduct of the Indians: "their conduct becomes outrageous in proportion to the impunity with which they offend." The Indians had added to the list of their offenses by seizing boats passing along the Detroit River. Matters had reached a climax when two of the dock-yard men had gone to collect a boat which had drifted toward Lake Erie. As they passed Elliott's farm a party of Indians fell upon them and seized the boat. The Indians were also again attacked for stealing horses, and Dewar stated that the whole problem was aggravated by the fact that the Indians were obtaining liquor from the soldiers.[11]

In the War of 1812, as in the Revolution, the British regulars were frequently embarrassed by the actions of their Indian allies.

The usual proceeding when such embarrassment occurred was to attack the officers of the Indian Department. The Indian Department was given practically an impossible task. Not only were they required to recruit Indian allies, they were also expected to maintain a standard of discipline alien to the normal methods of Indian warfare. Their task was frequently complicated by the ease with which the Indians obtained liquor from the troops. The army depended upon the service of these expert irregulars, but always seemed to hope that they would act with the discipline of regular troops. Elliott himself was long inured to the wartime activities of the Indians, and was also beginning to feel the effects of his age. The task of running about Amherstburg restraining small groups of drunken Indians from committing excesses (the task he had performed in Detroit before 1795) was not one to which he was now disposed to give excessive effort.

The regular troops became even more critical of the Indians after Major Adam Muir led an unsuccessful expedition against Fort Wayne in September 1812. At the beginning of September, news had reached Amherstburg that the Indians were besieging Fort Wayne. Procter wanted to send Elliott to restrain the Indians from excesses, but Elliott was ill with lumbago. Procter had to rest content with messages to that effect. A few days later, however, the Indians around Fort Wayne requested help from the British. Accordingly, Procter ordered three hundred and fifty troops and eight hundred Indians to go to their aid. Part of the expedition left Amherstburg on the night of September 14 (though Indians had been leaving for some days), and the remainder on the morning of September 15. Elliott was in command of the Indians. They had been reinforced a few days before by the arrival of two hundred warriors from Mackinac. Thomas McKee led these off on the morning of the fifteenth, to the accompaniment of a salute from the garrison. The expedition made slow progress, and it was not until September 25 that it reached a spot some forty miles from Fort Wayne. Muir had sent his heavy equipment by boat along the Maumee to Fort Defiance (at the Auglaize), and was now continuing the journey by land. On the twenty-fifth, about sunset, an advance party of British Indians captured an advanced party of Americans – from them they learned that an army of five thousand men was about four miles in their rear, and that another army of three thousand was marching down the Auglaize River and would meet the other at Fort Defiance. Although this was an overestimate of the numbers, Muir's party was in fact advancing toward the army of Brigadier General James Winchester, which had left Fort Wayne and was hoping to proceed along the Maumee to Fort Defiance and to the rapids. Winchester then hoped to give support to General William Henry Harrison, who was proposing to lead a surprise attack against Detroit by striking north from Fort Wayne to the St. Joseph's River and to the River Raisin.

Major Muir now prepared to meet the American force. Immediately after his scouts brought the news, he dispatched a messenger to Elliott, who was camped opposite Fort Defiance at that time with some six hundred Indians. Elliott immediately prepared to bring his Indians forward, and arrived at Muir's camp at about noon on September 26. Scouting parties went out in all directions, and a Wyandot brought back the news that the American camp was about eight miles away. The British were in a dangerous position, for they were outnumbered and had only two days provisions (the cattle had escaped from their herdsman). As soon as Elliott had brought the Indians to Muir's position, he hurried back along the Maumee to the rapids to try to secure more cattle and flour. By the twenty-seventh, Elliott had rejoined Muir, who had now withdrawn to Fort Defiance. The Americans were marching toward him under the careful scrutiny of the British Indian scouts. When the American force was within two miles, Muir sent for Elliott to find out the intentions of the Indians. Elliott consulted Round Head, a Wyandot and the principal chief present, and returned with the answer that Muir might choose any place on the plain which he thought best suited to the British guns, and the Indians would flank Muir's force. Muir chose a position and established it, but Elliott rode up to say that the Indians did not like the place he had chosen, and wanted him to withdraw into the woods. He proceeded to do this but, according to Muir, the spot the Indians had chosen for a stand was not satisfactory – it was a mere opening in the woods, and gave the guns insufficient range.

199

Muir therefore rejected it, and decided to send his guns and stores in boats to Amherstburg – this would make cooperation with the Indians easier, and would also mean that in case of precipitate retreat, he would not lose his guns to the Americans. That evening Muir went into council with the Indians. They gave him to understand that they intended to meet the enemy in the morning (September 28). About one hour before dawn Muir received a message from Elliott to the effect that the Indians had been in council all night, and that the Mackinac and Saginaw Indians were going to leave the camp. Muir now presumed a retreat had been agreed on, and ordered that the cattle and the baggage should be withdrawn. But thirty minutes later another message from Elliott announced that the Indians were determined to fight, and requested that Muir advance the troops. Muir immediately ordered them to march and reached the Indian camp in a matter of minutes. Elliott then asked Muir to wait, as the Indians were not ready, even though Muir then noticed the Indians moving off in small bands. Elliott told him that they were going to hide their possessions. At this point the reason for the utter confusion became apparent. The chief of the Mackinac Indians said the Indians were divided, and that he was going to take his young men home – he marched off with his band of some two hundred warriors. It became increasingly obvious that there had been considerable division among the Indians as to the advisability of fighting what appeared to be a considerably stronger American force. Elliott, in trying to keep unity, and in all probability reluctant to admit to Muir that the Indians were divided, added to the confusion by the limited amount of information he was giving to the commander.

Even though many of the Indians had left, Muir and Elliott went to inspect the ground on which they intended to fight – a spot about three miles above Fort Defiance. At this point Muir himself, who had sent off his guns, and who could see that there were only some three hundred and twenty or thirty Indians present, announced to Elliott that it would be madness to fight. Elliott told Muir that two of the Indian "Conjurors" had dreamed that the Indians would be successful on this day, and that the Indians were determined to meet the Americans. Muir replied that he would not throw away the lives of his troops on such a flimsy pretext. Elliott told this to Round Head, and the chief came to Muir to urge that they should fight in compliance with the dream of the "Conjurors." Eventually, however, Muir prevailed on the force to retreat, and rather ignominiously, the British force set off for Detroit, where they arrived at the beginning of October.[12]

This confused episode apparently stemmed from the Indian shock and surprise at encountering a superior American force when they thought they were going to assault a small American fort after it had been battered by British guns. Elliott tried to maintain unity among his Indian forces, but naturally became the scapegoat for the whole episode. The sensible military course might well have been swift retreat in the face of the American force, but this decision was not taken. Elliott's stock with the military now further deteriorated. At the time of Brock's capture of Detroit, Elliott's prestige had been at a high point, but Brock had left for the east soon after the capture of Detroit, and Elliott's relations with Colonel Procter were never good. Procter's comment on the Muir expedition was; "If I had not been already perfectly convinced of the necessity of an independent regular force to insure the effectual assistance of the Indians, the history of this expedition would have confirmed me in that opinion."[13]

Relations between Elliott and Procter deteriorated sharply after the Muir expedition. On October 30 Procter reported that the great defect of the Indian Department was the lack of a leader in the field. This was indeed the case. The lack was well-emphasized by the fact that Elliott, now over seventy, was having to lead his Indians in the field, rather than supervize them from Amherstburg. Thomas McKee, who should have been able to take the responsibility, was killing himself with drink. The Indians themselves were disgruntled after the Muir expedition. Early in October it was reported that an American party had been seen in the vicinity of the River Raisin, and Procter decided to dispatch a force of twenty-five militia and twenty Indians to secure the commissary at that place from disturbance. Elliott sent interpreters across to Brownstown to secure Indians for the task, but they refused to come. Lieutenant Edward Dewar personally went across to Brownstown on October 7, and that night managed to persuade Round Head and fourteen warriors to go with him to the River Raisin. This again did not improve relations between the Indian Department and the army, who were now perturbed by the fact that there were some eight hundred warriors in the vicinity of Amherstburg consuming provisions. [14]

It was decided that in order to lessen the pressure on the provisions, Elliott should lead the Indians away from Amherstburg and take them to the old gathering place at the foot of the Maumee rapids. The Indians would not go without Elliott. At the foot of the rapids there was a large quantity of corn which had been planted by the Americans, as well as cattle running wild in the area. Elliott finally left Amherstburg with his warriors on October 29. The move was certainly necessary, since he had only some two days supply of provisions in his stores. He reported to Claus that he intended to pitch his tent at the foot of the rapids, let the Indians feed on the corn, and then constantly send out parties to annoy General Winchester who was still in the region of Fort Defiance. This was an ambitious program for a man well over seventy. He also told Claus that it would be impossible to keep the Indians together much longer unless provisions were sent immediately. The Indians, Elliott reported, had now lost three crops of corn, and were now completely dependent upon the British. [15]

Elliott proceeded to the foot of the rapids by boat, and arrived there "after a most unpleasant passage" on the evening of November 7. When he wrote to George Ironside on the tenth, he had already seen signs of Americans in the vicinity, and asked Ironside to hurry the Indians who were still in the region of Amherstburg, since he had only some two hundred and fifty at the foot of the rapids. Elliott also wanted three hundred pounds of powder – one hundred and fifty pounds of the supply he had brought with him had been damaged in the vessel. Throughout a bleak November, Elliott stayed with his Indians at the foot of the rapids. His son Alexander scouted along the Maumee, and it was in this month that, with his Indian companions, he took prisoner a party of American Indians. On November 22, after being left unbound, they seized guns, shot five of the seven in the British party, and escaped. Alexander Elliott was among those killed. When Elliott's force retreated from the rapids on December 8, Elliott took his son's corpse with him. The tragedy was compounded when the boat foundered in the ice, but Elliott completed his self-appointed task. He returned to Amherstburg, and on December 17 his son was buried.[16]

Elliott was soon in action again. The Americans were naturally anxious to regain control of Detroit, and William Henry Harrison was in charge of this difficult task. Harrison had far more troops than Hull, but in the late fall and winter of 1812, he ran into the usual problems of supply and organization. He had divided his troops into four columns, and he hoped that three of them would converge on the rapids of the Maumee; Winchester via the Maumee, Brigadier General Edward Tupper via the road cut by Hull through Ohio, and Brigadier General Simon Perkins from the Sandusky River. At the same time, a column under Brigadier General Samuel Hopkins was to attack the Indian towns on the Wabash and Illinois Rivers. This last expedition failed, and the other three had considerable difficulties in October and November owing to the great difficulty in moving supplies. In December, Harrison, who was under considerable pressure to secure some success in the area, decided upon a risky winter expedition against Fort Malden. This expedition never took place, because before it effectively began, General Winchester committed a blunder which ended American hopes.[17]

Winchester had finally advanced to the Maumee rapids at the beginning of January 1813. Harrison hoped to join him there with additional men from the Sandusky River. But Winchester, under pressure from his officers, made a tragic mistake. Soon after the army arrived at the rapids, the French at Frenchtown on the River Raisin requested the Americans to come to their relief. They pointed out that there was only a small British garrison on the Raisin, and that there were a good many supplies there which could be taken by the Americans. The Frenchmen at the River Raisin had long disliked the British in Canada. On January 17 a force of some six hundred and fifty men under the command of Lieutenant-Colonel William Lewis was sent to the River Raisin. In an action on January 18 they defeated the British, who had a much inferior force of some fifty militia and two hundred Indians. Lewis then remained at Frenchtown with some six hundred effectives. The rest of Winchester's force joined him there by January 20, leaving only three hundred men at the rapids.[18]

The British General Procter, who has been considerably attacked for his part in the War of 1812, at least on this occasion acted with vigor. He heard of the British defeat on the night of January 18. He decided to attack, and by January 21 had led his force across the Detroit River to Brownstown. His force was about twelve hundred strong – he had nearly six hundred white soldiers and between six and eight hundred Indians under the command of Elliott. The Indian leader was again the Wyandot Round Head, since Tecumseh was absent attempting to recruit other Indians for the British cause. Procter camped that night at Stony Creek, only five miles from Frenchtown. The British attacked at dawn the next morning, with snow lying deep upon the ground. The first winter of the war gave Elliott no respite, in spite of his age. After a fierce action, Winchester was captured, and he feared that the Indians would carry out a general massacre if the battle continued. Many of the Kentuckians had already been scalped in the action that had captured Winchester – not all the Americans had been within the pickets of the town, and it was the group outside that yielded and finally fled after being flanked by Elliott's Indians. After his capture, Winchester suggested under flag of truce that his men within the pickets should surrender. Procter had promised him that they would be treated as prisoners of war.[19]

It was on the night of the victory that the real tragedy of the battle occurred. In the action itself, the British and Indians combined had probably not lost more than fifty men killed, the Americans not more than a hundred. After the engagement, Procter and Elliott rapidly retreated to Amherstburg, leaving the American wounded guarded by only a few interpreters. That night the Indians moved in among the wounded, and completed their work of earlier in the day by slaughtering some thirty of them. The reason for this event has never been satisfactorily explained. Procter had previously been worried by possible excesses of the Indians, and in spite of his American frontier reputation there is no evidence that Elliott had engaged in needless cruelty. The most likely explanation is that the quarrel between

Procter and Elliott which had developed throughout the fall, and which was growing worse, made it impossible for them to discuss matters of policy in an intelligent manner. Elliott himself had seen much cruelty, was inured to it, and had buried his eldest son only a month before. He had shown the previous summer that he was no longer prepared to keep a constant surveillance over the misdeeds of the Indians. In any event the responsibility was ultimately Procter's. He was the commander of the British force, and he had accepted the American surrender. It was his duty as commander to see that no harm was done to his prisoners. Doctor Robert Richardson, who was with the British forces at the battle, lamented the murder of the wounded men by the Indians. He said that within his hearing protection had been promised, and that if he had been the commanding officer he would have considered himself responsible for every one of them: "be assured we have not heard the last of this shameful transaction. I wish to god it could be contradicted."[20] It was not without irony that in the General Orders issued at Quebec on February 6, 1813, was an extract from an official dispatch of the Prince Regent praising the capture of Detroit:

> His Royal Highness has observed with Great satisfaction, that, the co-operation of the Indian Nations, led on by Col. Elliott and Captain McKee has been marked with humanity; such conduct is highly creditable to the Officers who commanded them, and to the System which has been adopted under your direction.[21]

The attack of Procter on Elliott continued throughout the late winter and spring of 1813, and his constant complaints began to have its effect on headquarters. When Robert Dickson was appointed a temporary Superintendent of Indian Affairs among the western Indians, it was stressed that he should not be under the authority of Elliott, and that he would only be subject to the immediate orders and instructions of Procter. Procter had informed headquarters that Elliott was jealous of Dickson, and that he thought Elliott would attempt to thwart Dickson's work. Procter could not get along with Elliott, and made every effort to damage his reputation with higher authorities. That May he suggested in a letter to Quebec: "I should be much gratified if Colonel Elliott from his Age and long Service was permitted to retire on his full Pay. He is past seventy and I have understood near eighty." It is difficult to judge the merits of the Procter-Elliott argument, but it would seem that Procter was exaggerating the decline of Elliott's powers because of his dislike of the Indian Department at Amherstburg.[22]

Despite Procter's attacks on his competence, Elliott was still capable of leading the Indians, although he was perhaps less able to maintain as tight a control over them as he had in earlier days. This stemmed not only from Elliott's age and perhaps increased bitterness owing to the death of his son, but also from the increased desperation of the Indians in their struggle against the Americans. By 1812 the Indians had lost much of their land in the Old Northwest to American pressure. They had every reason to hate the Americans who had deprived them of their homes and hunting grounds.

While Procter wasted the opportunity for attack which he had gained by his victory on the River Raisin, Harrison established his forces more securely in the region of the rapids of the Maumee. In February and March 1813, his men began the construction of what later was called Fort Meigs, slightly below the old battlefield of Fallen Timbers on the opposite side of the river. It was not until April that Procter finally decided to move against the Americans. Toward the end of that month he took a large force down the Maumee to attack Fort Meigs. Procter's force consisted of nearly one thousand white troops and twelve hundred Indians under Elliott and Tecumseh. Procter planned to take the fort by siege. The Indians surrounded the fort from the south, while the British artillery established themselves on the north bank of the river.[23]

After some skirmishes, the full bombardment of the fort began on May 1. The British batteries were aided by fire from two gunboats. The fort presented considerable difficulty to the besiegers, since the dilatoriness of Procter had allowed Harrison to build up its strength to some two thousand men. The situation seemed even better for the Americans when on May 4 news reached Harrison that Brigadier General Green Clay had reached the Glaize with a force of twelve hundred Kentuckians. Harrison decided to relieve pressure on the fort by an attack on the British forces. The main part of the attack would send some eight hundred men from Clay's force against the British batteries opposite the fort on the other side of the river. They were to destroy what they could, spike the guns, and retreat. The first part of the maneuver went smoothly, and Lieutenant-Colonel William Dudley led his men successfully against the British batteries. But they failed to retreat swiftly enough, and the British counter-attacked. The Indians under Tecumseh flanked Dudley's regiment, while the British troops drove into their center. The result was utter disaster for the Americans. About one hundred and fifty managed to retreat across the river by boat, but the rest were killed or captured. Dudley fell in the battle. The captured troops were then taken by the Indians, and with a small guard of British troops were led to the old British Fort Miami. Inside the fort another massacre took place. The Indians moved among the prisoners, and tomahawked those they selected; forty more Americans died as prisoners. Once again Procter failed to stop the slaughter, and eventually it was Tecumseh who put an end to the excesses. One of the prisoners described the scene: "Colonel Elliott and Tecumseh, the celebrated Indian chief, rode into the garrison .... Elliott was an old man; his hair might have been termed with more propriety, white than gray, and to my view he had more of the savage in his countenance than Tecumseh."[24]

Although in this fighting Harrison had more success in the sorties in the area of Fort Meigs, the disaster across the river had cost him half of his reinforcements. In the action of the fifth, the British claimed they had lost only fourteen killed, and forty-one prisoners, while the Americans had probably lost well over one hundred killed and over six hundred prisoners. In spite of this, Procter found that it was not within his power to take Fort Meigs. He was undoubtedly hindered by the attitude of the Indians and the militia. After the victory over Dudley, most of the Indians dispersed with their booty and prisoners, and the militia wanted to return home. The dispersal of the Indians was another event for which Procter could blame Elliott, although Elliott could do little about it. The Indians had won a victory, and they had little liking for attacking American fortifications. Both Procter and Elliott, however, must take partial blame for the killings at Fort Miami. It appears that no real

207

effort was made by these two leaders to curb the excesses of the warriors. Tecumseh succeeded where they had failed. With part of his force already dispersing, Procter withdrew the remainder on May 9. His expedition had not succeeded in its object, but the Americans had lost another engagement.[25]

The first year of the war had been a disastrous one for the Americans. They had expected to sweep into Canada, but they had met with nothing but disaster on the Detroit front – the loss of Detroit, defeat at the River Raisin, and the excessive losses in the defense of Fort Meigs had succeeded one another with painful regularity. In spite of Procter's complaints against Elliott's management of the Indians, the Indian forces of the Northwest had played a vital part in all three of these engagements. Moreover, in spite of Procter's assertions that Elliott was too inactive in his prosecution of Indian affairs, Elliott had led the Indian forces in all these actions, and had been highly complimented by Brock for his part in the capture of Detroit. Elliott had also, in spite of his age, taken the Indians from Amherstburg and lived with them throughout the cold November of 1812 near the rapids of the Maumee. This had successfully conserved provisions for the use of Procter's forces in Amherstburg. For the British on the Detroit frontier, the first year of the war brought a success which few could have predicted. The next year was to bring disaster.

Chapter 11

THE LAST DAYS

In July and August 1813, Procter made the last of his attempts to take the offensive south of Detroit. He was in a difficult position, since the shortage of provisions at Amherstburg made supplying the Indians increasingly difficult. As the provisions became scarcer, the danger of Indian dispersal increased. To ease the pressure, and in an attempt to snatch a victory, Procter yielded to Indian persuasion. In the middle of July he once again set out for the Maumee rapids with several hundred white soldiers and about one thousand Indians under Elliott. As Procter lacked the siege equipment to overwhelm Fort Meigs, his only hope was to lure the garrison out of the fort. The British arrived on the Maumee on July 20, and unsuccessfully attempted to entice the enemy during the following week. While this took place, Elliott and Tecumseh led a force eastward into Ohio and scouted for possible American reinforcements. By July 28, Procter decided that the fort could not be taken, and determined instead to attack the American posts along the Sandusky River.[1]

The British force now travelled by boat down the Maumee into Lake Erie, and along the coast to the mouth of the Sandusky. Their first objective was the American Fort Stephenson, located up the Sandusky at the head of navigation. Fort Stephenson was an extremely weak post, manned by only one hundred and sixty men. The commander of the post, Major George Croghan, had not obeyed General Harrison's order to abandon the post at the end of July (Harrison was at the Seneca Towns ten miles above Lower Sandusky on the Sandusky River). On August 1, Procter's force appeared before the fort, and Procter sent Elliott and Major Chambers to negotiate for its surrender. The American negotiator met Elliott and Chambers two hundred yards from the fort. Elliott stated that the British knew the weakness of the defenses, and he demanded an American surrender. He used the same arguments used by Brock to persuade Hull at the surrender of Detroit. If the fort fell by storm, Elliott warned, he would be unable to prevent the Indians killing everyone in it. The Americans refused to surrender and Procter, who did not have the necessary guns to take even the weak Fort Stephenson, was placed in another embarrassing position. In his later report of this affair, Procter as usual blamed most of his troubles on the Indians and on the Indian Department. This was becoming an all-too-familiar story.

On the morning of August 2, the members of the Indian Department, led by Elliott, told Procter that unless the fort were stormed the British would be unable to bring the Indian warriors into the field. The Indians had become accustomed to the idea that with the aid of British guns they could take fortified places that they could not storm alone. After the two unsuccessful attempts on Fort Meigs, and now with the doubt regarding Fort Stephenson, they were growing impatient at what they considered the British part of the operations. According to Procter, the Indians promised that they would attack one side of the fort if the British troops would attack the other. On the afternoon of August 2, after a bombardment, the attack began. The Indians scarcely began the assault before they retreated out of range, and the British troops were driven off with nearly one hundred casualties. The problem was that the Indians, who were now only two or three hundred strong, had never shown any relish or ability for attacking fortified strongholds, and both the Indians and the Indian Department were concerned that the British under the command of Procter were also showing little ability in this area. Although Procter tried to blame the whole episode on the weaknesses of the Indians and the Indian Department, commander in chief Prevost indicated later that he thought Procter's judgement also left something to be desired. On the night of August 2, the British retreated into their boats to return to Amherstburg, and the Indians travelled overland. Procter's campaign against Fort Meigs and Fort Stephenson was a singularly undistinguished one. The gulf between Procter and the Indian Department was now even greater.[2]

The turning point in this desultory struggle along the Detroit frontier came not on land but on the Great Lakes – the key to the supply system of Upper Canada. On September 10, 1813, at the battle of Put-in-Bay, an American fleet under Commander Oliver H. Perry defeated the British under the command of Captain Robert Herriot Barclay. The command of Lake Erie now rested with the Americans, and Procter's position at Amherstburg was untenable. However, if he could meet and defeat an American force before retiring, he could considerably improve his position and withdraw with honor. Moreover, this would also perform the essential task of keeping the allegiance of the Indians, to whom a retreat was a retreat, notwithstanding assurances that it was really a strategic withdrawal. By the fall of 1813, a great number of warriors had assembled at Amherstburg – possibly over three thousand with their families. This considerably increased Procter's strength (he had some eight or nine hundred other troops), but it put a severe strain on his provisions. This strain enabled Simon Girty, who was now nearly blind, to perform one of his last services for his old Indian friends. Elliott ordered the Indians to provision themselves from one of Girty's cornfields. (Girty subsequently claimed payment for this service.)[3]

When Harrison received news of Perry's victory, he immediately prepared to attack the British position at Amherstburg. Eventually, with liberal help from Kentucky, he managed to muster some five thousand men for the invasion. While a mounted force under the command of Richard M. Johnson advanced overland by way of the River Raisin to Detroit, Harrison's main force came by boat along Lake Erie to Middle Sister Island, only twelve miles from the Canadian shore. By September 25 they were ready to advance.[4]

While Harrison advanced, fully expecting to have to fight a battle in the region of Amherstburg, Procter was trying to decide what he should do. After the defeat of the British fleet on September 10, Procter gave orders that Fort Malden should be dismantled in preparation for the retreat of the British troops. The large number of Indians there became most perturbed at this order. They did not understand why the defeat of the British fleet had necessitated this move, and they were afraid that they

211

were being deserted. Tecumseh and other chiefs requested that Elliott and Procter should meet them in council. The council took place on September 17, and Tecumseh made a fiery speech in favor of defending Fort Malden. He said that if all the Indian supplies were handed out the Indians would defend it without British help: "We must compare our father's conduct to a fat animal that carries its tail upon its back, but when affrighted, it drops between its legs and runs off."[5]

There is no doubt that the entire British position in Upper Canada was sadly weakened by the mutual lack of faith between Procter and the Indian Department. Procter had consistently attacked Elliott and the Indians, but had depended on them for most of his support in each action he had fought. In answer to Tecumseh's plea not to retreat, Procter suggested that there should be only a partial retreat to the River Thames at Chatham. The Indians and Elliott had to be content with this, for Procter would not agree to stand and fight at Amherstburg, though even Harrison assumed that this would be done.

On September 23, the retreat from Amherstburg began. For Elliott it was a sad moment. He had built up the finest plantation in the whole region at the mouth of the Detroit River, and now it was all to fall into the hands of the American troops. He was never to see it again. His wife later wrote of how at the opening of the War of 1812 they had held extensive and cultivated estates at Amherstburg, "with all the advantages which wealth could afford." She estimated the income of the plantation to be at least £600 a year. As the British forces marched away from Amherstburg, nine waggons and thirty horses belonging to Elliott went with them. The waggons contained "only his plate and the most valuable part of his personal effects." The plate alone, Sarah Elliott claimed, was worth "upwards of fifteen hundred pounds." But it was all no use, for all of Elliott's effects subsequently fell into the hands of the Americans. Moreover, soon after Amherstburg had been evacuated, one hundred Kentuckians gutted the inside of Elliott's home, broke up the furniture, and destroyed his fences, barn, and storehouses.[6]

Procter retreated northward along the east bank of the Detroit River, and turned east along the southern shore of Lake St. Clair. Elliott was covering Procter's retreat with his Indians, and at first remained about two days march behind the main force. By the time the British reached the Thames River, the force of Indian warriors had been reduced to one thousand. Elliott bitterly complained to Claus later that this force would have been three thousand if the stand had been made at Amherstburg. The Potawatomis, Chippewas, and Ottawas had all left the British force. By October 1, the British had reached Dolson's; this was only three miles from Chatham, where Procter had promised to make his stand. Procter then went to scout the ground eastward to the Moravian Town (Fairfield) some twenty-six miles away. He also conducted his family to safety. He left his troops without real guidance at this critical point, and they continued their retreat; some suggesting that Procter should be replaced for neglect of duty. The Indians who had been expecting to make a stand at Chatham were now even more puzzled and disturbed. Elliott's task was becoming a more and more thankless one, for the Americans were now close in pursuit of the British force. Some of the Indians fought a rearguard action, but Elliott persuaded most of them to follow Procter's retreating force. As a result of Procter's failure to make an effective stand at Chatham, even more Indians (including the Wyandots and some of the Shawnees) deserted the British ranks.

The British and the Indians finally took up their defensive positions near the Moravian village of Fairfield. Even here there was disagreement. Procter drew up the troops in a wood, whereas both Elliott and Tecumseh told him that he was neglecting an excellent defensive position in the rear. The British troops were disgusted from the start, for few had faith in the abilities of Procter as a general. The Americans attacked on October 5, and the British troops quickly broke in confusion. Elliott later reported that "The conduct of the troops was shameful in the highest degree." The Indians fought desperately, and they suffered the shattering loss of Tecumseh, who was killed in the action. The Indians were still in the field when Procter's troops fled. The full collapse of British resistance, brought about by the lack of faith in Procter, was well-demonstrated by British losses of only twelve killed, thirty-six wounded, and nearly six hundred captured. The Indians left thirty-three dead on the field, and certainly carried away others. The American losses were twelve killed, and twenty or so wounded. The battle was a disaster for British arms, and for his conduct Procter was subsequently court-martialed, and sentenced to loss of rank and pay for six months. After that, as might be expected, he remained on the unattached list of the army. In some ways, Procter had been unfortunate. He certainly never had satisfactory support in troops or supplies, but he also showed insufficient enterprise or military skill to be a forceful and effective commanding officer. He tended to substitute vacillation and criticism of the Indian Department for effective military action.[7]

The morning after the defeat, Elliott overtook Procter and proceeded to make every arrangement in his power for the accommodation of the remaining Indians. He sent Captain William Elliott to meet the Indians who were retreating, and purchase provisions for them along the route. In all, Elliott gathered together some two thousand Indians (men, women, and children), and retreated to the head of Lake Ontario. He now made his headquarters at Burlington, on Burlington Bay, on the property he had purchased for Joseph Brant in 1796. Brant had died in 1807, but Elliott now made use of his home down near the beach to attempt to exercise some control over the western Indians.[8]

Elliott himself was in a precarious financial position at this time. His salary from the government was not high – £200 a year – and he had now lost the home and farm which had proved so profitable in the past. His wife, her sister, and servants had all retreated with him, and all their personal property had been lost at the Moravian Town. By October 1813, Elliott was once again reduced to petitioning the government. He sent a memorial to Sir George Prevost on October 24, pointing out that whereas the duties of the office, and not the pay, had interested him while he had his farm at Amherstburg, he now could not support his family owing to the retreat. The long campaign conducted against Elliott by Procter was well-reflected in the reply which announced that Prevost did not think an increase in pay was justified, and that any claim for indemnification for loss of property would have to be a matter for future consideration. The army was seldom enamored of Elliott, although the members of the Indian Department supported him as usual. William Claus reported in December that he believed Elliott's name had never appeared in general orders, "and that man had been out with the Indians upon Every occasion and no man worse paid has suffered more than he has." Claus complained in this report that the troops were always given credit for what was done by the Indians.[9]

The Detroit frontier was now secured to the Americans, and apart from those warriors who had followed Elliott to Lake Ontario, the Americans had little else to fear from the western Indians for the rest of the war. Tecumseh was dead, his confederacy broken. For Elliott, the war continued. His knowledge and command over the Indians was now to be used in the winter campaigns upon the Niagara frontier – though he was now about seventy-five years of age. The British had also suffered reverses on the Niagara frontier. The Americans had captured British Fort George, across the Niagara River from Fort Niagara, in May 1813, and the British command had retreated to the western end of Lake Ontario – the head of the Lake. Elliott now came under this command, and arrived in the region in time to take part in the offensive operations planned for the winter.

The first task was accomplished with little difficulty, except from the weather. The British had decided to retake Fort George, and early in December Colonel Murray led a force from the head of the Lake to accomplish this task. In the van were Elliott and seventy of his western Indians. Although they did not have to go into action, they made a forced march in "inclement weather." The American force at Fort George was insufficient to defend the fort, and on hearing of the approach of the British, the American commander abandoned his position, burning the town of Newark to the north, and part of the town of Queenston to the south. The Americans then crossed the river to Fort Niagara. The British entered Fort George on December 12 and gave the Americans little respite, for it was decided to launch an attack across the river against Fort Niagara.[10]

Elliott received his orders on December 17. He was to assemble the chiefs of his Indians together, and impress upon them in the strongest manner the necessity of abstaining from plunder, and from all acts of violence on women, children, and unarmed men. Also, if the Indians were to be employed, they would have to abstain from acts of violence against prisoners of war. The attack was to be led by a force under Colonel Murray, and Elliott and the Indians were to come with the reserve under Major General Riall. The reserve was to give support to Murray if needed, and also was to deliver an independent attack against Lewistown, which was south of Fort Niagara and across the river from Queenstown. The attack took place on the night of December 18; Murray's force of five hundred and fifty regulars surprised Fort Niagara, and took it with the loss of only eight killed and wounded. The American losses were sixty-seven killed, and eleven wounded – rather unusual proportions which reflected British anger at the burning of Newark and Queenstown – and took three hundred and fifty prisoners. Riall's force crossed immediately after Murray's, and as Elliott and the Indians were not needed in the attack on Fort Niagara, they turned against Lewistown. This was a ferocious attack and Lieutenant-General Gordon Drummond reported on December 20: "I am, however, extremely concerned to state, that, notwithstanding my most positive orders, and their own assurances (made me through Lieut.-Colonel Elliott, in a Council of their Chiefs) that they would refrain from outrage, several acts of violence were committed by the Indians." Drummond did not like this, but he immediately directed Elliott to send off an express to Michilimackinac (which was still in British hands) to announce the British success, and to assure the Indians that the British would shortly revisit them in power.[11]

Elliott was quickly in action again, for on December 29 Drummond ordered Major-General Riall to lead an attack against Black Rock and Buffalo, on the American side of the Niagara River above the falls. On the following night, Riall led a force of fifteen hundred men on this mission, including Elliott and his Indians. The expedition successfully accomplished its objectives, and burned the town, the public stores, two schooners, and a sloop. For this exploit Elliott was given praise that he had rarely, in recent times, received from the army:

> Lt. Colonel Elliott on this as well as other occasions
> is entitled to my highest commendations for his Zeal
> and activity as Superint. of the Indian Department, and
> I am happy to add that thro' his Exertions, & that of

his Officers no Act of Cruelty, so far as I could learn, was committed by the Indians towards any of their Prisoners.[12]

Elliott was coming back into favor. There were few vacillating judgements given about Elliott during his entire career; he was either well-liked or thoroughly disliked by those with whom he came into contact. He was a man with considerable force of character, and had little patience with those he thought weak or inefficient.

After the campaigns of December 1813, Elliott returned to Joseph Brant's old house at Burlington. From there Elliott kept up his contact with the Indians to the west in the early part of 1814. The Indian messengers he had sent to announce the successes on the Niagara frontier returned on January 31. They reported that the Indians were joyful at the British victories, and had demanded arms and ammunition. They wanted the British to send them forty men bearing the articles they required. Elliott reported this to the military, but the project proved unsuccessful.[13] Elliott met with the Indians in his vicinity at the beginning of March, but they refused to travel westward. Their argument was that the regular troops were not advancing to the west, and that they would be unable to protect their friends in the American area. If the Americans heard of the sending of the supplies, the consequences might then be fatal for the Indians within easy reach of the Americans. Rather than endanger the Indians and their families, they thought it would be better that the ammunition should not be sent. A party of British troops and Elliott had moved west to Delaware to facilitate the sending of supplies, but when the Indians refused to go, Elliott returned to Burlington.[14]

This unsuccessful attempt to send supplies to his old friends in the west coincided with the beginning of a serious illness for Elliott. He had served energetically for the past two years, and his exposure had reached a peak during the expeditions on the Niagara frontier in December 1813. His sickness persisted throughout March, although Elliott still kept up the business of the Indian Department from the beach at Burlington. He reported to Claus at the end of March that as soon as the weather became warmer, the British could expect many of the Indians to come and join them. Elliott was worried by a rumor that

217

the Americans were going to attack by way of Long Point when the navigation opened, and that the Wyandots, Delawares, and Shawnees were going to come with them. He estimated that these nations could send five or six hundred men, and still leave sufficient protection for their women and children. He told Claus that he was asking the other nations to try to avert this evil.[15]

At this time of Elliott's illness, the Indian Department was still attempting to obtain an increase in pay for him. Sir John Johnson urged this upon the British, pointing out the great losses Elliott had suffered at Amherstburg and the great services he had performed. At last, on April 20, Prevost agreed to give Elliott an additional £100 per year. Not knowing that this step had been taken, Lieutenant-General Drummond was at the same time urging the merits of some reward for Elliott: "his zealous exertions were so unremitting in keeping the Nations in our interest, that any addition, however great, to his present Salary, which his Excellency may be pleased to authorize, would prove a most advantageous expenditure to the British Government."[16]

The decline in Procter's military fortunes had produced another reassessment of Elliott's talents and his ability to control the Indians. But it was too late. The letter granting Elliott a pay increase left Montreal on April 20, and while it was on its way westward Elliott's situation became critical. On April 22, Elliott signed his last will and testament. It was a careful will, and provided well for his family. His "dearly beloved wife" Sarah, his half-Indian son Matthew Jr., and the two infants, Francis Gore and Robert Barclay, all were well-provided for out of the land at Amherstburg. In addition he left £500 in cash to Sarah, and £200 to her sister Mary, who had lived with the Elliott's at Amherstburg.[17]

On April 23, it was reported that Elliott's physicians had forbidden him to work, or to receive any communication that might excite him. The physicians had given up hope, and were content with the observation that "nature is so much worn out as to be unable to bear the struggle both of mind and body." Captain William Elliott (who was no relation) wrote from the scene, with some exaggeration, that Elliott's anxiety over the husbanding of provisions and the satisfaction of the Indians had been in great degree the cause of his illness. He thought that "posterity will be more just to his services than his contemporarys have."[18]

Elliott lingered on through the last days of April; his wife Sarah and his old friend George Ironside with him. He was no less tenacious in leaving the world than he had been while in it. Although despaired of shortly after the middle of April, it was not until May 7, 1814, that he died. He was buried on May 9 in Burlington, and among those paying their last tributes was a representative of the Moravians, Brother Dencke, who had visited him throughout his sickness.[19] The Irish immigrant had travelled from Donegal to western Pennsylvania, to the Scioto, the Great Miami, the Maumee, the Detroit, and finally the head of Lake Ontario. He died as appropriately in time as anyone could have died, for as the war came to an end in 1814, the frontier moved west beyond his old haunts. He could hardly have been happy with the scattered remnants of the once-great tribes that in the next generation would be driven sorrowfully westward. The Ohio he had known was finished. He did not live on to be a strange anomaly in a different world. His last winter, like many before, was spent in campaigning, and in planning for the future. He had lived a full life.

EPILOG

Matthew Elliott had died, but his young wife had most of her life still before her. She remained in exile for the rest of the war, and travelled into Lower Canada in an attempt to obtain relief from the government. Her neatly written appeals, couched in the sentimental idiom of the early nineteenth century, are abundant in the government files. There are some indications that Elliott may have escaped some rather harassing last years, as when Sarah commented on the sufferers from the western country: "I presume it is well understood that none have suffered in the smallest degree comparative to myself." Mrs. Elliott was given help for the rest of the war, and eventually returned to Amherstburg to spend her widowhood – some fifty years – on the banks of the Detroit River. The old Elliott home was repaired and lived in once again, and some years later, Sarah moved to another house nearby. The original Elliott home was lived in throughout the nineteenth century, but in the twentieth it was slowly allowed to fall to pieces. The shell finally collapsed in the 1950's, leaving the foundations and rubble amid a tangle of underbrush and trees. A road now separates the remnant of the house from the edge of the water, but the road is a quiet one along which one can still conjure up the days of Elliott and Tecumseh.[1]

Elliott's sons also lived on well into the nineteenth century. Matthew Jr. was at Amherstburg for many years, and as late as 1828, he and others who had served in the Department in the War of 1812 sent a memorial to the Secretary of State for the Colonies. Francis Gore became a clergyman of the Church of England, and as might be expected, lived near three score and ten. He did not die until 1880. Robert Herriot Barclay became "a gentleman farmer," and died in 1858. Sarah Elliott was more careful than her husband, and her will was drawn up some ten years before she died. She still had not lost the attitude which perhaps came from her early marriage into the Elliott prosperity. She wanted to be buried according to the rites of the Church of England, and desired "that my funeral be conducted in a manner corresponding with my Estate and station in Life." Prosperity sat a little more heavily on the daughter of Matthew Donovan than on Matthew Elliott. The frontier drama of the Georges had passed into the rural placidity of Victoria. It is perhaps as well that Matthew was not there to comment on Sarah's bequest to their son the Reverend Francis Gore Elliott of "one large picture known as 'King John Signing the Magna Charta.' "[2]

NOTES

Prolog

1 For these events of the fall of 1812, see Elliott to William Claus, October 28, to George Ironside, November 10, to Colonel St. George, November 11, Henry Procter to Major Evans, October 28, to Major-General Sheaffe, November 9, George Ironside to Claus, November 13, 1812, Series C, Military, RG 8, C 677, p. 157, 176-182, Canadian Public Archives, Ottawa; also Sarah Elliott to Noah Freer, November 10, 1814, *ibid.,* C 506, p. 18-19; note regarding Alexander Elliott's burial in Fort Malden archives, Amherstburg, Canada; Benjamin Drake, *Life of Tecumseh, and of His Brother the Prophet; with a Historical Sketch of the Shawanoe Indians* (Cincinnati, 1841), p. 57-58; Elias Darnell, *A Journal Containing an Accurate and Interesting Account of the Hardships, Sufferings, Battles, Defeat and Captivity of Those Heroic Kentucky Volunteers and Regulars, Commanded by General Winchester, in the Years 1812-1813* (Philadelphia, 1854), p. 35-36, 47.

Chapter 1: Wilderness Trader

1 Information on Elliott's life before he came to America must be gleaned from the later statements of Elliott and others. The most likely date for his birth is 1739, but he could have been born as early as 1735. See Audit Office, Claims, American Loyalists, No. 40, Evidence, 1785-87 Pennsylvania, p. 381-85, Public Record Office, London, microfilm in the Canadian Public Archives, Ottawa; see also Henry Procter to Captain M. Douall, May 14, 1813, Series C, Military, RG 8, C 678, p. 240-42; Ernest A. Cruikshank, *The Correspondence of Lieut. Governor John Graves Simcoe* (5 vols., Toronto, 1923-1931), I, 157 n. 1, mistakenly gives Maryland as the place of Elliott's birth.

2 For Pontiac's conspiracy, see Howard H. Peckham, *Pontiac and the Indian Uprising* (Princeton, 1947), and Francis Parkman, *The Conspiracy of Pontiac* (2 vols., Boston, 1917).

3 Thomas Guy and Henry Watson to Henry Bouquet, March 7, 1764, Sylvester K. Stevens and Donald H. Kent (eds.), *The Papers of Henry Bouquet, Series 21650,* Part II (Pennsylvania Historical Commission, Harrisburg, 1942), p. 48.

4 See *ibid., Series 21649,* Part II, 137; *Series 21650,* Part II, 147; *Series 21653,* p. 176; also Mary C. Darlington, *History of Colonel Henry Bouquet and the Western Frontiers of Pennsylvania, 1747-1764* (Privately printed, 1920), p. 144-45, 156-57, 179-80, 184-86, 205-6, 212.

5 Edward Moran to Evan Shelby, October 21, 1764, *Collections of the State Historical Society of Wisconsin* (31 vols., Madison, 1854-1931), VIII (1879), p. 237. For the advance of Bouquet into the Ohio country, see Lawrence H. Gipson, *The British Empire before the American Revolution, IX, The Triumphant Empire: New Respon-*

221

sibilities Within the Enlarged Empire, 1763-1766 (New York, 1956), p. 124-26.

6 David Jones, *A Journal of Two Visits Made to Some Nations of Indians on the West Side of the River Ohio, in the years 1772 and 1773* (Burlington, N.J.; reprinted New York, 1865), p. 50-87; also Elliott to Commissioners of Indian Affairs, August 31, 1776, Yeates Papers, Correspondence 1762-1780, Historical Society of Pennsylvania, Philadelphia.

7 John W. Harpster (ed.), *Pen Pictures of Early Western Pennsylvania* (Pittsburgh, 1938), p. 119-121 (Diary of David McClure); also Jones, *Journal,* 20.

8 For Dunmore's War and Elliott's role, see Virgil A. Lewis, *History of the Battle of Point Pleasant* (Charleston, W. Virginia, 1909), p. 55; Charles Whittlesey, *A Discourse Relating to the Expedition of Lord Dunmore against the Indian Towns upon the Scioto in 1774* (Cleveland, 1842), p. 25; E. O. Randall, *The Dunmore War* (Reprinted from the *Ohio Historical and Archaeological Quarterly,* Columbus, Ohio, 1902), p. 31-32; also Reuben G. Thwaites and Louise P. Kellogg (eds.), *Documentary History of Dunmore's War, 1774* (Madison, 1905).

9 E. W. Hassler, *Old Westmoreland: A History of Western Pennsylvania During the Revolution* (Cleveland, 1900), p. 14-16.

10 Max Savelle, *George Morgan: Colony Builder* (New York, 1932), p. 133.

11 Simon Gratz Collection, Case 4, Box 4, Historical Society of Pennsylvania, Philadelphia; also deposition of Elliott, March 5, 1793, *Michigan Pioneer and Historical Collections* (40 vols., Lansing, Michigan, 1877-1929), XXIV, 532.

12 Alexander Blaine to Elliott, August 9, 1775 (2 letters), Haldimand Papers, B 185-2 (Papers Relating to State Prisoners), 526-28, 532-35, 545-46, Canadian Public Archives, Ottawa.

13 Hassler, *Old Westmoreland,* 18-19; William Wilson to Elliott, October 7, 1775, Haldimand Papers, B 185-2, p. 536-37.

14 Blaine to Elliott, October 8, 1775, R. Connor to Elliott, October 31, 1775, Haldimand Papers, B 185-2, p. 538-40.

15 Blaine to Elliott, February 2, 1776, *ibid.,* 542-43.

16 Haldimand Papers, B 185-2, p. 547.

17 For the events of the spring and early summer of 1776, see Hassler, *Old Westmoreland,* 19-23; Savelle, *George Morgan,* 136-39, 167; Consul W. Butterfield, *History of the Girtys* (Cincinnati, 1890), p. 37-40; Yeates Papers, Correspondence 1762-1780.

18 Commissioners at Fort Pitt to William Wilson, August 3, 1776, George Morgan Letter Books, II, Carnegie Library, Pittsburgh; Commissioners to Wilson, August 11, 1776, Wilson to Commissioners, August 13, 1776, Yeates Papers, Correspondence 1762-1780.

19 Elliott to the Commissioners, August 31, 1776, Yeates Papers, Correspondence 1762-1780.

20 The committee letters of August 31 are in Yeates Papers, Correspondence 1762-1780, and in the George Morgan Letter Books, II.

21 Morgan to John Hancock, November 8, 1776, January 4, 1777, David Zeisberger to John Anderson, January 8, 1777, George Morgan Letter Books, I; Hassler, *Old Westmoreland,* 23.

22 Audit Office, Claims, American Loyalists, No. 40, Evidence, 1785-1787 Pennsylvania, p. 381-85.

23 A. Blaine to Elliott, September 30, 1776, Haldimand Papers, B 185-2, p. 555.

24 *Ibid.,* 556-57, E. Blaine to Elliott, October 15, 1776.

25 *Ibid.,* 558-59, 562-63, Elliott to A. Blaine, [c. October 17, 1776], W. Wilson to Elliott, November 19, 1776.

26 Audit Office, Claims, American Loyalists, No. 40, Evidence, 1785-1787 Pennsylvania, p. 381-85.

27 Elliott to A. Blaine, [c. October 17, 1776], Michael Capell to Elliott, January 31, 1777, Haldimand Papers, B 185-2, p. 558-59, 564.

28 Haldimand Papers, B 185-2, p. 544.

29 John Heckewelder, *A Narrative of the Mission of the United Brethren Among the Delaware and Mohegan Indians* . . . (Philadelphia, 1820), p. 147-49; David Zeisberger to George Morgan, November 21, 1776, George Morgan Letter Books, I.

30 Deposition of Michael Herbert, Haldimand Papers, B 185-2, p. 566.

31 The correspondence concerning Elliott's arrest and subsequent release is in the Haldimand Papers, B 185-2, p. 525-69; also *ibid.,* B 121, Guy Carleton to Hamilton, May 16, 1777; Rocheblave to Hamilton, May 8, 1777, Clarence W. Alvord (ed.), *Virginia Series,* vol. 1, *Cahokia Records, 1778-1790* (Illinois Historical Collections, II, Springfield, Illinois, 1907), p. XXXIV n. 2.

32 Hassler, *Old Westmoreland,* 38-43.

33 For accusations against Morgan, see Savelle, *George Morgan,* 148-51.

34 For McKee's early career, see Walter R. Hoberg, "Early History of Colonel Alexander McKee," *Pennsylvania Magazine of History and Biography,* LVIII (1934), p. 26-36; also Committee of Correspondence (Lancaster) to Alexander McKee, January 15, 1776, Yeates Papers, Correspondence 1762-1780; Hassler, *Old Westmoreland,* 44-45.

35 George Morgan to Henry Laurens, March 31, 1778, George Morgan Letter Books, III. Morgan had heard that Elliott had impressed McKee with the idea that he was in danger of assassination; also Hassler, *Old Westmoreland,* 46. Butterfield, *History of the Girtys,* is the best account of the Girty family. It would seem that McKee was thinking of the possibility of flight during the previous year, for in June 1777 he sold his farm at the mouth of Chartier's Creek to his brother James for £1500 in Pennsylvania currency. See McKee Papers, Burton Historical Collection, Detroit.

36 Reuben G. Thwaites and Louise P. Kellogg, *Frontier Defense on the Upper Ohio, 1777-1778* (Madison, 1912), p. 249-55.

37 Elliott's claim of August 1787 is in Audit Office, Claims, American Loyalists, No. 40, Evidence, 1785-1787 Pennsylvania, p. 381-85. His earlier estimate is in Haldimand Papers, B 185-2, p. 561, and the list he submitted to George Morgan is in *ibid.,* 559-60.

Chapter 2: War on the Frontier

1 White Eyes and John Kilbuck to George Morgan, April 6, 1778, Zeisberger to Morgan, April 6, 1778, George Morgan Letter Books, III; Heckewelder, *Narrative of the Mission of the United Brethren,* 170-71; Benson J. Lossing, *Pictorial Field Book of the Revolution* (2 vols., New York, 1860), p. 264; Hassler, *Old Westmoreland,* 46-47.

2 Hamilton to Carleton, April 25, 1778, Haldimand Papers, B 122, pp. 35-42.

3 Butterfield, *History of the Girtys,* 62; population of Detroit, April 26, 1778, Haldimand Papers, B 122, p. 195; John D. Barnhart, *Henry Hamilton and George Rogers Clark in the American Revolution, with the Unpublished Journal of Lieut. Gov. Henry Hamilton* (Crawfordsville, Ind., 1951) has successfully shown that Hamilton has been much maligned by historians.

4 *Colonial Records of Pennsylvania* (16 vols., Harrisburg, 1851-1853), II, 513-18.

5 Barnhart, *Henry Hamilton and George Rogers Clark* has the best brief account of this expedition. For Elliott's scouting activities, see *ibid.,* 164, 166. The question of currency in this period is a complicated one. The New York (York) shilling (20 to the pound) was worth half the sterling shilling, and the Halifax shilling was worth three quarters the sterling shilling. The dollar was worth eight York shillings. In Detroit, the rate from dollars to pounds was usually based on the York shilling. By February 1783, Elliott received ten shillings sterling per day. See Haldimand Papers, B 122, February 24, 1783.

6 There is a good description of the problem of the powder supply and of the Elliott-

Girty raid in Hassler, *Old Westmoreland,* 31-36, 54-59; also Butterfield, *History of the Girtys,* 110-11; Henry Shetrone, "The Indian in Ohio," *Ohio Archaeological and Historical Quarterly,* XXVII (1918), p. 380; De Peyster to (Haldimand), November 1, 1779, Haldimand Papers, B 122, p. 430; De Peyster to McKee, November 2, 1779, Claus Papers, MG 19, Series Fl, vol. 2, p. 139-41, Canadian Public Archives, Ottawa.

7 De Peyster to Haldimand, March 8, 1780, *Michigan Pioneer and Historical Collections,* X, 378; also Haldimand Papers, B 122, p. 443.

8 Correspondence relating to this campaign is in the Haldimand Papers, B 122, p. 484, 516, 527. A good brief account of the campaign is provided by Milo M. Quaife, "When Detroit Invaded Kentucky," *Burton Historical Collection Leaflet,* IV (November, 1925), p. 17-32; also Butterfield, *History of the Girtys,* 118-20.

9 There is an account of the affair of Mrs. La Force's slaves in William R. Riddell, *The Life of William Dummer Powell: First Judge at Detroit and Fifth Chief Justice of Upper Canada* (Lansing, 1924), p. 26-30; see also Quaife, "When Detroit Invaded Kentucky," 22-23, 31-32.

10 De Peyster to Brig. Gen. H. Watson-Powell, April 4, 17, 1781, *Michigan Pioneer and Historical Collections,* XIX, 614-15, 619-20.

11 The best account of the Moravians is Elma E. and Leslie R. Gray, *Wilderness Christians: The Moravian Indian Mission to the Delaware Indians* (Ithaca, N.Y., 1956).

12 In 1800 General Edward Hand formally thanked the Moravians for the information concerning war parties they had supplied during the Revolution, see Paul A. W. Wallace (ed.), *Thirty Thousand Miles with John Heckewelder* (Pittsburgh, 1958), p. 133-34; Zeisberger to Brodhead, August 18, 1781, Consul W. Butterfield (ed.), *Washington-Irvine Correspondence* (Madison, 1882), p. 58; Alexander Scott Withers, *Chronicles of Border · Warfare,* ed. by Reuben G. Thwaites (Cincinnati, 1912), pp. 316-17 n. 1; letter of Ephraim Douglass, August 29, 1781, "Notes and Queries," *Pennsylvania Magazine of History and Biography,* IV (1880), p. 247-48.

13 Heckewelder, *Narrative of the Mission of the United Brethren,* 232-36, 244-45, 277; Wallace (ed.), *Thirty Thousand Miles with John Heckewelder,* 170-71.

14 Bliss (ed.), *Diary of Zeisberger,* I, 3-8; Edmund de Schweinitz, *The Life and Times of David Zeisberger,* (Philadelphia, 1870), 493-96; Wallace (ed.), *Thirty Thousand Miles with John Heckewelder,* 171-75; Gray, *Wilderness Christians,* 65-66.

15 The events of the first weeks of September are contained in Heckewelder, *Narrative of the Mission of the United Brethren,* 276-77; Bliss (ed.), *Diary of Zeisberger,* I, 8-17; De Schweinitz, *Zeisberger,* 507-8; Gray, *Wilderness Christians,* 66-67.

16 McKee to De Peyster, September 26, 1781, Haldimand Papers, B 122, vol. 2. The Shawnee had withdrawn from their villages on the Scioto owing to their vulnerability to American attack.

17 De Peyster to Haldimand, October 5, 1781, McKee to De Peyster, October 10, 18, 1781, Haldimand Papers, B 122, vol. 2; Bliss, (ed.), *Diary of Zeisberger,* I, 18-30; Wallace (ed.), *Thirty Thousand Miles with John Heckewelder,* 182-83.

18 McKee to De Peyster, October 10, November 2, 1781, Minutes of the Detroit Council of November 9, 1781, Haldimand Papers, B 122, vol. 2; Bliss (ed.), *Diary of Zeisberger,* I, 30-32; Wallace (ed.), *Thirty Thousand Miles with John Heckewelder,* 183-88.

19 Gray, *Wilderness Christians,* 72-82; Wallace (ed.), *Thirty Thousand Miles with John Heckewelder,* 189-200.

20 The best account of the Crawford expedition is Consul W. Butterfield, *An Historical Account of the Expedition against Sandusky under Col. William Crawford in 1782* (Cincinnati, 1873); also Hassler, *Old Westmoreland,* 162-69.

21 Reuben G. Thwaites (ed.), *A Short Biography of John Leeth with an Account of*

his Life among the Indians (reprinted from the original edition of 1831, Cleveland, 1904), p. 46-47; Butterfield, *Sandusky Expedition,* 173-78,205-13. The battlefield was about three miles north of the present Upper Sandusky, Ohio.

22 Butterfield, *Sandusky Expedition,* 214-45, 259; John Turney to De Peyster, June 7, 1782, Haldimand Papers, B 122, vol. 2.

23 For torture of Crawford see Butterfield, *Sandusky Expedition,* 379-84; Butterfield, *History of the Girtys,* 178-182, 355-72; William Irvine to Washington, July 11, 1782, Butterfield (ed.), *Washington-Irvine Correspondence,* 126-27; Account of Colonel John Johnston, Draper Manuscripts, 11YY12, State Historical Society, Madison, Wisconsin. For British reaction see Haldimand to De Peyster, July 11, 1782, De Peyster to Haldimand, August 18, 1782, Haldimand Papers, B 122, vol. 2.

24 John Knight and John Slover, *Narrative of a late Expedition against the Indians; with an Account of the Barbarous Execution of Col. Crawford; and the Wonderful Escape of Dr. Knight and John Slover from Captivity, in 1782* (Philadelphia, 1783), *passim;* Butterfield, *History of the Girtys,* 184-85,193; Butterfield, *Sandusky Expedition,* 322, 344-53; Samuel M. Wilson, *Battle of Blue Licks, August 19, 1782* (Lexington, 1927), 16-17; Caldwell to McKee, July 4,1782, Claus Papers, MG 19, Series Fl, vol. 3.

25 Wilson, *Blue Licks,* 18-90; Butterfield, *History of the Girtys,* 194-98, 200-1; Milo M. Quaife, "Detroit Battles: The Blue Licks," *Burton Historical Collection Leaflet,* VI (November, 1927), No. 2, p. 17-32; W. Arundel to T. Williams, August 20, 1782, M. Agnes Burton, *Manuscripts from the Burton Historical Collection,* No. 8 (Detroit, July, 1918), p. 350; Caldwell to De Peyster, August 28, 1782, De Peyster to Haldimand, August 27, 1782, Haldimand Papers, B 122, vol. 2.

26 Butterfield, *History of the Girtys,* 201-2; W. Dawson to W. Arundel or T. Williams, November 6, 1782, Burton, *Manuscripts,* No. 8, p. 356; De Peyster to McKee, May 6, 1783, Claus Papers, MG 19, Series Fl, vol. 3, p. 217-18.

27 Merrill Jensen, *The New Nation: A History of the United States during the Confederation, 1781-1789* (New York, 1950), p. 67-68; Worthington C. Ford *et. al.* (eds.), *Journals of the Continental Congress, 1774-1789* (34 vols., Washington, 1904-1937), XXIV, 264, 319-20; Benjamin Lincoln to Brig. Gen. William Irvine, May 3, 1783, Butterfield (ed.), *Washington-Irvine Correspondence,* 188. The details of Douglass's trip, including his journal, are in Clarence M. Burton (ed.), "Ephraim Douglass and his Times," *Magazine of History with Notes and Queries,* extra numbers, vol. 3, no. 10 (New York, 1910); De Peyster to Brig. Gen. MacLean, September 15, 1783, Haldimand Papers, B 122, vol. 2.

Chapter 3: Landowner and Fur-Trader

1 Bliss (ed.), *Diary of Zeisberger,* I, 191; "Matthew Elliott's Village Lot," *Burton Historical Collection Leaflet,* vol. 11, no. 3 (January, 1924), p. 30-31.

2 For transactions of 1783-84 see Haldimand to Hay, April 26, 1784, Haldimand Papers, B 122, vol. 2; Francis Cleary, "History of Fort Malden and Amherstburg," *Essex Historical Society Papers and Addresses,* II (1915), 37-38; manuscript notes in Fort Malden archives, Amherstburg, Ontario.

3 See Gilbert C. Paterson, *Land Settlement in Upper Canada, 1789-1840* (16th Report of the Bureau of Archives for the Province of Ontario, 1920, Toronto, 1921), p. 22-24 and *passim* for an account of the general policy; Hay to Haldimand, July 22,

4 See Henry Bird to Castlereagh, August 27, 1805, Series C, Military, C 272,

4 See Henry Bird to Castlereagh, August 27, 1805, Series C, Military, C 272, p. 133-35; letter of December 16, 1795, in Claus Papers, MG 19, Series Fl, vol. 7, p. 121-22; Haldimand to Hay, August 14, 1784, *Michigan Pioneer and Historical Collections,* XX, 246; Memo from Hay to Ensign Fry, "Manuscript of the Minutes of the Meetings

of the Board to the Land Office for the District of Hesse, 1789-1794, with index of Names, *"Third Report of the Bureau of Archives for the Province of Ontario,* by Alexander Fraser (Toronto, 1906), p. 29-30. Each "acre in front" was the equivalent of just over 208 feet. The use of "acre in front" as a measure of length was common in French settlements.

5 Paterson, *Land Settlement in Upper Canada,* 24-32. Elliott had a home on his land opposite Bois Blanc by 1788, see "Narrative of a Captivity Among the Shawanese Indians, in 1788, of Thomas Ridout . . .," *Appendix* to Lady Matilda Edgar, *Ten Years of Upper Canada in Peace and War* (Toronto, 1890), 368; *Third Ontario Archives Report,* xcii-xciii. In July 1792 Upper Canada was divided into counties. Land on the Detroit River was now under the land board for the counties of Essex and Kent, and the Hesse land board came to an end, Paterson, *Land Settlement in Upper Canada,* 39, and *Third Ontario Archives Report,* cviii.

6 *Third Ontario Archives Report,* 2-3, 30-31.

7 *Ibid.,* 22; Alexander Fraser (ed.), *Grants of Crown Lands in Canada, 1787-1791* (Seventeenth Report of the Bureau of Archives for the Province of Ontario, 1928, Toronto, 1929), p. 181-82. Also see map in *Third Report of Ontario Archives,* xcvi.

8 Paterson, *Land Settlement in Upper Canada,* 33-34, 51, 57; see also *Sixth Report of the Bureau of Archives for the Province of Ontario,* 1909 (Toronto, 1911), ix-xi; Elliott's petition for land is in *Third Ontario Archives Report,* 159, 439; see also *ibid.,* 171, and petitions of Elliott to Lord Dorchester, April, 1792, Upper Canada Land Petitions, RG 1, L3, vol. 175, no. 21, Canadian Public Archives, Ottawa.

9 *Third Ontario Archives Report,* 187, 22-23; Alexander Fraser (ed.), *Grants of Crown Lands in Upper Canada,* 1792-1796 (Eighteenth Report of the Bureau of Archives for the Province of Ontario, 1929, Toronto, 1930), p. 22; Paterson, *Land Settlement in Upper Canada,* 34, 38, 46; D. W. Smith to A. McKee, January 12, 1793, Indian Affairs, Superintendent-General, RG 10, vol. 8, Canadian Public Archives, Ottawa.

10 *Eighteenth Ontario Archives Report,* 43-44; *Third Ontario Archives Report,* 248. A complete list of Elliott's land holdings at the time of his death can be obtained from his will, dated April 22, 1814, copy in Fort Malden archives, Amherstburg.

11 See Audit Office, Claims, American Loyalists, No. 40, Evidence, 1785-1787 Pennsylvania, p. 381-85; Bliss (ed.), *Diary of Zeisberger,* I, 181-82, 184.

12 See memorial of Elliott to Haldimand (and endorsements), July 1784, Haldimand Papers, B 185-2, p. 568-69. The best account of British policy after 1783 is Alfred L. Burt, *The United States, Great Britain, and British North America from the Revolution to the Establishment of Peace after the War of 1812* (New Haven, 1940).

13 The trading activities of Elliott and Caldwell can be pieced together from materials in the Burton Historical Collection of the Detroit Public Library. The most useful collections are the John Askin Papers (1704-1788 Box), and the Solomon Sibley Papers (1750-1786 Box); also the Macomb Papers (1780-1784 Letterbook).

14 For a discussion of American Indian policy after 1783 see Reginald Horsman, "American Indian Policy in the Old Northwest, 1783-1812," *William and Mary Quarterly,* Third Series, XVIII (January, 1961), 35-53. For Shawnee raids of 1784 see Butterfield, *History of the Girtys,* 233-34. The prisoner (James Moore) who was given to Elliott and then reclaimed eventually found his way back to Virginia.

15 *Journals of the Continental Congress,* XXVIII, 125-26, 172-73, 180-81, 330-33, 460-62, 486-87; *Michigan Pioneer and Historical Collections,* XXIV, 21-22. For the British council at Sandusky see *ibid.,* XX, 176-77, and for speech of Captain Johnny, *ibid.,* XXV, 691-93.

16 For refusal of tribes to come, see message to the Americans, September 20, 1785, Draper MSS, 23U27. For the events of the treaty council see Richard Butler, "Journal

of General Butler," Neville B. Craig (ed.), *The Olden Time* (Pittsburgh, 1848; reprinted Cincinnati, 1876), II, 453-525. The treaty is in *Statutes at Large of the United States of America,* VII (Boston, 1853), 26-27. The boundary was drawn from the forks of the Great Miami westward to the River de la Panse (Wildcat Creek), and down that river to the Wabash.

17 Report of Philip Liebert, July 20, 1786, is in William H. Smith (ed.), *The St. Clair Papers* (2 vols., Cincinnati, 1882), II, 16-17, n. 1; Shawnee message to the British, April 29, 1786, *Michigan Pioneer and Historical Collections,* XXIV, 25-26; Butterfield, *History of the Girtys,* 226.

18 See Leonard C. Helderman, "The Northwest Expedition of George Rogers Clark 1786-1787," *Mississippi Valley Historical Review,* XXV (December 1938), p. 326; *Journals of the Continental Congress* XXXI, 656-58 (St. Clair's speech).

19 Helderman, 327-28; Harmar to the Secretary of War, November 15, 1786, Smith (ed.), *St. Clair Papers,* II, 18-19; *Michigan Pioneer and Historical Collections,* XXIV, 34-39.

20 The collapse of Elliott and Caldwell in 1787 can be traced in the manuscript material in the Sibley Papers, 1750-1786 Box, and 1787 to 1796 Box.

21 Elliott's successful claim is in Audit Office, 12, vol. 66, p. 63, and vol. 109, p. 136; for his appointment as a J. P. see *Michigan Pioneer and Historical Collections,* XI, 622; for residents objection see *ibid.,* 632.

22 For Indian message see *American State Papers, Indian Affairs,* vol 1 (Washington, 1832), p. 8-9; also *Michigan Pioneer and Historical Collections,* XI, 470-72; The Fort Harmar treaties are in *Statutes at Large,* VII, 28-35.

Chapter 4: Renewal of War

1 Butterfield, *History of the Girtys,* 246; Smith (ed.), *St. Clair Papers,* II, 146-48, 162-63; *American State Papers, Indian Affairs,* I, 92-93, 100.

2 England was anxious to maintain good relations with the United States at this time owing to the danger of war with Spain, see Samuel F. Bemis, *Jay's Treaty: A Study in Commerce and Diplomacy* (New York, 1924), p. 67.

3 For the west wing of the attack see Gayle Thornbrough, *Outpost on the Wabash, 1787-1791* . . . (Indiana Historical Society Publications, vol. 19, Indianapolis, 1957), p. 259-64. For Harmar's attack see *ibid.,* 268-69; *American State Papers, Indian Affairs,* I, 104; "Military Journal of Major Ebenezer Denny, *Memoirs of the Historical Society of Pennsylvania,* VII (Philadelphia, 1860), 345-53.

4 See McKee to Sir John Johnson, October 18, 1790, *Michigan Pioneer and Historical Collections,* XXIV, 106; Elliott to McKee, October 23, 1790, and information of Elliott, October 28, 1790, Series Q Colonial Office (transcripts), Q 50-1, Canadian Public Archives, Ottawa. For actual American Losses, see *American State Papers, Military Affairs,* I (Washington, 1832), p. 20-35.

5 Elliott's report of October 28 was enclosed in Dorchester to Grenville, January 23, 1791, Series Q, Colonial Office (transcripts), Q 50-1. The development of the idea of British mediation is discussed in Bemis, *Jay's Treaty,* 109-33; Dorchester to Sir John Johnson, February 10, 1791, Douglas Brymner (ed.), *Report on the Canadian Archives, 1890* (Ottawa, 1891), p. 169; Dorchester to Colonel Gordon and Major Smith, Ernest A. Cruikshank (ed.), *The Correspondence of Lieut. Governor John Graves Simcoe* (5 vols., Toronto, 1923-1931), I, 19.

6 Bliss (ed.) *Diary of Zeisberger,* II, 153-54. Elliott's change of heart caused the Moravians some embarrassment, for in the English translation of George Henry Loskiel's history of the Moravian missions which was due to appear in the early 1790's (it

eventually appeared in 1794) bitter comments had been made about Elliott. David Zeisberger now had to request that Elliott's name (along with McKee's and Girty's) be omitted, see Gray, *Wilderness Christians,* 87.

7 Bliss, (ed.) *Diary of Zeisberger,* II, 173-75, 179-81 203-5, 210-11; Gray, *Wilderness Christians,* 88-89.

8 For the events of 1791-92 see Bliss (ed.), *Diary of Zeisberger,* II, 220-53 *passim;* also Gray, *Wilderness Christians,* 90-92.

9 Cruikshank (ed.), *Simcoe Correspondence,* I, 25; *Michigan Pioneer and Historical Collections,* XXIV, 276-79; Bliss (ed.), *Diary of Zeisberger,* II, 174-75, 181.

10 *Michigan Pioneer and Historical Collections,* XXIV, 243, 247-48; Bliss (ed.), *Diary of Zeisberger,* II, 187-89.

11 McKee's speech to the nations at the foot of the rapids is in Cruikshank (ed.), *Simcoe Correspondence,* I, 36. For the boundary line proposed to Dorchester see *ibid.,* I, 55; see also Bliss (ed.), *Diary of Zeisberger,* II, 198-99; Bemis, *Jay's Treaty,* 116; Grenville to George Hammond, September 2, 1791, Bernard Mayo (ed.), *Instructions to the British Ministers in the United States, 1791-1812* (American Historical Association, *Annual Report,* 1936, III, Washington, 1941), p. 13-17; Henry Dundas to Dorchester, September 16, 1791, Cruikshank (ed.), *Simcoe Correspondence,* I, 66-68.

12 See *American State Papers, Indian Affairs,* I, 112-13; Smith (ed.), *St. Clair Papers,* II, 200-1, 203.

13 For Scott's expedition, see *American State Papers, Indian Affairs,* I, 131-32, and for Wilkinson's expedition, *ibid.,* I, 133-35. For flight of Indians and remarks of Elliott and the British officer, see Bliss (ed.), *Diary of Zeisberger,* II, 205-6.

14 See Smith (ed.), *St. Clair Papers,* II, 243-46, 262-67; "Journal of Ebenezer Denny," *Memoirs of the Historical Society of Pennsylvania,* VII, 367-79; Bliss (ed.), *Diary of Zeisberger,* II, 228.

15 The hopes of the British government for mediation, and the project of a neutral barrier state, are treated in Burt, *United States, Great Britain,* 106-24, and in Bemis, *Jay's Treaty,* 109-33; Grenville's letter to Hammond is in Mayo, *Instructions to British Ministers,* 25-27.

16 *Sixth Report of the Bureau of Archives for the Province of Ontario,* 1909 (Toronto, 1911), ix-x.

17 Speech of the Shawnees, Delawares, Ottawas, Chippewas, Potawatomis, Munsees, and other western nations to Elliott, May 16, 1792, Indian Affairs, Superintendent-General, RG 10, vol. 8.

18 See England to Le Maistre, July 5, 1792, *Michigan Pioneer and Historical Collections,* XXIV, 427, and Series C, Military, C 546, p. 18-19; England to Simcoe, July 24, 1792, Cruikshank (ed.), *Simcoe Correspondence,* I, 181. Elliott even purchased from the Indians a supposed captured American soldier, William May (who later turned out to be a spy), and employed him on the schooner that carried supplies from Detroit along the Maumee, see *American State Papers, Indian Affairs,* I, 243; Cruikshank (ed.), *Simcoe Correspondence,* I, 330.

19 For the McKee-Simcoe talks see Cruikshank (ed.), *Simcoe Correspondence,* I, 164-65, 171-74.

20 Simcoe to McKee, August 30, September 24, 1792, Cruikshank (ed.), *Simcoe Correspondence,* I, 207-9, V, 41-42. The suggestion that the Indians should request British mediation had originated with George Hammond in Philadelphia, see Bemis, *Jay's Treaty,* 130.

21 See Simcoe to Hammond, September 27, 1792, Cruikshank (ed.), *Simcoe Correspondence,* I, 214-17.

22 For the proceedings of the fall 1792 council, see *ibid.,* I, 218-29; also B.H. Coates

(ed.), "A Narrative of an Embassy to the Western Indians from the Original Manuscript of Hendrick Aupaumut," *Memoirs of the Historical Society of Pennsylvania,* II (Philadelphia, 1827), 115-21. For the request of the Indians to the British, see Cruikshank (ed.), *Simcoe Correspondence,* I, 256-60. For Hammond's negotiations, see Simcoe to Hammond, November 17, 1792, January 21, 1793, Hammond to Simcoe, November 27, 1792, *ibid.,* I, 262, 267-69, 277-78.

23 For the Spencer incident, see Oliver M. Spencer, *Indian Captivity: A True Narrative of the Capture of the Rev. O. M. Spencer by the Indians, in the Neighbourhood of Cincinnati* (New York, 1834), *passim;* also Cruikshank (ed.), *Simcoe Correspondence,* I, 262, 270-71.

24 Simcoe to Hammond, January 21, 1793, to McKee (extract), January 23, 1793, Cruikshank (ed.), *Simcoe Correspondence,* I, 277-79. McKee recommended that a large quantity of supplies (including 1500 bushels of corn, 100 barrels of pork, and 100 barrels of flour) should be requisitioned for the coming American-Indian treaty. This was all approved by Simcoe, *ibid.,* I, 296.

25 See McKee to Simcoe, January 30, 1793, *ibid.,* I, 282.

26 Knox to the Western Indians, December 12, 1792, *ibid.,* I, 270. In this reply, the United States agreed to meet the Indians at the rapids of the Maumee rather than at Sandusky, as requested by the Indians. This offended the Indians, and the United States claimed that it was owing to an interpreter's mistake. Eventually Knox corrected this error, and it was agreed to meet the Indians at Sandusky, *ibid.,* I, 283-84, 295.

27 Western Indians to the Five Nations, February 27, 1793, Claus Papers, MG 19, Series Fl, vol. 5, p. 87-89. The Six Nations had given the request for the treaty to the Americans, see Cruikshank (ed.), *Simcoe Correspondence,* I, 256-60.

28 Brant to McKee, March 23, 1793, Claus Papers, MG 19, Series Fl, vol. 5, p 95-97; Simcoe to Alured Clarke, April 1, 21, 1793, to McKee, April 29, 1793, Cruikshank (ed.), *Simcoe Correspondence,* I, 308-9, 317-18, 322-24.

29 Simcoe to McKee, April 29, 1793, Cruikshank (ed.), *Simcoe Correspondence,* I, 322-24.

30 Jefferson to Charles Pinckney, November 27, 1793, H.A. Washington (ed.), *The Writings of Thomas Jefferson* (9 vols., New York, 1854), IV, 85-86; see also Washington to Charles Carroll, January 23, 1793, John C. Fitzpatrick (ed.), *The Writings of George Washington* (39 vols., Washington, 1931-44), XXXII, 312-13.

31 The instructions to the commissioners, dated April 26, 1793, are in *American State Papers, Indian Affairs,* I, 340-42; for cabinet discussions preceding the sending of instructions see Fitzpatrick (ed.) *Writings of Washington,* XXXII, 348-49; Washington (ed.), *Writings of Jefferson,* IX, 136-38; Clarence E. Carter (ed.), *The Territorial Papers of the United States,* II, *The Territory Northwest of the River Ohio, 1787-1803* (Washington, 1934), 440-41, 447-49. Knox to Wayne, April 20, 1793, Richard C. Knopf (ed.), *Anthony Wayne: A Name in Arms: Soldier, Diplomat, Defender of Expansion Westward of a Nation: The Wayne-Knox-Pickering-McHenry Correspondence* (Pittsburgh, 1960), p. 221-25.

32 See *American State Papers, Indian Affairs,* I, 342-48; also Benjamin Lincoln, "Journal of a Treaty Held in 1793, with the Indian Tribes North-West of the Ohio, by Commissioners of the United States," *Collections of the Massachusetts Historical Society,* Third Series, V (Boston, 1836), 122-37.

33 R. G. England to Littlehales, April 16, 1793, Cruikshank (ed.), *Simcoe Correspondence,* I, 314; McKee to England, May 16, 1793, Selby to McKee, May 20, 1793, England to Simcoe, May 22, 1793, *ibid.,* V, 40-41, 43-44, I, 333-34; Elliott to McKee, May 20, 1793, England to McKee, May 21, 1793, Claus Papers, MG 19, Series Fl, vol. 5, p. 129-30, 133-36.

34 Joseph Brant's Journal, Cruikshank (ed.), *Simcoe Correspondence*, II, 5; Brant to McKee, May 17, 1793, *ibid.*, V, 41; A. Clarke to McKee, May 27, 1793, *ibid.*, I, 337; England to McKee, May 27, 1793, *ibid.*, V, 44-45; Chiefs at the Glaize to McKee, May 27, 1793, Indian Affairs, Superintendent-General, RG 10, vol. 8.

35 Elliott to McKee, June 19, 1793, Indian Affairs, Superintendent-General, RG 10, vol. 8; also *ibid.*, Elliott to McKee, June 11, 14, 1793, England to McKee, June 10, 18, 1793; Elliott to McKee, May 20, June 5, 1793, Claus Papers, MG 19, Series Fl, vol. 5, p. 129-30, 149-50.

36 Elliott to McKee, June 19, 1793, Indian Affairs, Superintendent-General, RG 10, vol. 8; Cruikshank (ed.), *Simcoe Correspondence*, I, 361; Claus Papers, MG 19, Series Fl, vol. 5, p. 161.

37 Elliott to McKee, June 24, 25, 28, 1793, England to McKee, June 26, 1793, Indian Affairs, Superintendent-General, RG 10, Vol. 8; McKee to Simcoe, June 29, 1793, England to McKee, June 29, 1793, Cruikshank (ed.), *Simcoe Correspondence*, I, 371-73; Thomas Duggan to McKee, July 3, 1793, England to McKee, July 5, 1793, Elliott to McKee, July 13, 1793, Claus Papers, MG 19, Series Fl, vol. 5, p. 199, 203, 205-6.

38 Joseph Brant's Journal, Cruikshank (ed.), *Simcoe Correspondence*, II, 5-7; McKee to Simcoe, June 29, July 1, 1793, *ibid.*, I, 371-72, 374.

39 Simcoe to McKee, June 2, 1793, Claus Papers, MG 19, Series Fl, vol. 5, p. 145-48; Simcoe to Alured Clarke, June 14, 1793, Cruikshank (ed.), *Simcoe Correspondence*, I, 354-55; *ibid.*, I, 329.

40 Cruikshank (ed.), *Simcoe Correspondence*, I, 365-66, 368.

41 *Ibid.*, V, 50-53. Simcoe and McKee not only envisioned an Indian buffer state northwest of the Ohio, but also thought that Great Britain should retain Detroit, *ibid.*, I, 173.

42 *Ibid.*, I, 377-83, V, 55-56.

43 Thomas Talbot to McKee, June 30, 1793, *ibid.*, I, 373-74; Simcoe to England, June 28, 1793, Joseph Bunbury to McKee, July 16, 1793, Claus Papers, MG 19, Series Fl, vol. 5, p. 183-86, 255.

44 *American State Papers, Indian Affairs*, I, 351; "Journal of a Treaty Held in 1793," *Collections of the Massachusetts Historical Society*, Third Series, V, 141-43; Elliott to McKee, July 16, 1793, Thomas Duggan to McKee, July 17, 1793, Claus Papers, MG 19, Series Fl, vol. 5, p. 239, 259-60; Commissioners of the United States to McKee, July 21, 1793, Cruikshank (ed.), *Simcoe Correspondence*, I, 395.

45 Brant's account of the council is in Cruikshank (ed.), *Simcoe Correspondence*, II, 7-12; see also Western Indians to the Commissioners of the United States, July 27, 1793, *ibid.*, I, 401-2.

46 *American State Papers, Indian Affairs*, I, 352-54; Wallace (ed.), *Thirty Thousand Miles with John Heckewelder*, 315-18; Cruikshank (ed.), *Simcoe Correspondence*, I, 405-9, II, 29-30.

47 Cruikshank (ed.), *Simcoe Correspondence*, I, 402-3; England to Simcoe, July 18, 1793, Simcoe to Clarke, July 29, 1793, *ibid.*, I, 391-93; Simcoe to McKee, July 23, 1793, Claus Papers, MG 19, Series Fl, vol. 5, p. 243-44.

48 Brant to Joseph Chew, September 26, 1793, Brant to Simcoe, September 2, 1793, William J. Chew to Joseph Chew, November 26, 1795, Simcoe to Brant, August 8, 1793, Cruikshank (ed.), *Simcoe Correspondence*, II, 68-69, 47, IV, 145, II, 4-5.

49 See Brant to McKee, August 4, 1793, Claus Papers, MG 19, Series Fl, vol. 5, p. 285-88; Brant's account of the council is in Cruikshank (ed.), *Simcoe Correspondence*, II, 12-15.

50 Cruikshank (ed.), *Simcoe Correspondence*, II, 16-17; Wallace (ed.), *Thirty Thousand Miles with John Heckewelder*, 315-16; Burt, *United States, Great Britain*, 130,

accepts McKee's rather than Brant's account of these proceedings.

51 Cruikshank (ed.), *Simcoe Correspondence,* II, 17-20.

52 *American State Papers, Indian Affairs,* I, 357; Joseph Bunbury to Doctor Cole, August 17, 1793, Claus Papers, MG 19, Series Fl, vol. 5, p. 295; Cruikshank (ed.), *Simcoe Correspondence,* II, 17.

53 McKee to Simcoe, August 22, 1793, Indian Affairs, Superintendent-General, RG 10, vol. 8; Simcoe to Hammond, September 8, 1793, Butler to Joseph Chew, March 1, 1795, Cruikshank (ed.), *Simcoe Correspondence,* II, 49-50, III, 313.

Chapter 5: American Victory

1 The main outlines of Wayne's campaign can be followed from his correspondence in Richard C. Knopf (ed.), *Anthony Wayne, a Name in Arms.*

2 See the letters of Thomas Smith, Thomas Duggan, Matthew Elliott, and Lieut. Colonel Richard England in the Claus Papers, MG 19, Series Fl, vol. 6, p. 31-33, 41-43, 49-53, 57-58, 61-62.

3 "Journal of Colonel Alexander McKee," in Cruikshank (ed.), *Simcoe Correspondence,* II, 126-29.

4 Claus Papers, MG 19, Series Fl, vol. 6, p. 43.

5 *Ibid.,* 49-53, 57-58, 61-62.

6 Cruikshank (ed.), *Simcoe Correspondence,* II, 149-50. The best discussion of the policies of Lord Dorchester and of the diplomatic background of these events is contained in Burt, *United States, Great Britain,* 106-40.

7 McKee to Joseph Chew, February 1, 1794, Cruikshank (ed.), *Simcoe Correspondence,* II, 138-39.

8 Report of Elliott to McKee, February 11, 1794, Indian Affairs, Superintendent-General, RG 10, vol. 8.

9 Cruikshank (ed.), *Simcoe Correspondence,* II, 154, 179-80.

10 *Ibid.,* II, 200-1, 209, 211-12, 225-26.

11 *Michigan Pioneer and Historical Collections,* XXIV, 656.

12 Cruikshank (ed.), *Simcoe Correspondence,* II, 202-4.

13 McKee to Joseph Chew, May 8, 1794, *ibid.,* II, 234-35.

14 England to Simcoe, May 29, 1794, Thomas Duggan to Joseph Chew, May 30, 1794, *ibid.,* II, 252-53.

15 McKee to Joseph Chew, May 30, June 3, 10, 1794, Simcoe to McKee, June 15, 1794, *ibid.,* II, 253-54, 258-59, 262-63, 268.

16 The material in this paragraph, and the account of the attack on Fort Recovery which follows is based on "Diary of J.C., an officer at the Glaize," Claus Papers, MG 19, Series Fl, vol. 6, p. 163-74. This diary was apparently written as a report to McKee.

17 Elliott to McKee, June 20, 1794, *ibid.,* vol. 6, p. 181.

18 McKee to R.G. England, and to Simcoe, July 5, 1794, Cruikshank (ed.), *Simcoe Correspondence,* II, 305-6, V, 95-6.

19 McKee to R.G. England, July 10, 1794, *ibid.,* II, 315.

20 Thomas Duggan to Joseph Chew (extract), July 10, 1794, *ibid.,* II, 317.

21 Simcoe to McKee, July 16, 1794, Claus Papers, MG 19, Series Fl, vol. 6, p. 199-201.

22 Simcoe to R.G. England, July 16, 1794, Cruikshank (ed.), *Simcoe Correspondence,* II, 320-21.

23 Dundas to Simcoe, July 4, 1794, *ibid.,* II, 300.

24 England to Simcoe, July 22, 1794, *ibid.,* II, 333-34.

25 *Ibid.,* II, 344-45.

26 McKee to R.G. England, August 10, 1794, *ibid.,* II, 365.

27 Simcoe to McKee, Private, August 6, 1794, Claus Papers, MG 19, Series Fl, vol. 6, p. 203-4.

28 *Ibid.,* vol. 6, p. 205; Cruikshank (ed.), *Simcoe Correspondence,* II, 385-86.

29 *Ibid.,* II, 366-67, 371, 376-77, 379, 387-88, III, 12; also John Askin to McKee, August 17, 1794, Thomas Duggan to McKee, August 18, 1794, to Prideaux Selby, August 23, 1794, Indian Affairs, Superintendent-General, RG 10, vol. 8.

30 Cruikshank (ed.), *Simcoe Correspondence,* II, 371-74, 387.

31 The account of the battle of Fallen Timbers in this and the following paragraphs is based on material in *ibid.,* II, 395-98, 402-5, 414-15, III, 7-14, 29-30, 99-100, 147-48; also journal of Wayne's march in Leonard Covington Correspondence, Burton Historical Collection, Detroit Public Library; Dwight L. Smith (ed.), *From Greene Ville to Fallen Timbers: A Journal of the Wayne Campaign, July 28-September 14, 1794* (Indiana Historical Society Publications, vol. 16, no. 3, Indianapolis, 1952); Reginald C. McGrane (ed.), "William Clark's Journal of General Wayne's Campaign" *Mississippi Valley Historical Review,* I (December, 1914), p. 418-44.

32 *American State Papers, Indian Affairs,* I, 494.

33 McKee to Joseph Chew, August 27, 1794, R.G. England to Simcoe, August 23, 1794, W. Jarvis to Rev. Samuel Peters, September 3, 1794, Cruikshank (ed.), *Simcoe Correspondence,* II, 413-15, III, 7-8, 29-30; Bliss (ed.), *Diary of Zeisberger,* II, 372.

34 Cruikshank (ed.), *Simcoe Correspondence,* II, 404-9.

35 Bliss (ed.), *Diary of Zeisberger,* II, 378-79.

36 McKee to R.G. England, August 30, 1794, Cruikshank (ed.), *Simcoe Correspondence,* III, 23.

37 See William Campbell to McKee, August 30, 1794, Campbell to Elliott, September 3 and 12, 1794, Indian Affairs, Superintendent-General, RG 10, vol. 8; Elliott's return of Indians at Swan Creek (September 15), and recommendation for six months provisions are in Claus Papers, MG 19, Series Fl, vol. 6, p. 215; for McKee's request and Simcoe's approval see Cruikshank (ed.), *Simcoe Correspondence,* III, 156-58.

38 Cruikshank (ed.), *Simcoe Correspondence,* III, 48, 96. England had already expressed his displeasure at the Indian conduct at Fallen Timbers: "The Indians on this occasion have forfeited every pretension to a Warlike or Gallant Character. They behaved excessive ill in the action at the Falls and afterward fled in every direction." See England to Simcoe, August 30, 1794, *ibid.,* III, 20-22.

39 *Ibid.,* III, 71, 73, 85, 95.

40 *Ibid.,* III, 74-78.

41 Speech of Simcoe (October 10) is in William L. Stone, *Life of Joseph Brant* (2 vols., New York, 1838), II, 392-93; also for the proceedings of this council see *Michigan Pioneer and Historical Collections,* XXV, 40-46, and memoranda by William Mayne, Cruikshank (ed.), *Simcoe Correspondence,* III, 78.

42 Brant to Joseph Chew (extract), October 22, 1794, Cruikshank (ed.), *Simcoe Correspondence,* III, 140-41.

43 Smith's reports to McKee are in *ibid.,* III, 128-31.

44 Claus Papers, MG 19, Series Fl, vol. 6, p. 241-44.

45 England to Simcoe, December 31, 1794, Cruikshank (ed.), *Simcoe Correspondence,* III, 244-45.

46 See *American State Papers, Indian Affairs,* I, 526-28, 559-60; Cruikshank (ed.), *Simcoe Correspondence,* III, 252-53, 275-76, 279-80, 287-91; *Michigan Pioneer and Historical Collections,* XX, 389-91.

47 Cruikshank (ed.), *Simcoe Correspondence,* III, 274-76.

48 Sarah Ainse to Brant, February 5, 1795, Brant to Joseph Chew, February 24, 1795, *ibid.,* III, 287-88, 310.

49 Dorchester to McKee, December 26, 1794, George Ironside Papers, L5: 1794-1813, Burton Historical Collection, Detroit Public Library.

50 See McKee to Joseph Chew, March 27, 1795, Cruikshank (ed.), *Simcoe Correspondence,* III, 335; also *ibid.,* IV, 1-2.

51 Elliott to McKee, March 29, 1795, Indian Affairs, Superintendent-General, RG 10, vol. 9.

52 England to Selby, April 10, 1795, to Littlehales, July 10, August 9, 1795, to Simcoe, July 13, 1795, Cruikshank (ed.), *Simcoe Correspondence,* V, 135-36, IV, 41-42, 58, 43-44.

53 The proceedings of the Greenville treaty council are in *American State Papers, Indian Affairs,* I, 564-82.

54 Brant to John Butler, June 28, 1795, England to Simcoe, July 13, 1795, Cruikshank (ed.), *Simcoe Correspondence,* IV, 33, 43-44; Elliott to McKee, July 13, 1795, Series C, Military, RG 8, C 248, p. 261-62.

55 The Treaty of Greenville is in *Statutes at Large,* VII, 49-54.

56 Elliott to McKee, August 21, 1795, Indian Affairs, Superintendent-General, RG 10, vol. 9; McKee to Joseph Chew, September 4, 1795, Series C, Military, RG 8, C 248, p. 289-90.

57 The arrangements for Chenail Ecarte can be followed in Cruikshank (ed.), *Simcoe Correspondence,* III, 224-25, IV, 42, 96, and in McKee to Chew, September 4, 1795, Selby to Chew, October 13, 1795, Series C, Military RG 8, C 248, p. 289-90, 337-38; McKee to Chew, October 24, 1795, Indian Affairs, Superintendent-General, RG 10, vol. 9.

58 Selby to Chew, October 13, 1795, Series C, Military, RG 8, C 248, p. 337-38; England to McKee, November 30, 1795, Claus Papers, MG 19, Series Fl, vol. 7, p. 117-18; Portland to Simcoe, December 5, 1795, Cruikshank (ed.), *Simcoe Correspondence,* IV, 154-55.

59 England to Simcoe, September 8, 1795, McKee to Chew, September 14, 1795, January 29, 1796, Cruikshank (ed.), *Simcoe Correspondence,* IV, 91-93, 186; Alexander McKensie to Elliott, January 13, 1796, Claus Papers, MG 19, Series Fl, p. 157-58.

60 Dorchester to Simcoe, January 24, 1796, Selby to Chew, January 30, 1796, McKee to Chew, April 14, July 1, 1796, Cruikshank (ed.), *Simcoe Correspondence,* IV, 179-80, 178-88, 245, 323; George Ironside to Selby, July 7, 18, 1796, Elliott to Selby, July 13, 1796, Claus Papers, MG 19, Series Fl, vol. 7, p. 277-78; Elliott to Selby, July 28, 1796, Council at Chenail Ecarte, August 30, 1796, Indian Affairs, Superintendent-General, RG 10, vol. 9.

61 For preparations see Cruikshank (ed.), *Simcoe Correspondence,* IV, 122-23, 210, 243, 259, 275-76, 283, 285-86, 289; Thomas Duggan to Selby, June 3, 1796, Claus Papers, MG 19, Series Fl, vol. 7, p. 221-23; F. Clever Bald, *Detroit's First American Decade, 1796-1805* (Ann Arbor, Michigan, 1948), p. 18-19.

62 See Cruikshank (ed.), *Simcoe Correspondence,* IV, 152-53, 330, 335-36, 343.

63 *Ibid.,* IV, 293-95; also Series C, Military, RG 8, C 249, p. 220-221.

64 See Portland to Prescott (extract), December 13, 1796, and additional instructions to Upper Canada, December 15, 1796, Series Q Colonial Office (transcripts), Q 229, p. 264-67. For Simcoe's earlier complaints and suggestions see Cruikshank (ed.), *Simcoe Correspondence,* III, 61-63, 71, 318-24, IV, 3-4. These were rejected, *ibid.,* III, 340-41, IV, 36-37, 89-90.

Chapter 6: A Quick Downfall

1 For the actions of Simcoe and Butler prior to Elliott's purchase, see Cruikshank (ed.), *Simcoe Correspondence,* IV, 101-2, 106, 119, 144-45, 191, 208, V, 141. Dorchester had issued detailed additional instructions regarding the purchase of land on December 26, 1794, *ibid.,* III, 241-42. Elliott's part in the transactions can be followed in Claus Papers, MG 19, Series Fl, vol. 7, p. 305-7, and in Series C, Military, RG 8, C 249, p. 370-73, 418, 350-51.

2 See Cruikshank (ed.), *Simcoe Correspondence,* IV, 344. Colonel England was transferred from the Detroit River in July 1796 when the establishment was reduced.

3 There is a collection of George Ironside Papers in the Burton Historical Collection of the Detroit Public Library, though there is little material for the pre-1812 period. There is a sketch of him in Milo M. Quaife (ed.), *The John Askin Papers* (2 vols., Detroit, 1928-1931), I, 332 n. 77.

4 See Isaac Weld, *Travels through the States of North America and the Provinces of Upper and Lower Canada during the Years 1795, 1796, and 1797* (London, 1799), p. 343-359.

5 *Ibid.,* 359, 417.

6 McKee to Selby, December 2, 1796, Claus Papers, MG 19, Series Fl, vol. 7, p.325-27; Selby to Chew, October 4, 1796 (extract), Series C, Military, C 249, p. 419.

7 Advertisement is in Quaife (ed.), *Askin Papers,* II, 83; Elliott's protest is in Series C, Military, C 250/2, p. 415-17.

8 Series C, Military, C 250/2, p. 411-12, 418-19, 550-53.

9 Ernest A. Cruikshank (ed.), *The Correspondence of the Honourable Peter Russell,* I (Toronto, 1932), p. 172-73, 213; Series Q, Colonial Office (transcripts), Q 79/1, p. 160-61.

10 For the England affair, see Series C, Military, C 238, p. 203-5.

11 *Ibid.,* C 250/1, p. 223; Mayne to Elliott, June 5, 1797, *ibid.,* C 250/2, p. 533-35, 537-38.

12 *Ibid.,* C 250/1, p. 233-38.

13 *Ibid.,* C 250/1, p. 118-20.

14 McLean to Green, August 18, 23, 1797, *ibid.,* C 250/1, p. 123-29; *Michigan Pioneer and Historical Collections,* XX, 529.

15 McLean to Ironside, September 11, 12, 1797, Ironside to McKee, September 12, 13, 1797, Indian Affairs, Upper Canada, Civil Control, RG 10, vol. 1; Ironside to Lees, September 13, 1797, Series C, Military, C 250/1, p. 239-40.

16 See Indian Affairs, Upper Canada, Civil Control, RG 10, vol. 1, p. 101-8.

17 *Ibid.,* vol. 1, 101-4; Series C, Military, C 250/1, p. 145-52.

18 McLean to Russell, September 21, 1797, Series Q, Colonial Office (transcripts), Q 299, p. 243-45; McLean to Green, September 23, 1797, Series C, Military, C 250/1, p. 197-200.

19 McLean to Green, September 23, 1797, Series C, Military, C 250/1, p. 197-200.

20 Mayne to Green, September 28, October 2, 1797, *ibid.,* C 250/1, p. 220-21, 224-26.

21 For the Wilkinson-Day affair, see Elliott to McKee, October 3, 1797 (enclosing statement of James Day), Claus Papers, MG 19, Series Fl, vol. 8; Wilkinson to McLean, September 28, 1797, McLean to Green, October 9, 1797, Indian Affairs, Upper Canada, Civil Control, RG 10, vol. 1.

22 Prescott to Russell, October 9, 1797, Indian Affairs, Upper Canada, Civil Control, RG 10, vol. 1.

23 Selby to Elliott, October 12, 1797 (enclosing list of Indians), McKee to Elliott,

October 13, 1797, McKee to Russell, February 7, 1798, Series Q, Colonial Office (transcripts), Q 299, p. 273-76, 296-300.

24 Elliott to McKee, October 14, 1797, Indian Affairs, Superintendent-General, RG 10, vol. 8; Elliott's requisition of October 14, Indian Affairs, Upper Canada, Civil Control, RG 10, vol. 1; McLean to Green, October 18, 1797, Series C, Military, C 250/1, p. 296-303.

25 Elliott to McKee, October 16, 1797, McLean to Elliott, October 20, 21, 23, 1797, Indian Affairs, Upper Canada, Civil Control, RG 10, vol. 1; Elliott to McKee, October 24, 1797, Series Q, Colonial Office (transcripts), Q 299, p. 246-49.

26 This whole correspondence from October 26 to November 19 is contained in Indian Affairs, Upper Canada, Civil Control, RG 10, vol. 1; Series Q, Colonial Office (transcripts), Q 299, p. 263, 270-72; Series C, Military, C 250/2, p. 351-62, 374-78.

27 See Indian Affairs, Upper Canada, Civil Control, RG 10, vol. 1; Prescott to the Duke of Portland, December 27, 1797, Series C, Military, C 250/2, p. 394-96.

28 For the affidavits see Series Q, Colonial Office (transcripts), Q 299, p. 294-95; McKee's letters to Russell and Fisher's affidavit are in *ibid.,* 273-76, 292-93, 302-3. Although affidavits were obtained at this time saying that there had been no trade or barter with Indian store goods, a leading Detroit merchant, John Askin, later stated in another connection that he had bartered for articles from the Indian store when Elliott was in charge of it. He also stated that Elliott had barter accounts with almost all the merchants of Detroit. See John Askin to Solomon Sibley, September 2, 1807, and September 17 1808, Solomon Sibley Papers.

29 See Series Q, Colonial Office (transcripts), Q 299, p. 301; also Series C, Military, C 251, p. 22-25.

Chapter 7: Peace and Prosperity

1 See McLean to Green, May 11, 13, July 18, 1798, Series C, Military, C 251, p. 90-95, 150-53.

2 McLean to Green, September 13, November 24, 1798, June 20, July 17, July 29 (with enclosure), 1800, *ibid.,* C 251, p. 236-39, C 223, p. 63-64, C 253, p. 140-46, 153-57.

3 Portland to Prescott, June 8, 1798, *ibid.,* C 251, p. 179-80; Elliott to Russell, July, 1798, Series Q, Colonial Office (transcripts), Q 299, p. 277-78.

4 See Russell to McKee, October 13, 1798, Series Q, Colonial Office (transcripts), Q 299, p. 305.

5 Elliott to Portland, December 20, 1798, to Prescott, January 28, 1799, to Sir John Johnson, April 20, 1799, Series Q, Colonial Office (transcripts), Q 299, p. 288, 279-82; Elliott to Simcoe, January 22, 1799, Brant to Simcoe, January 22, 1799, *ibid.,* Q 57-2. For death of McKee see McLean to Green, January 16, 1799, Series C, Military, C 252, p. l.

6 For Elliott's Shawnee wife and family, see John Johnston to Lyman C. Draper, July 10, 1848, Draper MSS, 11YY33; affidavit of Alexander Elliott, February 8, 1812, Secretary of State, Commissions of Advocates, 1811-1816, RG 4, B 8, vol. 19, Canadian Public Archives, Ottawa.

7 See affidavit of Alexander Skakel, February 8, 1812, *ibid.,* RG 4, B 8, vol. 19.

8 Russell to Selby, February 2, 1799, Claus Papers, MG 19, Series F1, vol. 8, p. 81-87; Chairman of the Council to Peter Russell, February 1, 1799, State Papers, Upper Canada, RG 1, E 3, vol. 12, p. 41, Canadian Public Archives, Ottawa.

9 See T. McKee to McLean, July 15, 1799, McLean to T. McKee, July 16, 1799, McLean to Green, August 8, 27, Series C, Military, C 252, p. 213-16, 223-27, 233-37.

10 Johnson to (Hunter), September 30, 1799, affidavit of Elliott, September 26, 1799, *ibid.*, C 252, p. 248-53. Lieut. - Gen. Peter Hunter became Lieut. - Governor of Upper Canada and Commander in Chief of the military forces in all Canada in August 1799.

11 Johnson to Hunter, September 30, 1799, Series C, Military, C 252, p. 249-53.

12 See Thomas Ridout's narrative of his captivity by the Shawnees in Lady Edgar (ed.), *Ten Years of Upper Canada*, p. 370.

13 Johnson to Claus, December 11, 1799, Claus Papers, MG 19, Series Fl, vol. 8, p. 111-118.

14 Simcoe to Elliott, April 9, 1800, Series Q, Colonial Office (transcripts), Q 299, p. 314-15.

15 Elliott to Edward, Duke of Kent, June 20, 1800, *ibid.*, Q 299, p. 283-85; W. Gordon to Hunter, July 26, 1800, Series C, Military, C 252, p. 217-22.

16 Elliott to Portland, June 24, 1801, Series Q, Colonial Office (transcripts), Q 299, p. 289-90.

17 *Sixth Ontario Archives Report*, 1909, p. 174-75; Thomas Smith to John Askin, July 24, 1800, Quaife (ed.), *Askin Papers*, II, 298-99.

18 There is a brief sketch of Thomas McKee in Quaife (ed.), *Askin Papers*, I, 376.

19 Journal of the first session of the third Parliament is in *Sixth Ontario Archives Report, 1909*, p. 169-245.

20 Journals of the 1802, 1803, and 1804 sessions of the third Parliament are in *ibid.*, 247-481. The 1804 election results are in Alexander Fraser (ed.), *Eighth Report of the Bureau of Archives for the Province of Ontario, 1911*, Part II (Toronto, 1912), p. 4. Elliott eventually voted for a school bill in 1807, *ibid.*, p. 164.

21 For grant of land in 1801, see Attorney - General of Upper Canada to John Joseph, August 14, 1847, Upper Canada, Land Petitions, RG 1, L3, vol. 182, Canadian Public Archives, Ottawa.

22 Vincent to Green, December 13, 1802, Series C, Military, C 108, p. 61-63; Vincent to Green, March 20, 1803, *ibid.*, C 254, p. 102-4. Also Alexander Campbell to Green, October 21, 1805, *ibid.*, C 109, p. 147-48; Lieut. - Col. Grant to Green, July 26, 1806, *Michigan Pioneer and Historical Collections*, XV, 36.

23 For Elliott's land transactions see action in Council Chamber, June 16, 1804, Upper Canada, Land Petitions, RG 1, L 3, vol. 176.

24 Johnson to Elliott, August 16, 1804 (with enclosure), Smith to Earl Camden, August 17, 1804, Series Q, Colonial Office (transcripts), Q 299, p. 241-42, 316-20.

25 Elliott's memorial to Earl Camden, summer 1804, Prescott to E. Cooke, September 30, 1804, Elliott to Camden, October 1804, *ibid.*, Q 299, 308-12, 341-42, 240.

26 Journals of the 1805, 1806, and 1807 sessions are in *Eighth Ontario Archives Report*, part II, 1-186. Address on Trafalgar is in *ibid.*, 61.

27 Elliott's petition of February 22, 1806, and the subsequent action is in Upper Canada, Land Petitions, RG 1, L 3, vol. 176, no. 17.

28 Articles of the Agreement (June 26, 1806) are in Secretary of State, Commissions of Advocates, 1811-1816, RG 4, B 8, vol. 19.

29 McKee to Selby, August 12, 1804, *Michigan Pioneer and Historical Collections*, XXIII, 31-32.

30 *Ibid.*, XXIII, 42.

Chapter 8: Frontier Crisis

1 There is considerable information regarding the impact of the *Chesapeake* affair in Ernest A. Cruikshank, "The *Chesapeake* Crisis as it Affected Upper Canada, *"Ontario Historical Society Papers and Records*, XXIV (1927), 281-322. See also Isaac Brock to Thomas Dunn, July 17 and 23, 1807, and Brock to Castlereagh, July 25, 1807,

Ferdinand B. Tupper, *Life and Correspondence of Major General Sir Isaac Brock* (2nd ed., London, 1847), p. 60-63.

2 See Claus to McKee, October 7, 1807, McKee to Claus, October 18, 1807, Indian Affairs, Superintendent-General, RG 10, vol. 11.

3 The whole case of the escaped slaves, the attempt to recover them, and the ensuing difficulties can be followed in William Wirt Blume (ed.), *Transactions of the Supreme Court of the Territory of Michigan, 1805-1814,* vols. I and II (Ann Arbor, 1935), I, 86-88, 98-99, 108-109, 135, 142-43, 151-52, 402, 405, 412, 414-22, 454-55, II, 155-56, 212-19, 275-76. See also Solomon Sibley Papers, Boxes for 1807. For the Negro militia see also Alexander Grant to James Green, August 17, 1807, Series C, Military, C 673, p. 106-9. The whole question of the slave in Upper Canada is discussed in William R. Riddell, "The Slave in Upper Canada," *Journal of Negro History* (Lancaster, Pa.), IV (October, 1919), p. 372-395.

4 The Askin-Elliott case can be followed in Blume(ed.), *Transactions of the Supreme Court of the Territory of Michigan,* I, 95,396, 403-5, 411, 423, 430, 438, II, 150-54. There is also a good deal of material in the Solomon Sibley Papers, Boxes for 1807, 1808, and 1809.

5 Blume (ed.,), *Transactions of the Supreme Court of the Territory of Michigan,* II, 215-16.

6 *Ibid.,* I, 420; II, 212-15.

7 *Ibid.,* II, 217.

8 For decision see *ibid.,* I, 414-18; for later indictments see *ibid.,* I, 108-9, 135, 142-43, 151-52, 454-55, II, 275-78.

9 Series C, Military, C 255, p. 139-40; also McKee to Selby, December 4, 1807, *Michigan Pioneer and Historical Collections,* XXIII, 42-43.

10 Craig to Gore, December 6, 1807, Douglas Brymner(ed.), *Report on the Canadian Archives, 1896* (Ottawa, 1897), Note B, 31.

11 Craig to Gore, December 28, 1807, *Michigan Pioneer and Historical Collections,* XXV, 232-33.

12 Gore to Craig, January 5, 1808, *Report on Canadian Archives, 1896,* Note B, 36.

13 Johnson to Claus, December 11, 1807, Gore to Craig, January 8, 1808, Indian Affairs, Upper Canada, Civil Control, RG 10, vol. 2.

14 Gore to Claus (Secret), January 29, 1808, Indian Affairs, Superintendent-General, RG 10, vol. 11.

15 *Eighth Ontario Archives Report,* part II, 199.

16 The secret instructions, dated January 29, 1808, are in Indian Affairs, Superintendent-General, RG 10, vol. 11.

17 Craig to Gore, February 10, 1808, Canada, Miscellaneous Documents, vol. 8, p. 179, Canadian Public Archives, Ottawa.

18 Claus to Gore, February 14, 1808, Series C, Military, C 255, p. 141-43; Claus to Gore, February 27, 1808, Claus Papers, MG 19, Series F 1, vol. 9, p. 177-82.

19 Claus to Selby, February 16, 17, 1808, Claus Papers, MG 19, Series Fl, vol. 9, p. 171-75. On April 2, James Girty was appointed interpreter at Amherstburg on Gore's order, George Ironside Papers, L5 1794-1813.

20 Claus to Selby, March 25, 1808, and "Proceedings of a Private Meeting with the Shawenoes," *Michigan Pioneer and Historical Collections,* XV, 45-46, XXV, 242-45; Gore to Craig, April 8, 1808, *ibid.,* XXV, 245.

21 Claus to Gore, April 20, 1808, *ibid.,* XV, 47-48.

22 Claus to Selby, May 3, 1808, *ibid.,* XV, 49; also Claus to Gore, May 22, 1808, *ibid.,* XXIII, 62. For Fisher's appointment see Gore's order, January 25, 1808, George Ironside Papers. For his activities at Greenville from 1806 see the account of John

Johnston, Draper MSS, 11YY17; also *ibid.,* 1YY24, 2YY6, and 3YY60.

23 Craig to Gore, May 11, 1808, Indian Affairs, Upper Canada, Civil Control, RG 10, vol. 2, p. 328-31; see also Craig to David M. Erskine, May 13, 1808, Craig to Edward Cooke, July 15, 1808, *Report on Canadian Archives, 1893,* p. 10, 13.

24 Claus to Gore, May 22, 1808, *Michigan Pioneer and Historical Collections,* XXIII, 62; also Diary of Claus, May 16, June 11, 13, 14, 1808, *ibid.,* 50, 53-54.

25 *Ibid.,* XXIII, 54; Gore to Craig, June 5, 1808, Indian Affairs, Lower Canada, Civil Control, RG 10, vol. 486, p. 388-94; reappointment of Elliott, June 6, 1808, Indian Affairs, Upper Canada, Civil Control, RG 10, vol. 2, p. 354; Gore to Claus (Secret), June 6, 1808, Cruikshank, "The *Chesapeake* Crisis," *Ontario Historical Society Papers and Records,* XXIV, 304.

26 Claus to Gore, June 15, 1808, *ibid.,* 304-5.

27 Claus to Selby, June 19, 1808, Claus Papers, MG 19, Series Fl, vol. 9, p. 235; also *ibid.,* 209; Gore's order re Ironside (July 16, 1808) is in Indian Affairs, Super-intendent-General, RG 10, vol. 11.

28 See *Michigan Pioneer and Historical Collections,* XXIII, 54-57. Gore's speech of July 11 and Indian reply of July 13, 1808, are in Indian Affairs, Superintendent-General, RG 10, vol. 11; also *ibid.,* Gore to Craig, July 27, 1808.

29 *Ibid.,* Gore to Craig, July 27, 1808.

30 Claus to Selby, January 18, 1809, Series C, Military, C 256, p. 4-5; Gore to Craig, February 20, 1809, *Michigan Pioneer and Historical Collections,* XV, 53. In January 1809, Elliott visited the Moravians at Fairfield and gave them one hundred pounds of lead and twenty-five pounds of powder from the Indian Department stores, see Fred C. Hamil, *The Valley of the Lower Thames, 1640-1850* (Toronto, 1951), p. 41.

31 Castlereagh to Craig, April 8, 1809, Series C, Military, C 256, p. 26-28.

32 See Elliott to Major Halton, May 19, 1809, Indian Affairs, Upper Canada, Civil Control, RG 10, vol. 3, p. 52; also Cruikshank, "The *Chesapeake* Crisis," *Ontario Historical Society Papers and Records,* XXIV, 307.

33 Elliott to Claus, June 28, 1809, Indian Affairs, Superintendent-General, RG 10, vol. 11.

Chapter 9: Prelude to War

1 There is considerable information on the dispute at St. Joseph's in Indian Affairs, Upper Canada, Civil Control, RG 10, vol. 3, p. 125-220, and in Series C, Military, C 256, p. 62-69, 73-79.

2 For the February-March, 1810, session of the Assembly see *Eighth Ontario Archives Report,* part II, p. 279-381. For the family of Matthew Donovan, see Matthew Donovan Papers (one item), Burton Historical Collection, Detroit Public Library. See also the note on Sarah Donovan in M. Agnes Burton (ed.), *Governor and Judges Journal. Proceedings of the Detroit Land Board* (Detroit, 1915), p. 165-66 n., and Sister Mary Rosalita, *Education in Detroit Prior to 1850* (Lansing, 1928), p. 29-30. There is also geneological information on Matthew, Sarah, and their children in the Fort Malden archives.

3 Elliott to Claus, July 9, 1810, Series Q, Colonial Office (transcripts), Q 114, p. 66-67.

4 Harrison to the War Department, July 18, 1810, *American State Papers, Indian Affairs,* II, 799.

5 Elliott to Claus, October 16, 1810, also substance of the Indian speeches at the council, Series Q, Colonial Office (transcripts), Q 114, p. 70-73. For the Brownstown Council see William Hull to John Johnston, September 27, 1810, United States Office

for Indian Affairs, Fort Wayne Agency, Letterbook, 1809-1815, p. 47-53, William L. Clements Library, University of Michigan.

6 Tecumseh's speech, November 15, 1810, is in Series Q, Colonial Office (transcripts), Q 114, p. 77-79, see also Elliott to Claus, November 16/18 (same letter), 1810, *ibid.,* 74-75.

7 Elliott to Claus, November 16/18, 1810, *ibid.,* Q 114, p. 74-75. For answer to Elliott's request for instructions, see Gore to Claus, February 26, 1811, *ibid.,* p. 108-9, transmitting Craig's instructions of February 2, *ibid.,* 80-82.

8 Brock to Craig, February 27, 1811, Tupper, *Life and Correspondence of Brock,* 94-96. Brock, who had been in Canada since 1802, became a major general in June 1811, and in October, after the departure of Gore for England, he was given complete command in Upper Canada.

9 See Augustus Foster to James Monroe, December 28, 1811, William R. Manning (ed.), *Diplomatic Correspondence of the United States: Canadian Relations, 1784-1860* (4 vols., Washington, 1940-1945), I, 608-9. See also Foster to Monroe, June 7, 1812, *ibid.,* 612-13.

10 Series Q, Colonial Office (transcripts), Q 114, p. 65.

11 Craig to Gore, February 2, 1811, *ibid.,* Q 114, p. 80-82; Craig to Brock, February 4, 1811, David B. Read, *Life and Times of Major-General Sir Isaac Brock* (Toronto, 1894), 69-70.

12 Gore to Claus, February 26, 1811, Series Q, Colonial Office (transcripts), Q 114, p. 108-9.

13 Brock to Taylor, March 4, 1811, Tupper, *Life and Correspondence of Brock,* 96-98.

14 Harrison to the War Department, February 6, 1811, *American State Papers, Indian Affairs,* II, 800.

15 For session of the Assembly see *Eighth Report of the Ontario Archives,* part II, 383-487. For the Moravian comment see H. E. Stocker (trs.), "The Autobiography of Abraham Luckenbach," *Transactions of the Moravian Historical Society,* X (1913-1916), p. 395. The appointment of Matthew Elliott, Jr., dated June 13, 1811, is in the George Ironside Papers. The proceedings by which Alexander was admitted to the bar are in Secretary of State, Commissions of Advocates, 1811-1816, RG 4, B 8, vol. 19.

16 See *Michigan Pioneer and Historical Collections,* XV, 54-61, 63-66, 68-83, 85-87, for letters detailing this activity from August 1811 to May 1812. See also Tupper, *Life and Correspondence of Brock,* 147-78, for information on Brock's preparations for war.

17 Series Q, Colonial Office (transcripts), Q 114, p. 110.

18 Brock to Prevost, December 2, 1811, Tupper, *Life and Correspondence of Brock,* 123-30. In January, Elliott sent Brock an account of the Detroit defenses which he had obtained from visitors to Detroit. He seemed to think Detroit could be taken, and stated that once its capture was accomplished "we would have nothing to dread, and we could open communication with the Indians," Elliott to Brock, January 11, 1812, Series C, Military, C 728, p. 61-61b.

19 Prevost to Brock, December 24, 1811, *ibid.,* 133-35; cf. Craig to Gore, December 6, 1807, *Report on Canadian Archives, 1896,* Note B, 30-32.

20 See Draper MSS, 4YY *passim* for Tecumseh's visit to the southern tribes; also Drake, *Life of Tecumseh,* 144. There is a description of Harrison's Tippecanoe campaign in Alec R. Gilpin, *The War of 1812 in the Old Northwest* (East Lansing, 1958), p. 8-21.

21 Series C, Military, C 728, p. 62-65.

22 See Series Q, Colonial Office (transcripts), July 28, 1811, Q 114, p. 110; Prevost to Liverpool, January 13, 1812, *Michigan Pioneer and Historical Collections,* XXV, 291. See also Manning (ed.), *Diplomatic Correspondence: Canadian Relations,* I, 613 n.

23 Brock to Prevost, February 25, 1812, William H. Wood (ed.), *Select British Documents of the Canadian War of 1812* (4 vols., Toronto, 1920-28), I, 426-27.

24 See Tupper, *Life and Correspondence of Brock,* 159-61, 171-72; *Report of Canadian Archives, 1896* Note B, 67-68; *Michigan Pioneer and Historical Collections,* XV, 85-86; Francis L. Bickley (ed.), *Report of the Historical Manuscripts Commission on the MSS of Earl Bathurst* (London, 1923), p. 174-75.

25 The Journal of this session of the Assembly is in Alexander Fraser (ed.), *Ninth Report of the Bureau of Archives for the Province of Ontario 1912* (Toronto, 1913), part III, 1-97. Brock's address is in *ibid.,* 5.

26 Prevost to Brock, March 31, 1812, *Report on Canadian Archives, 1896,* p. 67-68; also Read, *Life and Times of Brock,* 96.

27 Ernest A. Cruikshank, "The Military Career and Character of Major-General Sir Isaac Brock," New York State Historical Association *Proceedings,* VIII (1909), p. 73; statement of Robert Dickson, December 3, 1812, Wood (ed.), *Select British Documents,* I, 426-27.

28 Confidential letter to Dickson, February 27, 1812, John B. Glegg to Baynes, November 11, 1812, Wood (ed.), *Select British Documents,* I, 423, 421; Dickson replied on June 18, *ibid.,* 424. For American action at Chicago, see Matthew Irwin to the Secretary of War, May 15, 1812, Clarence E. Carter (ed.), *The Territorial Papers of the United States,* vol. XVI, *The Territory of Illinois, 1809-1814* (Washington, 1948), 221-22; deposition of Francis Reheaum, May 1, 1812, *ibid.,* vol. XIV, *The Territory of Louisiana-Missouri, 1806-1814* (Washington, 1949), 574-75; Ninian Edwards to the Secretary of War, May 26 and August 4, 1812, Ninian W. Edwards, *History of Illinois from 1778 to 1833: and Life and Times of Ninian Edwards* (Springfield, Ill., 1870), p. 324. The North West and South West Fur Companies had also offered their aid in the area west of Lake Michigan in the event of war with the United States. See A. Gray to Prevost, January 13, 1812, *Michigan Pioneer and Historical Collections,* XV, 70-72; memoranda from the North West and the Michilimackinac Companies, January 13, and 31, 1812, *ibid.,* 68-69; Brock to Edward Baynes, February 12, 1812, Read, *Life and Times of Brock,* 93.

29 Claus to Brock, June 16, 1812, Series C, Military, C 676, p. 144-46; B. F. Stickney to Hull, June 20, 1812, United States Office for Indian Affairs, Fort Wayne Agency, Letterbook, p. 95.

Chapter 10: American Defeat

1 See Gilpin, *War of 1812,* p. 29-61.

2 J. B. George to Brock, July 8, 10, 1812, Elliott to Claus, July 15, 1812, Series C, Military, C 676, p. 134-43, 180-82. Elliott actually held two positions. As well as serving as Superintendent of Indian Affairs he was also a Lieutenant-Colonel in the Essex militia.

3 See Alexander C. Casselman (ed.), *Richardson's War of 1812* (Toronto, 1902), p. 26-32; Milo M. Quaife (ed.), *War on the Detroit: The Chronicles of Thomas Verchères de Boucherville, and The Capitulation by an Ohio Volunteer* (Chicago, 1940), p. 88-93; also Milo M. Quaife, "The Story of Brownstown," *Burton Historical Collection Leaflet,* IV (May, 1926), p. 65-80.

4 See Casselman (ed.), *Richardson's War of 1812,* p. 33-36; Quaife (ed.), *Chronicles of Verchères de Boucherville,* 93-103.

5 Gilpin, *War of 1812,* p. 98-105.

6 *Ibid.,* 105; "Charles Askin's Journal of the Detroit Campaign," in Quaife (ed.), *Askin Papers,* II, 716; District General Orders, August 14, 1812, Ernest A. Cruikshank (ed.), *The Documentary History of the Campaign upon the Niagara Frontier, 1812-1814* (Lundy's Lane Historical Society, *Publications,* III, parts I-IX, 1902-1908) III, 179-80.

7 See Casselman (ed.), *Richardson's War of 1812*, p. 49 ff; District General Orders, August 15, 1812, Cruikshank (ed.), *Documentary History*, III, 180-81.

8 Brock to Prevost, August 17, 1812, Series C, Military, C 688-A, p. 183-91; "Charles Askin's Journal," Quaife (ed.), *Askin Papers*, II, 717-21; Casselman (ed.), *Richardson's War of 1812*, p. 49-92; Tupper, *Life and Correspondence of Brock*, 247-48.

9 "Charles Askin's Journal," Quaife (ed.), *Askin Papers*, II, 722-24. John Richardson, who also fought in these actions in the Detroit region, later stated that Elliott and the officer in command at Amherstburg tried every possible means to soften the warlike habits of the Indians. See Casselman (ed.), *Richardson's War of 1812*, p. 7.

10 "Charles Askin's Journal," Quaife (ed.), *Askin Papers*, II, 725-26.

11 *Ibid.*, II, 727; Chambers to Procter, August 24, 1812, Ernest A. Cruikshank (ed.), *Documents Relating to the Invasion of Canada and the Surrender of Detroit, 1812*, (Ottawa, 1912), p. 176-77; Dewar to Procter, August 28, 1812, Series C, Military, C 688-A, p. 222-24.

12 For the Muir expedition, see Procter to Brock, September 9, 1812, *Michigan Pioneer and Historical Collections*, XV, 145; "Charles Askin's Journal," Quaife (ed.), *Askin Papers*, II, 728-29; Casselman (ed.), *Richardson's War of 1812*, p. 93-103; Muir to Procter, September 26, 1812, Series C, Military, C 677, p. 97-99, 102-10.

13 Procter to Brock, October 3, 1812, Series C, Military, C 677, p. 111-12. Brock himself had some doubt of Elliott's influence, Brock to Procter, September 17, 1812, Tupper, *Life and Correspondence of Brock*, 310-11.

14 Procter to Sheaffe, October 30, 1812, Dewar to McDonnell, October 19, 1812, Series C, Military, C 677, p. 163-65, 136-39.

15 Elliott to Claus, October 28, 1812, *ibid.*, 176-77.

16 Elliott to Ironside, November 10, 1812, to Colonel St. George, November 11, Procter to Sheaffe, November 9, Ironside to Claus, November 13, Series C, Military, C 677, p. 178-82; Sarah Elliott to N. Freer, November 10, 1814, *ibid.*, C 506, p. 18-19; Note re Alexander's burial, December 17, 1812, in Fort Malden archives; Drake, *Life of Tecumseh*, 57-58; Elias Darnell, *A Journal*, 35-30, 47.

17 See Gilpin, *War of 1812*, p. 144-58; Henry Adams, *History of the United States* (9 vols., New York 1889-1891), VII, 75-85.

18 Adams, *History*, VII, 87-90; Gilpin, *War of 1812*, p. 163-165.

19 See Casselman (ed.), *Richardson's War of 1812*, p. 132-47; Gilpin, *War of 1812*, p. 166-71.

20 See Richardson to Askin, February 7, 1813, Quaife(ed.), *Askin Papers*, II, 749-50; *Michigan Pioneer and Historical Collections*, XV, 239-40. See also Adams, *History*, VII, 72-98 for the whole River Raisin affair.

21 Series C, Military, C 1203-1/2 F, p. 209-12.

22 Noah Freer to Sir John Johnson, March 27, 1813, Series C, Military, C 1220, p. 260-61; Procter to Captain M. Douall, May 14, 1813, *ibid.*, C 678, p. 240-42.

23 The siege of Fort Meigs can be followed in Casselman (ed.), *Richardson's War of 1812*, p. 148-76; Gilpin, *War of 1812*, 173-92; Adams, *History*, VII, 103-8.

24 Horace S. Knapp, *History of the Maumee Valley* (Toledo, 1877), p. 172; also for massacre see Draper MSS, 12YY63-64.

25 See Gilpin, *War of 1812*, p. 188-191.

Chapter 11: The Last Days

1 Casselman (ed.), *Richardson's War of 1812*, p. 177-79; A. Battersby to Colonel Baynes, July 31, 1813, Series C, Military, C 679, p. 517-20; Gilpin, *War of 1812*, 202-5.

2 The Fort Stephenson affair can be followed in Casselman (ed.), *Richardson's War*

of 1812, p. 179-88; Journal of Joseph H. Larwill, Larwill Papers, Burton Historical Collection, Detroit Public Library; Gilpin, *War of 1812,* p. 205-8.

3 Girty to Colonel Foster, March 8, 1815, Series C, Military, C 88, p. 1; for estimate of Indian force, see Elliott to Claus, October 24, 1813, Claus Papers, MG 19, Series Fl, vol. 10, p. 111-13.

4 Adams, *History,* VII, 128-30; Gilpin, *War of 1812,* 217-19.

5 For this council see Casselman (ed.), *Richardson's War of 1812,* p. 204-7, and Elliott to Claus, October 24, 1813, Claus Papers, MG 19, Series Fl, vol. 10, p. 111-13; cf. Quaife (ed.), *Chronicles of Verchères de Boucherville,* 141-43.

6 Memorial of Sarah Elliott, August 29, 1814, Series Q, Colonial Office (transcripts), Q 318-2, p. 532-35; Sarah Elliott to N. Freer, October 26, 1814, to Colonel Foster, April 10, 1815, Series C, Military, C 506, p. 16-17, 24-25; *Michigan Pioneer and Historical Collections,* I, 412; Butterfield, *History of the Girtys,* 310-11.

7 See Elliott to Claus, October 24, 1813, Claus Papers, MG 19, Series Fl, vol. 10, 111-13; Casselman (ed.), *Richardson's War of 1812,* p. 204-42; Col. Claus to Lieut. Claus, May 11, 1814, Cruikshank (ed.), *Documentary History of the Campaigns on the Niagara Frontier,* VIII, 168; also C. O. Ermatinger, "The Retreat of Procter and Tecumseh," *Ontario Historical Society Papers and Records,* XVII (1919), p. 11-21.

8 Elliott to Claus, October 24, 1813, Claus Papers, MG 19, Series Fl, vol. 10, p. 111-13; John Vincent to Major General De Rottenburg, October 18, 1813, Series C, Military, C 680, p. 261-63. Captain William Elliott who was with Matthew Elliott on this retreat has caused considerable confusion. He has often been identified as Elliott's son, although he was in fact no relation (or at best a distant one). William Elliott was born in England in 1775 and emigrated to Sandwich in Upper Canada in 1802. He was a lawyer. He married Sophia Bouchette in 1806, and had ten children, see material in Fort Malden archives.

9 Memorial of Elliott, October 24, 1813, Series C, Military, C 257, p. 165-66; N. Freer to Major General De Rottenburg, November 6, 1813, *ibid.,* C 1221, p. 223; Report of William Claus, December 4, 1813, Claus Papers, MG 19, Series Fl, vol. 10, p. 87-110. Elliott had appeared in General Orders in regard to the capture of Detroit, Series C, Military, C 1203-1/2 F, p. 209-12.

10 Murray to Major-General Vincent, December 12, 1813, Series C, Military, C 681, 4/1813; also Cruikshank (ed.), *Documentary History of the Campaigns on the Niagara Frontier,* IX, 32; Prevost to Bathurst, December 22, 1813, Series C, Military, C 1219, p. 160-61; Adams, *History,* VII, 202-3.

11 J. Harvey to Elliott, December 17, 1813, Drummond to Prevost, December 18, 20, 22, Series C, Military, C 681, 4/1813; Prevost to Bathurst, December 22, 1813, *ibid.,* C 1219, p. 160-61.

12 Riall to Drummond, January 1, 1814, *ibid.,* C 682, p. 5-8.

13 Elliott to J.B. Glegg, January 31, 1814, *ibid.,* C 682, p. 100-3; also Prevost to Drummond, February 17, 1814, *ibid.,* C 1222, p. 48-50.

14 Elliott to A. Stewart, March 4, Stewart to Riall, March 5, 11, 1814, Drummond to Prevost, March 11, 1814, *ibid.,* C 682, p. 190, 192-95, 208-10.

15 J. Le Breton to Foster, March 8, 1814, *ibid.,* C 682, p. 233-35; Gray *Wilderness Christians,* 253; Elliott to Claus (extract), March 25, 1814, Indian Affairs, Upper Canada, Civil Control, RG 10, vol. 3, p. 383-84. Claus expressed doubt that these nations could raise such a force, Claus to Captain Loring, March 28, 1814, *ibid.,* 381-82.

16 Letter of Sir John Johnson, April 14, 1814, Prevost to Johnson, April 20, 1814, Indian Affairs, Superintendent-General, RG 10, vol. 12; Drummond to Freer, April 21, 1814, Series C, Military, C 257, p. 239-40; also Freer to Drummond, April 26, 1814, *ibid.,* C 1222, p. 110-12.

17 There is a copy of Elliott's will in the Fort Malden archives.

18 W. Elliott to Major Glegg, April 23, 1814, Series C, Military, C 257, p. 248-49.

19 Claus to Captain Loring, May 2, 8, 1814, Indian Affairs, Upper Canada, Civil Control, RG 10, vol. 3, p. 405-7, 416; Order of William Claus, May 2, 1814, Series C, Military, C 688-D, p. 36; Drummond to Prevost, May 3, 1814, *ibid.*, C 257, p. 250-52; Prevost to Drummond, May 7, 1814, *ibid.*, C 1222, p. 117-18; Gray, *Wilderness Christians,* 253.

Epilog

1 The travels and appeals of Sarah Elliott can be followed in Indian Affairs, Upper Canada, Civil Control RG 10, vol. 3, p. 499-500, 521-22, vol. 4, p. 144-55; Department of Indian Affairs to Military, 1816, RG 10, vol. 488; Series C, Military, C 506, p. 12-13, 16-20, 24-29; *ibid.*, C 258, p. 516-19; *ibid.*, C 1223, p. 35; *ibid.*, C 1224, p. 181-82; Series Q, Colonial Office (transcripts), Q 318-2, p. 527-28, 530-35. The quotation is from Sarah Elliott to N. Freer, September 24, 1814, Series C, Military, C 506, p. 13.

2 Information on Elliott's descendents (including a copy of Sarah Elliott's will, March 28, 1859) is available in the Fort Malden archives. See also Series Q, Colonial Office (transcripts), Q 350-1 (for the memorial of Matthew Elliott Jr. and others in summer, 1828).

BIBLIOGRAPHICAL NOTE

PRIMARY SOURCES

Manuscripts

Canada. The most important source of manuscript material for Matthew Elliott is the Canadian Public Archives in Ottawa. There is, however, no one collection of Matthew Elliott papers, and material has to be obtained from a variety of collections. Information on Elliott is scattered throughout the over twelve hundred volumes in the Series C. Military (Record Group 8), and this series is indispensable for the study of Elliott and British Indian relations. Also indispensable is the information in RG 10; volumes 1-4 contain Indian Affairs, Upper Canada, Civil Control (1796-1816), and volumes 8-12 contain Indian Affairs, Superintendent-General (1791-1816). These last five volumes are particularly valuable, and there is also material in RG 10, vol. 486, Lower Canada, Civil Control (1801-1808), and in RG 10, vol. 488, Department of Indian Affairs to Military (1816). A most important collection is the ten volumes of Claus Papers (MG 19), which covers the period 1760-1816 (the main emphasis is on the period after the Revolution). For Elliott's land ownership at the mouth of the Detroit River there is information in RG 1, L 3, vols. 175-176, 182, Upper Canada, Land Petitions. There is material on Elliott's son Alexander in RG 4, B 8, vol. 19, Secretary of State, Commissions of Advocates, 1811-1816, and this record group also is useful for Elliott's trading activities in the 1780's (RG 4, B 17, vols. 13-14, Suits, 1787, 1788). Other material can be found in RG 1, E 3, vols. 12-13, State Papers, Upper Canada, C 1796-1825, and in Canada, Miscellaneous Documents, vol. 8, 1808-1825.

The Canadian Public Archives also contain transcripts of great value. The Haldimand Papers (the originals are in the British Museum) have information on Elliott in the Revolution; particularly valuable is B 185-2, Papers Relating to State Prisoners, 1777-

1784. Series Q, which consists of transcripts of Colonial Office material in the Public Record Office in London, also has much useful material on Elliott; of particular interest are Q 50-1, 57-2, 79-1, 114, 299, 314, 318-2, and 350-1. Also from the Public Record Office in London, and on microfilm in the Canadian Public Archives, is the valuable material on Elliott's pre-Revolutionary status contained in Audit Office, Claims, American Loyalists, Nos. 40, 66, 109.

There is also some material in manuscript form at the Fort Malden Historic Park in Amherstburg, Ontario. This is for the most part a small collection of clippings, jottings etc. relating to the area, but there is also some useful geneological material, and copies of the wills of Matthew and Sarah Elliott.

United States. The most valuable material on Elliott in the United States is to be found in the Burton Historical Collection of the Detroit Public Library. The John Askin Papers are a mine of information on the Detroit region in this period, and the two-volume published edition of these papers contains only a small part of the whole collection. There is also much useful information on Elliott in the Solomon Sibley Papers. Sibley was a prominent Detroit lawyer, and there is information in the papers on the trading activities of Caldwell and Elliott. Other collections of interest are the George Ironside Papers, the Macomb Papers, the Robison Papers, the Larwill Papers, the Heward Papers, the Woodbridge Papers, and the Leonard Covington Correspondence. The Alexander McKee Papers (4 items) contain a copy of the will made by McKee before the battle of Fallen Timbers.

There is also material on Elliott in several of the Pennsylvania libraries. The Historical Society of Pennsylvania in Philadelphia has scattered information; the Yeates Papers (1762-1780 Correspondence) proved of value for Elliott at the beginning of the Revolution, and there is something of use in the Simon Gratz Collection (Indian Wars and Indians, Case 4, Box 4), the Baynton, Wharton, and Morgan Papers, and the Papers of Major-General Edward Hand. The Pennsylvania State Library, Division of Public Records, in Harrisburg also has a good collection of Baynton, Wharton, and Morgan Papers, and the Papers of Major-General Edward Hand. The Pennsylvania State Library, Division of Public Records, in Harrisburg also has a good collection of Baynton, Wharton, and Morgan, 1765-1767 ("Fort Pitt Day Book") is of interest for trading activities in the 1760's.

The Draper Manuscripts in the State Historical Society of Wisconsin in Madison contain a great amount of material on this whole period. Most useful for this study were the Tecumseh MSS (YY, 13 vols.). The William L. Clements Library of the University of Michigan at Ann Arbor has of course an excellent collection on the Revolutionary period, but the most valuable aid for this study proved to be the Fort Wayne Agency, Letter Book, 1809-1815 (United States Office for Indian Affairs).

Printed Source Materials

There is an abundance of printed source material for these events in which Elliott took part from 1763 to 1814. Only a small proportion of it, however, contains material on Elliott himself, and I have merely included those works which proved of direct use for Elliott's activities.

American State Papers. Class II, Indian Affairs, I. Washington, **1832.**
John D. Barnhart, *Henry Hamilton and George Rogers Clark in the American Revolution, with the Unpublished Journal of Lieut. Gov. Henry Hamilton.* Crawfordsville, Ind., 1951.

Eugene F. Bliss(trs. and ed.), *Diary of David Zeisberger: A Moravian Missionary among the Indians of Ohio.* 2 vols., Cincinnati, 1885.

William Wirt Blume, *Transactions of the Supreme Court of the Territory of Michigan, 1805-1814.* I and II, Ann Arbor, 1935.

Douglas Brymner, Arthur G. Doughty, and Gustave Lanctot (eds.), *Report on the Canadian Archives.* Ottawa, 1872-

Clarence M. Burton (ed.), "Ephraim Douglass and his Times," *Magazine of History with Notes and Queries,* extra numbers, vol. 3, no. 10. New York, 1910.

M. Agnes Burton (ed.), *Governor and Judges Journal. Proceedings of the Land Board of Detroit.* Detroit, 1915.

——, *Manuscripts from the Burton Historical Collection,* collected and published by C. M. Burton Nos. 1-8. Detroit, October, 1916-July, 1918.

Consul W. Butterfield (ed.), *Washington-Irvine Correspondence.* Madison, Wis., 1882.

Clarence E. Carter (ed.)., *The Territorial Papers of the United States.* Washington, 1934-

Alexander Clark Casselman (ed.), *Richardson's War of 1812: With Notes and Life of the Author.* Toronto, 1902.

B.H. Coates (ed.), "A Narrative of an Embassy to the Western Indians from the Original Manuscript of Hendrick Aupaumut," *Memoirs of the Historical Society of Pennsylvania,* II, 61-133. Philadelphia, 1827.

Collections of the State Historical Society of Wisconsin. 31 vols., Madison, 1854-1931.

Colonial Records of Pennsylvania, 1683-1790. Vols. I-X, Minutes of the Provincial Council; Vols. XI-XVI, Minutes of the Supreme Executive Council. 16 vols., Harrisburg, 1851-1853.

Neville B. Craig (ed.), *The Olden Time.* 2 vols., Pittsburgh, 1848; reprinted Cincinnati, 1876.

Ernest A. Cruikshank and A. F. Hunter (eds.), *The Correspondence of the Honourable Peter Russell* 3 vols., Toronto, 1932-1936.

——, *The Correspondence of Lieut. Governor John Graves Simcoe.* 5 vols., Toronto, 1923-1931.

——, *The Documentary History of the Campaigns upon the Niagara Frontier, 1812-1814.* Lundy's Lane Historical Society, *Publications,* 111, parts 1-1X, 1902-1908.

——, *Documents Relating to the Invasion of Canada and the Surrender of Detroit, 1812.* Ottawa, 1912.

Elias Darnell, *A Journal Containing an Accurate and Interesting Account of the Hardships, Sufferings, Battles, Defeat and Captivity of those Heroic Kentucky Volunteers and Regulars, Commanded by General Winchester, in the Years 1812-1813.* Philadelphia, 1854.

Ebenezer Denny, "Military Journal of Major Ebenezer Denny," *Memoirs of the Historical Society of Pennsylvania,* V11, 237-409. Philadelphia, 1860.

Lady Edgar (ed.), *Ten Years of Upper Canada in Peace and War, 1805-1815; being the Ridout Letters.* Toronto, 1890.

"Matthew Elliott's Village Lot," *Burton Historical Collection Leaflet,* vol II, no. 3, p. 30-31. Detroit, January, 1924.

Logan Esarey (ed.), *Messages and Letters of William Henry Harrison.* 2 vols., Indianapolis, 1922.

Alexander Fraser (ed.), *Report of the Bureau of Archives for the Province of Ontario.* Toronto, 1903-

John W. Harpster (ed.), *Pen Pictures of Early Western Pennsylvania.* Pittsburgh, 1938.

John Heckewelder, *A Narrative of the Mission of the United Brethren among the Delaware and Mohegan Indians, from . . .1740, to . . .1808.* Philadelphia, 1820.

David Jones, *A Journal of Two Visits Made to Some Nations of Indians on the West Side of the River Ohio, in the years 1772 and 1773.* Burlington, N.J., 1774; reprinted

New York, 1865.

John Knight and John Slover, *Narratives of a Late Expedition against the Indians; with an Account of the Barbarous Execution of Col. Crawford; and the Wonderful Escape of Dr. Knight and John Slover from Captivity, in 1782* (Philadelphia, 1783).

Richard C. Knopf (ed.), *Anthony Wayne: A Name in Arms: Soldier, Diplomat, Defender of Expansion Westward of a Nation: The Wayne-Knox-Pickering-McHenry Correspondence*. Pittsburgh, 1960.

Benjamin Lincoln, "Journal of a Treaty Held in 1793, with the Indian Tribes North-West of the Ohio, by Commissioners of the United States," *Collections of the Massachusetts Historical Society, Third Series*, V, 109-176. Boston, 1836.

William R. Manning (ed.), *Diplomatic Correspondence of the United States: Canadian Relations* 1784-1860, vol. 1 (1784-1820). Washington 1940.

Michigan Pioneer and Historical Collections. 40 vols., Lansing, Michigan, 1877-1929.

Pennsylvania Archives. Samuel Hazard and others comps., 9 series. Philadelphia and Harrisburg, 1852-1931.

Milo M. Quaife (ed.), *The John Askin Papers*. 2 vols., Detroit, 1928-1931.

———, *War on the Detroit: The Chronicles of Thomas Verchères de Boucherville and The Capitulation by an Ohio Volunteer*. Chicago, 1940.

William H. Smith (ed.), *The St. Clair Papers*. 2 vols., Cincinnati, 1882.

Oliver M. Spencer, *Indian Captivity: A True Narrative of the Capture of the Rev. O.M. Spencer, by the Indians, in the Neighborhood of Cincinnati*. New York, 1834.

Sylvester K. Stevens and Donald H. Kent (eds.), *The Papers of Col. Henry Bouquet*. 17 vols., Harrisburg, Pa., 1940-1943.

Gayle Thornbrough, *Outpost on the Wabash, 1787-1791*. Indianapolis, 1957.

Reuben G. Thwaites (ed.), *A Short Biography of John Leeth with an Account of his Life among the Indians*. Reprinted from original edition of 1831, Cleveland, 1904.

Reuben G. Thwaites and Louise P. Kellogg, *Documentary History of Dunmore's War, 1774*. Madison, 1905.

———, *Frontier Defense on the Upper Ohio, 1777-1778*. Madison, 1912.

———, *The Revolution on the Upper Ohio, 1775-1777*. Madison, 1908.

Ferdinand B. Tupper, *Life and Correspondence of Major General Sir Isaac Brock, K.B.* 2nd ed., London, 1847.

Paul A.W. Wallace (ed.), *Thirty Thousand Miles With John Heckewelder*. Pittsburgh, 1958.

Isaac Weld, *Travels Through the States of North America and the Provinces of Upper and Lower Canada during the Years 1795, 1796, and 1797*. London, 1799.

William H. Wood (ed.), *Select British Documents of the Canadian War of 1812*. 4 vols., Toronto, 1920-1928.

SECONDARY ACCOUNTS

Books

As in the case of the printed source material, the list which follows is selective. It includes only those accounts which proved of greatest use in the preparation of the biography.

Thomas P. Abernethy, *Western Lands and the American Revolution*. Charlottesville, 1937.

Henry Adams, *History of the United States of America during the Administrations of Jefferson and Madison*. 9 vols., 1889-1891.

F. Clever Bald, *Detroit's First American Decade, 1796-1805.* Ann Arbor, 1948.

Francis F. Beirne, *The War of 1812.* New York, 1949.

Samuel F. Bemis, *Jay's Treaty: A Study in Commerce and Diplomacy.* New York, 1924.

Solon J. and Elizabeth H. Buck, *The Planting of Civilization in Western Pennsylvania.* Pittsburgh, 1939.

Alfred L. Burt, *The United States, Great Britain, and British North America, from the Revolution to the Establishment of Peace after the War of 1812.* New Haven, 1940.

Clarence M. Burton, "Matthew Elliott." Typewritten MSS. 20 pp. Burton Historical Collection, Detroit Public Library.

Consul W. Butterfield, *An Historical Account of the Expedition against Sandusky under Col. William Crawford in 1782.* Cincinnati, 1873.

——, *History of the Girtys.* Cincinnati, 1890; reprinted Columbus, Ohio, 1950.

Donald G. Creighton, *The Commercial Empire of the St. Lawrence.* Toronto, 1937.

Randolph C. Downes, *Council Fires on the Upper Ohio; a Narrative of Indian Affairs in the Upper Ohio Valley until 1795.* Pittsburgh, 1940.

——, *Frontier Ohio, 1788-1803.* Columbus, Ohio, 1935.

Benjamin Drake, *Life of Tecumseh, and His Brother the Prophet; with a Historical Sketch of the Shawanoe Indians.* Cincinnati, 1841.

Alec R. Gilpin, *The War of 1812 in the Old Northwest.* East Lansing, 1958.

Lawrence H. Gipson, *The British Empire before the American Revolution,* IX, *The Triumphant Empire: New Responsibilities within the Enlarged Empire, 1763-1766.* New York, 1956.

Elma E. Gray and Leslie Robb Gray, *Wilderness Christians: The Moravian Indian Mission to the Delaware Indians.* Ithaca, N. Y., 1956.

Charles A. Hanna, *The Wilderness Trail.* 2 vols., New York, 1911.

E. W. Hassler, *Old Westmoreland: A History of Western Pennsylvania During the Revolution.* Cleveland, 1900.

Virgil A. Lewis, *History of the Battle of Point Pleasant.* Charleston, W. Va., 1909.

Benson J. Lossing, *Pictorial Field Book of the Revolution.* 2 vols., New York, 1860.

——, *Pictorial Field Book of the War of 1812.* New York, 1869.

Sir Charles P. Lucas, *The Canadian War of 1812.* Oxford, 1906.

Robert B. McAfee, *History of the Late War in the Western Country.* Lexington, 1816; reprinted Bowling Green, Ohio, 1919.

Walter H. Mohr, *Federal Indian Relations, 1774-1788.* Philadelphia, 1933.

Gilbert C. Paterson, *Land Settlement in Upper Canada, 1789-1840.* Sixteenth Report of the Bureau of Archives for the Province of Ontario, 1920, Toronto, 1921.

David B. Read, *Life and Times of Major-General Sir Isaac Brock, K.B.* Toronto, 1894.

Max Savelle, *George Morgan: Colony Builder.* New York, 1932.

Edmund De Schweinitz, *The Life and Times of David Zeisberger, the Western Pioneer and Apostle of the Indians.* Philadelphia, 1870.

William L. Stone, *Life of Joseph Brant.* 2 vols., New York, 1838.

Samuel Wilson, *The Battle of Blue Licks, August 19, 1782.* Lexington, 1927.

Articles

Francis Cleary, "History of Fort Malden and Amherstburg," *Essex Historical Society Papers and Addresses,* II (1915).

Ernest A. Cruikshank, "The *Chesapeake* Crisis as it affected Upper Canada," *Ontario Historical Society Papers and Records,* XXIV (1927), p. 281-332.

——, "The Employment of Indians in the War of 1812," American Historical Association, *Annual Report,* 1895 (Washington, 1896), p. 319-335.

——, "The Military Career and Character of Major-General Sir Isaac Brock," *New York State Historical Society Proceedings,* **VIII** (1909), p. 67-90.

Randolph C. Downes, "George Morgan, Indian Agent Extraordinary, 1776-1779," *Pennsylvania History,* I (October, 1934), p. 202-216.

C.O. Ermatinger, "The Retreat of Procter and Tecumseh," *Ontario Historical Society Papers and Records,* **XVII** (1919), p. 11-21.

Reginald Horsman, "The British Indian Department and the Abortive Treaty of Lower Sandusky, 1793," *Ohio Historical Quarterly,* 70 (July, 1961), p. 189-213.

——, "British Indian Policy in the Northwest, 1807-1812," *Mississippi Valley Historical Review,* XLV (June, 1958), p. 51-66.

Orpha E. Leavitt, "British Policy on the Canadian Frontier, 1789-1792," Wisconsin Historical Society, *Proceedings.* 1915 (Madison, 1916), p. 151-85.

Milo M. Quaife, "Detroit Battles: The Blue Licks," *Burton Historical Collection Leaflet,* V 1, No. 2, (November, 1927), p. 17-32.

——, "The Story of Brownstown," *Burton Historical Collection Leaflet,* IV, No. 5, (May, 1926), p. 65-80.

——, "When Detroit Invaded Kentucky," *Burton Historical Collection Leaflet,* IV, No. 2, (November, 1925), p. 17-32.

George F. G. Stanley, "The Indians in the War of 1812," *Canadian Historical Review,* 31 (June, 1950), p. 145-65.

INDEX

This manuscript was edited by
Richard Dey. The book was designed by
John Vise. The type face for the text is
Linotype Baskerville designed in 1790. The
display face is Goudy Heavyface designed by
Frederich Goudy for Monotype Corporation
in 1926.
The book is printed on S. D.
Warren Paper Company's Olde Style Antique
and bound in Holliston's Zeppelin cloth
over boards. Manufactured in the United
States of America.